THE GENOCIDE PARADOX

# THE GENOCIDE PARADOX

Democracy and Generational Time

ANNE O'BYRNE

Fordham University Press

NEW YORK   2023

Fordham University Press has no responsibility for the persistence or accuracy of URLs for external or third-party Internet websites referred to in this publication and does not guarantee that any content on such websites is, or will remain, accurate or appropriate.

Fordham University Press also publishes its books in a variety of electronic formats. Some content that appears in print may not be available in electronic books.

Visit us online at www.fordhampress.com.

Library of Congress Cataloging-in-Publication Data available online at https://catalog.loc.gov.

Printed in the United States of America

25 24 23   5 4 3 2 1

First edition

To James, Marie, and Vincent
Ní bheidh a leithéid arís ann

# Contents

Introduction: Democracy and *Genos*                                        1

Generational Being, 10 • Genocidal Violence, 18 • Ontology
and Judgment—On Method, 23 • A Note on *Genos*, 31

1   *Genos*                                                                 33

Introduction, 33 • The Tree of Porphyry: The Pleasure of
Order, 36 • Linnaeus: The Sane Systematizer, 40 • Darwin:
Heredity and the Temporal Order, 48 • The Unstable Clade
and the Naturalization of Generational Being, 57

2   How Much Kin Does a Person Need?                                        64

Introduction, 64 • Absolute Belonging: *Atavus* and
Beyond, 64 • The Life of Blood, 73 • The Evidence
of DNA, 77 • Genealogical Thinking, 81 • Creating Kin, 93
• Genocide as Aenocide, 98

3   What's Wrong with Genocide?                                            103

Introduction, 103 • Genocide and the End of Ethics, 107
• Genocide beyond the End of Ethics, 114 • Genocidal Life:
The Case of Sexual Violence, 117 • Ontology and Politics, 119

4   Democracy of Generational Beings                                       126

The Democratic Paradox and the Genocide Paradox, 126
• *Genos* and *Cosmos*, 131 • *Genos* and *Demos*, 136 • The Problem
of Time for Democracies, 141

Conclusion: The Antigenocidal Democracy                    151

Acknowledgments                                            165
Notes                                                      167
Bibliography                                               203
Index                                                      221

THE GENOCIDE PARADOX

# Introduction: Democracy and *Genos*

Democracies are remarkable for being founded on nothing other than themselves. They are supported by no divine or natural right, and those who belong to a democracy do so by virtue of belonging to the people. Yet a democratic people is a people in a peculiar way: The *demos*, specifically and above all, is not a *genos*. Faced with the violence and ambition of the aristocratic Athenian families who claimed power by virtue of inheritance and the constant, hysterical scrutiny of the rolls to see who did and did not belong to the citizenry of Athens, Kleisthenes in 508 BCE invented the *demos* to cut through the categories of family, clan, and tribe and redistribute power across the country. This is not meant metaphorically. The demes were expanses of land in the countryside, stretches of coastline, and city districts, and a man became a member of the *demos* by virtue of his belonging to a deme. If democracy had been born as a matter of law under Solon, it was born again as a matter of place under Kleisthenes. Politically speaking, *genos* could now become a thing of the past.

In that same moment, the problem of democratic time took shape. The *genos*, in all its possible translations as tribe, family, or nation, is the embodiment of its own temporal principle. *Genos* describes a structure of relations by which one generation generates another, not only in the paradigmatic manner of bearing and begetting but also in terms of bequest and inheritance, teaching and learning, tradition and renewal. If democracy required its citizens to identify themselves based on where they chose to belong, how would it itself maintain continuity over time? Would deme membership be constantly reconstituted as each citizen made his choice as he came of age? In 508, every man who had any claim to Athenian citizenship chose his deme. What, then, of their sons, the newcomers by birth? What of those other newcomers who might arrive from elsewhere? Kleisthenes's democratic interruption turned out to be just that. It was an interruption that reorganized and recalibrated the pattern of descent but did not replace it; after the generation of 508 BCE, everyone belonged to the deme of his father, and the *demotoi* of each deme could decide on the roles permitted other sorts of newcomers.

Yet when we speak of democracies—Athenian democracy, modern democracy, our democracy—we have in mind both the interruptive revolutionary impulse that undoes the old order and also a way of living together that persists beyond the actions of the founding generation. We have in mind a set of institutions, practices, allocations of power, and distributions of violence that emerge from the contingencies of a specific democratic intervention but then, somehow, reproduce themselves over time. They sustain themselves according to law—as Aristotle notes, a polity is the same as a past polity insofar as it shares the same constitution—and, as Kleisthenes's solution of the problem of the second generation shows, they sustain themselves according to the reproductive or generative principle of *genos*. What would it mean for a democracy to instead sustain itself *democratically*? The world needs new young people if it is to survive, and newcomers enter the *cosmos* every day, each one generated in and by a *genos*. How can they regenerate a *demos*? The question points us to the temporal version of the democratic paradox.

Most often, democracy's paradoxes are traced to the modern confluence of democracy and liberalism and are most often thought in spatial terms. When sovereign power no longer resided in the person of the monarch and rule was no longer underwritten by a transcendental authority, democracy placed the people in the place left empty by their disappearance.[1] The people became the only source of legitimate rule, and the prize offered by its self-rule is individual freedom.[2] That is to say, collective rule is meant to deliver the freedom that will be a constant threat to collectivity. Put another way, self-rule requires sharing the work and responsibility of creating the rule to which all will be equally subject, even though we experience the very requirement that we be involved in the work of ruling as an infringement of the freedom that the rule promises.[3] Indeed, in the face of clashing ideas of freedom, we might, as Rousseau warned, have to be forced to be free. At the same time, it was Rousseau who also grasped that, in order to rule, the people must be something other than a collection of individuals and certainly something other than the collection of *all* individuals. Legitimate rule will not be achieved by people, or the people, but by *a* people, and, crucially, this people capable of self-rule is not found but must be created.

Essential to this creation is a boundary or criterion of belonging, and this produces another formulation of the paradox. Carl Schmitt points to the distinction between friend and enemy as the essential political distinction, and the inability of any liberal democracy to provide a liberal, democratic criterion for belonging demonstrates the problem with the form; for him, this was not a paradox but a contradiction that doomed the democratic project to failure and led him to a theologized politics and a fascist affirmation of *genos*-thinking.[4] The contradiction is avoided by *cosmos*-thinking, by which I mean the various forms of cosmopolitanism that might acknowledge the existence of peoples, and even the strategic necessity of creating peoples, but that also argue that, in all cases, a people's political existence can be governed by universal rules. From this point of view, peoples are at bottom indistinguishable from people-as-such when it comes to political arrangements. In its classical formulations, this is because we leave difference behind when we think ourselves into the public realm, the prepolitical original position, or the ideal speech situation.[5] Contemporary cosmopolitan thinkers are increasingly attuned to the fact that difference is both stickier and more precious than these formulations suggest. They acknowledge that the distinctions we make among ourselves are graduated—we regard some as close, others less so—and overlapping—a difference that is significant in one circumstance is imperceptible in another—without any being a fundamental distinction.[6] Yet *in*distinction before universal law remains fundamental. *Cosmos*-thinking rests on the assumption that, even if we are not all the same, we can always see the world from the other fellow's point of view.

Radical democratic theory responds to Schmitt's version of *genos*-thinking, on the one hand, and *cosmos*-thinking, on the other, by taking on the democratic paradox as what follows when social existence is fully acknowledged as part of political life. Indeed, it embraces it as a life-giving paradox. Social identities rely on the existence of others against whom to demonstrate their distinctness—us, not them—in turn creating the political challenge of discovering a mechanism that can ensure that an identity will avoid the drive to create enemies, to marginalize, exclude, and eliminate those very others, whether inside or outside the boundaries of the state. How will we prevent a single social or national identity filling the empty form of democratic citizenship or the abstract form of universal citizenship with its own contingent content? Can we uncouple *cosmos*-thinking from its roots in the particularities of European enlightenment and imperialism? William Connolly writes: "The depth grammar of a political theory is shaped, first, by the way in which it either acknowledges or suppresses this paradox, and, second, by whether it negotiates it pluralistically or translates it into an aggressive politics of exclusive universality."[7]

The tension also has a temporal form. Democracy lacks its own temporal principle, and this takes concrete shape in the problem of time for democracies. Some effort is needed to uncover its contours. After all, Kleisthenes's solution of following the democratic interruption with a return to *genos*-time remains codified in the democratic nation-state, where the institutional time of the state and the generational time of the *genos*—in the form of the nation—together ensure that the problem of a distinctively democratic time never arises. The state's perpetual claim to the whole of its territory grants citizenship to those born on that territory, according to *jus soli*; the generational life of the nation grants citizenship to children born of citizens, according to *jus sanguinis*; in both cases, the point is to translate the accident of birth into a matter of essential belonging and, at the same time, secure a future citizenry. No one chooses to be born, and none of us chose our parents or the where and when of our birth, yet these initial facts of existence are taken up by the naturalized, biologized version of *genos*-thinking as the ultimate determinants of our lives, establishing our place in an ordered *cosmos* and setting us into the generational flow of past into future. It is a powerful principle, even if the satisfaction it offers is complicated and dangerous. It fulfills our desires for categories into which to organize our experience, relationships that let us feel that we belong, patterns of signification that stabilize meaning and lodge us in a world, and a sense of time that allows us to feel sheltered and carried forward rather than exposed to the nothingness of destruction and oblivion. It shields us from the ruination that Lewis Gordon points to as signaling the human paradox: "Not to be ruined means to be a god. But that means not to be human."[8] All this, transmitted in what would seem to be the merely natural fact of generation. Generation is indeed a matter of nature, but all this epistemological, existential, and political work is carried out not by a natural phenomenon but by a technology of knowledge that emerges historically, across various lifeworlds, and is illuminated by various disciplines.

Approached from the tradition of *cosmos*-thinking, *genos* is irrelevant to politics (as it is to ethical life), and cosmopolitanism gives us formal principles of political organization that set aside family, tribal, and national existence. This also means setting aside the problem of history and of time. Once instituted, every political form strives to sustain itself over time; every institution needs to reinstitute itself or justify itself to new generations.[9] Despite everything, the *genos* is not nothing in political life.[10] It was not nothing for Kleisthenes, and it is not nothing for today's nation-states and their citizens. The starkest yet most neglected indication of this is the fact that, even now, the name for the worst, most awful thing, the greatest evil—worse than war, worse than other forms of mass violence and destruction—is *genocide*, the murder of the *genos*.

Invented in 1943 to name what was perpetrated upon Armenians in Turkey in 1915 and what was being done to the Jews of Europe right at that moment, *geno-cide* unites the Greek *genos* with the Latin *-cide* to name massive violence directed against people because of whom they belonged with, that is, because of who they were. We are familiar with the images: emaciated corpses lying in piles, human skulls stacked in heaps, thousands of people on the road carrying children and belongings, men peering through barbed-wire fences. We know the exemplary cases: Armenians, the Holocaust, the Rwandan genocide of 1994. Yet, though it names an extreme horror, we are not always able to account for what horrifies us, and there was and still is little agreement about the definition. The UN Convention on Genocide of 1948 describes attacks "committed with intent to destroy, in whole or in part, a national, ethnical, racial or religious group, as such," but what this means was a matter of dispute in the years before ratification and has continued to be ever since. Genocide is violent, but with what sort of violence? On what sort of group? *By* what sort of group? It is massive, but how much destruction counts? How enormous does it have to be? From one point of view, we seemed to need to move toward a more perfect definition that would be more theoretically satisfying and more legally effective; from another, the encroaching perfection would leave us at the mercy of a definition that is never adequate to the phenomenon.

What concerns me here is not precisely the phenomenon of genocide, or the efforts to define it, or even the correctness or otherwise of the judgment that violence that targets a *genos* is as bad as bad can be. After all, we can compare sufferings and evils and coherently assert that any given large-scale civil war was worse than this or that small-scale genocidal attack. Indeed, scholars of genocide have also argued against labeling genocide the ultimate crime.[11] Yet it is a judgment that persists in the world, and that fact is a point of access to the shared sense that genocide is *particularly* bad, that is, bad in a way different from other sorts of violence.[12] This judgment about genocide is the impetus for the analysis I give here of genocide as an attack on generational groups, that is, groups made up of old and young connected by patterns of generational inheritance. Biological genetic inheritance provides the model, but it is not the definition.

I will return to this often. Biological inheritance is essential to the story of generational being but is not the whole story. My argument is that genocide is an attack on generations and generational being, and it is abhorrent like nothing else because we value generational being like nothing else. We value the generational structure of our lives and our generational belonging to those who came before and those who will come after. We value the mode of being in time that anchors us in the past and in the future, that is, among those of us who have been and those of us who might yet be. Genocidal violence attacks the existential structure by which we live together, generationally, in a shared world.

This is why it is impossible to grasp what genocide is and what genocidal violence does if we approach it solely in the moral terms of the harm one person can do another or in terms of the relations between individuals. We are singular plural, which is just to say that the fact that we live our lives and are who we are, with and among others, is not an incidental feature of human existence but utterly essential. As an attack on a group *as such* by another group, genocide targets the way we exist together *plurally*, and, for this reason, political and social thinking must find a way to countenance it. It looks like a moral problem—genocidal situations generate terrible moral problems, and there is no denying that the atrocities committed by genocidal attackers demand the most vociferous moral condemnation—but moral thinking can also be a bar to understanding. By taking a different approach, I hope to open up a space of thought around the horror rather than drowning in it.

Genocide is a complex legal problem that, since the genocidal violence in Rwanda and the former Yugolavia in the 1990s, has prompted the development of a set of legal devices and challenged the deepest principles of jurisprudence. Genocide can be approached as an ethical, legal, or political problem, but it is also a problem *for* ethics because ethics cannot come up with a conclusive demonstration of why it is wrong, a problem *for* law because of the difficulty of developing a legal framework that can encompass it, and a problem *for* politics because politics—by which I will always mean democratic politics—does not make the *genos* redundant and the concept of genocide meaningless. In identifying genocide as a distinctive evil, perhaps the worst there is, we reinforce our commitment to the *genos* and thus reinforce one of the conditions that produce genocidal violence.[13] Note that the convention was generated by and addressed to the united *nations* of the world and that the contracting parties, for the most part, consider themselves *nation-states*.

Others have pointed to the nation as an inherently genocidal structure and the nation-state as an efficient mechanism for the distribution of genocidal violence. If the *genos* were the only way we knew to organize ourselves and understand our existence, there might be violence of tribe against tribe, nation against nation, wars of domination and annihilation, and we might be horrified by the suffering inflicted, but we would have no specific category of genocide; there would be nothing special about violence that attacks a *genos*. This also holds true for *cosmos*-thinking, though in a different way. War and violence, whatever their motivations and whomever they target, are already an affront to the highest cosmopolitan value, that is, our shared humanity. Insofar as this is valued as a timeless ideal, cosmopolitanism need not address the fact of generational being or the phenomenon of generational groups nor consider that there is anything particular about violence that targets a group. It is war that is abhorrent as an affront to our humanity, and nothing is added by specifying some attacks as attacks on a *genos*.

But note that many of the contracting parties to the convention considered themselves—and consider themselves—democracies. When we approach violence against the *genos* from the point of view of democratic values, the concern sharpens into a paradox. On one side, the *demos* is the anti*genos*, the group of whomever, formed without appeal to a criterion of birth and inheritance. Indeed, historically, it was formed in pointed opposition to the *genos*, making the values of the *genos* anachronistic and anathema to it. On the other side, the *demos* is never accounted for by its relation to a timeless, cosmopolitan ideal. Yet it does not have its own distinctively democratic mode of being in time, and, in its absence, democracies lapse into the structure of generational time. The problem is not that we continue to value the *genos* like nothing else but that, without its own temporal principle, the *demos* is experienced as a sort of *genos*. *Demos*-thinking, which dwells on the conscious affirmation and reaffirmation of the group of whomever, struggles against *genos*-thinking, which sees its membership as unfolding naturally over generational time. It is an uneven struggle, and democracies respond with a sort of doublethink that disavows *genos*-thinking while continuing to cherish the forms of *genos*-life; they identify genocidal violence, abhor it, but also perpetuate and disguise it. This is another formulation of the democratic paradox—call it the genocide paradox. What will it take to acknowledge it? To negotiate it pluralistically? *What will it take to envision an antigenocidal democracy?*

Aristotle taught us that politics is a matter of deciding how to live together well, and democracy is how we do so as people who need have no more than *being together* in common; politics is the work of *demos* rather than *genos*. Real existing democracies do as a matter of history take on the *genos* structures that they find ready to hand, and in doing so they evade the problem of democratic time; yet, at the same time, they remain committed to the democratic impulse and in various ways resist resolving its revolutionary drive back into the category of *genos*. The tension is never more apparent than when genocidal violence erupts in some part of the world and the world's democracies find themselves responding with fierce ambivalence. Democracies are no strangers to violence—like any state system, democratic states are mechanisms for the distribution of violence—but, on the one hand, genocidal violence must be construed as utterly far removed, exotic, and atavistic, the assertion of a value quite irrelevant to the democratic principle that thought to replace *genos*-thinking. Genocidal tendencies must be regarded as endemic to *those* societies, *those* places where *genos* identity remains available as a default when *demos* identity and democratic institutions are absent, weak, or in crisis. On the other hand, there is an accompanying acknowledgment of the special horror of attacks on people who become targets because of whom they belong with, that is, people linked together according to the temporality of generations, often—though not necessarily or exclusively—connected by biological descent, and engaged in the ongoing care of a distinctive shared world. *Genos*-thinking remains embedded in *demos* life.

The distancing/fascination effect has more than one source: It springs from the fact that, alongside our democratic commitments, we also sustain deep attachments to just such groups beyond our *demos* life and from the knowledge that the *demos* itself borrows the generational form and exists according to generational time. As a result, democracies are always at risk of having *demos* collapse into *genos*. Indeed, as we will see, the collapse was routinely courted—enforced—in the founding of modern democracies like the United States, where the celebration of revolutionary violence that spilled the blood of (imperial) tyrants and (colonizing) patriots masked genocidal violence against indigenous peoples and racialized, enslaved people. It continued and continues to be courted in the insistence on cultural assimilation as essential for political cohesion, in the ignorance and refusal of founding genocidal violence, and in the specific efforts by globally powerful democracies to export, institute, and sustain the democratic system.[14] Democracies and democratic theory both require an ongoing and painstaking decolonization.[15] Meanwhile, the structures of democratic life themselves turn out to be capable of obscuring varieties of violence that produce genocidal results in the form of social death, slow death, and forms of suffering that democracy cannot name.

From a sufficient distance, a genocide can be made to appear to belong to another world, one beset by a sort of violence our policies could not have prevented and that our foreign intervention surely would have no hope of stopping, a violence so foreign that it could surely never erupt here. For the democracies of Western Europe, the genocidal wars that destroyed Yugoslavia were often understood as spurred by a resurgence of old tribal thinking, *genos* against *genos*. In order to place the phenomenon of genocide in the past and far away, the Balkans would be remade as a marginal zone of Europe/not-Europe and as a throwback to the old Europe of belligerent nationalisms that had otherwise been replaced by the new Europe of federated commerce. Yet embedded in the horrified response was the knowledge that it was not so long ago or so far away. Democracy did not and does not make the *genos* irrelevant; it holds *genos* and *demos* in tension at its core. This is the oldest version of the democratic paradox, as old as Kleisthenes's invention of the *demos*, and it is what this book is about.

To begin, we must think about what it is to *be generationally*. We must try to understand what is meant by *genos* and how we value it, and by the activity of generating and how we value *it*. Here, *we* is not an authorial device; I mean the *we* quite seriously. If we are to shed light on the phenomena of genocide and genocidal violence we all—scholars, researchers, citizens, people—need to turn our attention to *genos* and generation. This is essential if we are to arrange our thinking and actions so that there will be less genocidal violence rather than more.

Rhetorically, this is far from satisfying. After 1943, we—scholars, people—began to say "Never again"; in 1948, the United Nations articulated its condemnation in the form of the Genocide Convention. Yet genocide did happen again, and if we keep cultural existence (the object of the deleted Article III) within the ambit of the concept, genocidal violence turns out to be insidious, running through our societies and taking deadly hold of generational groups and communities and their distinctive ways of being with a terrible tenacity. Instead of a rallying cry—though we will need those too—this research aims to get at the specific structures of existence that shape our judgments of genocide and genocidal violence. *Genos* and generation are two such structures, which we value as elements of generational being in ways that make it impossible simply to jettison them in the face of the affirmation that genocide must never happen again. Yet this does not put them beyond critical interrogation. The consensus around the judgment that genocide is evil makes it hard to see it *as a judgment*, which means that it will take some time to allow the deeper values supporting the consensus to open themselves for critical examination.

The structures I have in view are not structures we encounter in an objective way, yet they are also not merely subjective, personal, or psychological. They are not open to observation in the mode of the natural or political sciences, nor are they accounted for by singular first-hand experience alone. They are the existential structures of us and our shared world. They are the ways beings like us exist, which is to say that the claims I will argue for here are ontological, though offered as quasi-transcendental claims, characterized by the antidogmatic hesitation of critical phenomenology, already understood as socialized, and subject to the operations of power and biopower.[16] They will require observation that starts from the midst of things in the natural attitude, but with an eye to the fact that the things among which we find ourselves are always experienced in specific, contingent, historical arrangements. The structures that come into question bring us into question too: the observers and questioners, perpetrators, sufferers, bystanders, survivors, inheritors, commemorators, forgetters, all of us generational beings.[17]

Before the end of this chapter, I will consider questions of method in more detail, and in the final chapter I address the question of what the antigenocidal democracy could look like. First, we need a sense of what we talk about when we talk about generational being and genocidal violence.

## Generational Being

We come to be between past and future. It's not that we enter into a place between, or set ourselves up in the eye of a storm, but rather that we exist in the movement between past and future, generated and generational. Brought into the world, each of us somebody's child, we grow, some of us have children, a new generation emerges, and the *genos* is perpetuated. We sustain shared worlds, where sustaining means also holding them open for ways of being we have not anticipated. We send something of ourselves—genes, knowledge, ways of speaking, ways of being—into a future that is otherwise foreclosed for us mortals, and we do so knowing that we cannot control what will become of it but expecting that it will be valued and remain in some way recognizable as ours. My great-grandmother could not have known that there would be me. My being here is not a matter of her having extended herself into the future world but, rather, of her having had children and thereby having held open the possibility of something else, something more, perhaps something other, perhaps her wildest dreams, perhaps something that would shock or disappoint her, perhaps something she might be happy to acknowledge as hers. Built into generation is an anticipation that we might somehow remain for a while in memory, postponing oblivion and continuing to be part of the world. This means that we would destroy our own best hope of worldly immortality if we thought of the new generation as though they were clones or if we dreamed of clones that would repeat me, me, and more me. This courts the same danger that is embedded in all tradition, the risk of striking from the hands of the new their chance to renew the world.

Nietzsche was not wrong: Oblivion awaits us all, since a time will come when it will be as though none of us had ever been.[18] But we don't need Nietzsche to tell us that one day we each will die. Somewhere between grasping my own mortality and confronting the eventual death of us all, we come to value generational life. Arendt was also not wrong when she wrote that by virtue of being born we each owe the world a death, since by dying we make way for others. Between the death that makes way for others and the death that ends it all, there is a movement of living and dying. Between the realization of my own mortal finitude and the realization of human finitude as such, a space opens that we fill with the banal activities—eating, working, having sex, dancing—as well as the existential activities of making meaning, judging, and valuing. They are often the same thing.[19]

We know something of what it is to be mortal. We undergo it in the deaths of others, the sensations of growth and aging, the anxiety or sorrow or joy brought on by consciousness that our time is short. Philosophy has not ignored this. Plato showed us the condemned Socrates making his friends laugh with his remark that philosophers spend their lives practicing death. Heidegger drew twentieth-century philosophy back into the question of Being through an analysis of our being-toward-death. Yet mortality is not the whole story, and we also know something of what it is to be natal from the arrival of new ones, our need of care, and the realization that we were not always here. We may not know what it was like to come into the world, but we do know about being here, with others, in a world that's older than we are and that somehow makes demands of us. I may exist in the anticipation of my own death, but I am also oriented toward a world that surpasses and will surely outlive me.[20] We inherit, bequeath, and belong, terms that do not exclude the possibilities of refusal, disinheritance, neglect, and estrangement.[21] This—all of it—belongs to generational being.

World, mortality, natality, being-with, history, responsibility; phenomenology has long studied the elements of generational existence without making it a theme. Taking up phenomenology's terms now—inheriting them—means entering a conversation that is already highly developed but that earns its sophistication by constantly reexamining its terms. The aim here is not to establish whether generational being is fundamental or should rather be derived from a different, still more primitive ontological category. Questions of whether we are historical because we are generational, or generational because worldly, or worldly because natal, and so on, are less relevant than the experiment of attending to generational experience and finding a way to talk about it as lived experience rather than as a mere object of study. These six related terms—world, mortality, etc.—together provide a register for talking about the activity of generating and then the generational mode of being, which in turn will show up our worldliness as unfolding in time according to a generational structure, our mortality and natality as the passing and rising of generations, and so on. Since it is a mode of being *with*, what emerges is inevitably a social ontology, which is also properly a socialized ontology; since it is temporal, it is historical and properly historicized.[22]

*World.* This, here, now—our world's haecceity—is a pinprick, an infinitesimal, and *beyond* does not refer to another world but to this one in which we came to be without knowing it and into which we might extend ourselves. It will always be a matter of *this* world. Even as we project ourselves upon our deaths, we might experience a desire for another world, or a hope for life after life, and we certainly figure other worlds or other lives poetically all the time, but these are themselves all worldly pursuits. It is not a matter of extending beyond the world but beyond our individual existence in it. Moreover, worldliness locates whatever meaning there is to find in or give to a phenomenon in our attentive experience of it. If we begin by applying the models of genetic research, or treat *genos* as if it were a matter of natural kinds, we will end up with a biological account of generation, as if we lived in a merely natural world. This is a point I will return to in different ways. We *are* natural beings, and the biological description of our existence—Heidegger, after Husserl, calls it a regional ontology—provides a remarkably accomplished, internally coherent account of who we are. Yet it cannot account for the varieties of our experience. Only a worldly approach will acknowledge the struggle for coherence that is part of existential experience thanks to our being subject to time, or, more precisely, to our temporal being. We are brought into the world and are here for the ones who were here before us even before we are here for ourselves; we are their generational being, their struggle to hold open an existence they did not choose and that in turn sustains the world they thought of as theirs but must now become theirs *and* ours. Each generational gesture, each effort at self-extension, now takes on meaning as part of the work of sustaining the world *as meaningful*, even if, as Arendt suggests, it sometimes looks like pious preservation and at other times like destructive revolution.[23]

We lose the world in two opposing ways: in the face of chaos and in the face of totality. In both cases we lose hope of finding or making meaning, either because the background continuity against which any figure would stand out is missing or because continuity is so thoroughgoing and complete that there is no gap for critique, question, or action.[24]

*Mortality.* The knowledge that we will one day die bears down on us. We spend hours and years utterly absorbed by what is immediately in front of us—the person who needs care, the job that needs to be done, the entertainment that gives us pleasure—and, with some luck and a lot of effort, we could in principle pass from one absorption to another and hold the consciousness of mortality at bay indefinitely. Yet even a life spent shirking (as Heidegger put it) is lived on a mortal arc.[25] We may seldom extract ourselves from the matter at hand in order to think of our lives as a whole, and we may only occasionally be conscious of projecting ourselves upon our own death, but every decision we make orients and reorients us toward a mortal future. Every change we experience as our bodies grow and age is a reminder of our mortal being. Every time we step out into the world we do so under the certainty that we will die and the uncertainty of when it will happen to us. After all, we are vulnerable to mortal harm from the very beginning; as soon as we are born, we are old enough to die. Every time we face the loss of someone we love or see another of the old ones die, we encounter mortality and the riddle of mourning: What are the dead to us now?[26]

One element of genocidal violence is its capacity to make the full experience of human mortality impossible.[27] The purpose of Auschwitz was to produce dead bodies; the victims of Nazism were annihilated there, and their ends were in no sense the culmination of a fulfilled life in the passage into the ontological state of having-been-there.[28] If the killers had their way, the victims would die along with all their kind: There would be none to mourn, grieve, commemorate, or remember, no one for whom the victims would have been. We know something about the ghetto of Lodz and the Luboml shtetl because someone wrote their memorial Yizkor books, but what of the communities whose place on the earth has been erased and whose very names are lost?[29]

*Natality.* Our existence may involve projecting ourselves into the future onto our own deaths, but what transforms this projecting into action is natality. No one asked to be born. Our coming to be, our being thrown into the world, is utterly passive while also being quite particular and wholly universal. That is to say, the time and place of my birth is mine alone; we all share that uniqueness, and our very newness means we are the sorts of beings who are capable of doing what has not been done before. For Arendt, birth is the signal of our capacity for action, and our sharing this capacity is the signal of human plurality. Our arrival is not a matter of a new drop being added to the ocean of humanity. We are brought as new becoming beings into the old world, into a world we did nothing to make and whose past we cannot change but that is nevertheless the place where our actions will play. We appear in the world, and our actions will be performed here before others.

From the point of view of the perpetrators of genocidal attacks, birth is what perpetuates types. From an Arendtian point of view, natality both perpetuates and upsets them. We may reclaim natality from those who would naturalize it and reduce it to a determination by releasing it from the natural givenness and studying its history. Natality is denied in circumstances where we remain invisible, unacknowledged, and unrecognized by the world; in such cases, we are deprived of the condition for the possibility of enacting our natal newness. Also, if I cannot claim the attention of those who brought me into the world in particular, I am natally alienated, as Orlando Patterson will put it in his analysis of slavery, and I am prevented from establishing intergenerational relations of responsibility.[30]

*Being-with.* None of us came into the world alone, and our being here is always a matter of being with others. We are exposed and vulnerable to one another; we act with others, in concert with them, against them, in front of them. In every case I act into the world, delivering my actions over to others, not knowing what will become of them. Spontaneous though the act may be, the actor cannot know if it will be carried forth or stymied, ignored or honored, developed or distorted. Acting is acting with; our being is being-with. Self-extension is not a matter of stretching my ego beyond my mortal life but of experiencing my being as it reaches and projects toward, into, with others even as others project toward, into, and with me. This is what it means to be in relation, to be singularly, plurally.[31]

This has been taken up as the model for community. Being-with means being in relation across the distance that separates us and embracing the dynamic by which that space shrinks and expands in the change of relation. The danger is that the being-with of community will collapse into the being-one of a group—family, nation, people—and the movement of inclusion and exclusion will stop with the construction of a border or the institution of a shibboleth. Community dies in too close an intimacy or too close a communion.

*History, or having been generated.* At the moment of my birth, the world stood in a distinct configuration that was changed forever by my entering into it. How does it become my world? How does the past come to belong to me? We may have the opportunity to identify heroes whom we might choose as models for our own futural projections. This is a sliver of the story, but an important one. Those who brought us into the world and/or those who sustained us in it—a group that includes but is not exhausted by those who begat and bore us and those who fed and sheltered us— expose us to *their* heroes, and handing down the world to us is the process of having us choose our own. Insofar as our precursors have worked to make the world their own, they will not merely let it pass to us; since they brought us into the world only partially made, they—some among them—must make us. How they make us, that is, the upbringing and education they give us, is both their remaking of the world and their making of us as the beings to whom they will hand down and hand over that world. The old ones leave the world, leaving it to us, and leaving us to it.

But what about the still older ones? For all our natal newness and our futural temporality, we find ourselves working hard to find something of ourselves in the old world that is our inheritance. We naturalize our relation to it in the search for our roots, sometimes imagined as the strands of DNA that extend into the blood of the past, sometimes as the trails of evidence found in the historical archive, sometimes in the details of family lore. By approaching it as a phenomenon, we make clear the willfulness of the project, the decisions we must make in order to find meaning in it and the modern ancestry worship that disposes us to recognize and value something of ourselves in those who have already been.

We are denied our historicity by too much handing down as well as too little. Arendt describes the education of the young men of ancient Rome as a process of teaching the glorious deeds of their forefathers, accompanied by the constant exhortation that they be worthy of such ancestors. Newness was not to be desired. All that was needed was respectful reception and faithful repetition of their heroic example, with no room for what I have been calling action; history is given. Yet too little knowledge and the violent disruption of practices of handing down are devastating. In the late nineteenth and early twentieth century, residential schools for Native American children dismantled communities already pushed to the edge of annihilation by the settler-colonial project of replacement. Men and women enslaved in the plantation system of the United States could at any moment be separated from those who knew and could transmit the culture of their forebears. Poverty, sometimes by slow degrees and sometimes in the sudden events of famine or migration, can weaken and break the link between generations, blocking the transmission of generational knowledge.

*Responsibility.* In a text far removed from the discussions of the state of nature in *Leviathan*, Hobbes offers this insight: The only right in the state of nature is the right a mother has over her child. However, it does not arise directly from her having given birth to him but from the fact that, typically, she is the first to see the child and so the first to choose whether or not to feed him.[32] In the case of each of us, someone responded to our initial demand—perhaps our mothers, perhaps other members of our family, but inevitably someone who came before—setting in train a complex of nonreciprocal, overlapping calls and responses that make up the structure of generational responsibility. Feeding a child is an act, and, like other acts, it is undertaken in the impossibility of knowing what will come of it, and it is the pivotal moment of generational responsibility.[33] This disrupts our understanding of responsibility as moral or legal; I will argue here that it is above all a matter of plural, worldly, political responsibility. We are generationally responsible (it is always a matter of a "we") and take that on when, with our contemporaries and with the generations that came immediately before us, we assume joint responsibility for the world. It fails when we confuse it with moral responsibility—"We didn't do it, so we are not responsible for it"—or legal responsibility—"I didn't intend such harm" or "I need not pay for my father's crimes"—but also when we are cut off from those who came before as a worldly generation. Unable to make a claim on those who came before, we struggle to hear the claims of those who come after.

This transforms our understanding of what it is to extend ourselves, to have something of ourselves persist in or as the world. Before the middle of the eighteenth century, living beings did not reproduce; they were *engendered*.[34] Reproduction—the physical begetting and bearing that is part of the process of generation—is not insignificant. Far from it. It is the material condition of all the rest, and everything I write here is premised on the assumption that people will, one way or another, keep having babies. But, as Hobbes reminds us, it is not identical with the act of taking responsibility, which, generationally speaking, is the act of feeding, raising, and educating, the political act of bequeathing that holds open the possibility of both revolution and conservatism, renewal and preservation.[35] If we can only hold open the world, the day might yet come when the generations of the defeated and the dead will be redeemed.[36]

*Generating.* Even on the level of begetting and bearing, *reproduction* is a misnomer. It is never a matter of the production again of the same, and *generation* and *generating* capture far more pointedly the contingency of every arrival and the radical uncertainty of who he will be. We don't *make* the ones who come after so much as make them *possible*. Remembering this lets another dimension of the depravity of genocidal sexual violence come into focus. When people are bred as slaves or raped and impregnated as part of a genocidal attack, the attackers act as if they know what they are doing, as though they could know what the product of their violence would be: a slave, a bastard, a mix. From this point of view, the identification of the child is complete even before she is born; everything she could do is already accounted for by her parentage, and all she will ever be is exhausted by the identities of her mother and father in a context with no room for contingency, where all one is can be determined by descent and where *genos* means *race*. Remembering this brings us back to the genocide paradox.

*Generational being.* To be, generationally, is to be in a set of overlapping, mostly asymmetrical, rarely reciprocal, particular, temporal relations of creation and responsibility, both along a vertical axis between generations and a horizontal axis by which we are related to our peers. It means belonging to a generated group—a *genos*—that is longer-lived than I am and that gives the context for my most fundamental experience of mortal, natal, historical, responsible existence. Note that generational being is an inescapable ontological condition. Note that we encounter the *genos* in many ways: as a species, kinship group, family, tribe, race, community, people, nation, *phalanstère*, commune, clade, or polity, indeed any group or type insofar as it is linked according to a generational principle. Yet note also that conscious generational being means nurturing an awareness of the worldly, created character of any one of these forms and the uncertain, contingent, inoperative character of each of them.

If we get philosophical about mortality, natality, and being-with, it should not be in order to take refuge in abstraction but to see more clearly what is at stake in the generational structure of our existence. If mortality closes life experience, natality is the reminder that experience was once somehow opened for us. Generational being is not different from being mortal and natal; it is their inevitable relation. Our struggles to hold this existence open, to find ourselves in relations that go beyond what is here, now, that extend into a world that was here before we were and that allow us to think that we might extend beyond ourselves, if only a little, are all signals of generational being.[37] Sometimes it surges into consciousness in experiences of fulfillment and joy, as when we watch the work we do bear fruit or our children make their creative way in the world. But often it is experienced in the destruction of worlds and the violent rupture of the ties that bind generations together. The greatest challenges will come from the latter, from examining genocidal situations in which individuals and communities can*not* count on either survival or remembrance.[38]

## Genocidal Violence

Philosophical contributions to the conversation on genocide often exhaust themselves in the work of definition.[39] To be sure, courts and tribunals need definitions if they are to do their work, and a distinct philosophical tradition works to specify the terms that will be effective there.[40] Defining genocide becomes part of the work of policing its use, given the fear that broadening the definition will dilute the value of the term, making it less effective in the work of motivating us to action against genocidal violence. There is a danger in using the term too loosely, according to this logic, because a time will come when we will have need of it with all its motivating power intact. Yet it remains the case that the decision to use *genocide* to name a violent episode in another jurisdiction does not inevitably trigger intervention.[41] Meanwhile, we live in generational ways that give us reassurance and joy and also produce harm and violence. We could continue to cherish the term *genocide* in anticipation of a moment of great need, but its power in such a moment remains uncertain, and, meanwhile, we risk blinding ourselves to the insidiously genocidal structures of our own states, institutions, and democratic ways of living.

Article II of the 1948 Convention on Genocide states:

> In the present Convention, genocide means any of the following acts committed with intent to destroy, in whole or in part, a national, ethnical, racial or religious group, as such:
>
> (a)  Killing members of the group;
> (b)  Causing serious bodily or mental harm to members of the group;
> (c)  Deliberately inflicting on the group conditions of life calculated to bring about its physical destruction in whole or in part;
> (d)  Imposing measures intended to prevent births within the group;
> (e)  Forcibly transferring children of the group to another group.

Killing people, causing them bodily and mental harm, stealing their children, preventing their having children, making their lives unlivable and their deaths ungrieveable: These are all terrible things and were already terrible before Lemkin introduced his new category. What the Convention added in the aftermath of the horrors of the Nazi annihilation camps was a schema for characterizing their peculiar wrongness. These were *acts* of violence that are committed with *intent* to destroy *a group*. Every element of the schema is controversial. Which specific groups count, or is it a matter of groups as such? Is it a matter of the killing of individuals or destruction of the bonds that create a group, producing social death? Is a particular sort of intention required? On whose part? Is genocidal violence a matter of particular sorts of acts? Is it necessarily a matter of acts at all?

*Which groups?* More usefully, which sort of group must be the target of violence for it to count as genocidal? If we were to rewrite the Convention today, would we add political groups? Or groups identified on the basis of gender or sexual orientation? Which particular groups are susceptible?[42] Our genocide intuitions might be broadly shared—that is, there may be an identifiable basic public concept of genocide today, as the US delegation asserted there was at the time of the initial negotiations—but it is impossible to make good on those intuitions philosophically. One source of this difficulty is built into the term *genocide* itself. When he selected the Greek root of *geno-, genos*, Lemkin clearly had in mind *race* and *tribe*, and the term carries these meanings and more: birth, descent; race, family, kindred; descendant, child; sex, gender; one's own country; kind, species; generation.[43] That is to say, an understanding of *genocide* that taps into the deepest roots of the word is: killing, where a person belongs to the group that is singled out for death *by birth*. Birth emerges as the standard of genocide susceptibility and our intuitions are preserved. But birth is less than helpful when it comes to pinning down definitions because we are far from being able to define birth itself or those things for which it stands: bloodline, generation, race. The recourse to birth slips beneath the philosophical radar because we think of it not as an existential structure but as a fact to be studied by the regional ontology of biology. Philosophers need not define it, the thought goes, because biologists have already done so using the tools appropriate to the phenomenon, and controversies can be settled by a DNA test. But while DNA analysis gives us information, it does not give us meaning. The same is true of birth, which is one element of the existential and political condition of human natality, whose meaning we are far from grasping and that (for reasons to do with generational life) continue to resist definition. "I belong to this group by birth" misleads us because it has the form of a claim that can be verified—or at least falsified—by empirical data, whereas it is a testimony of lived experience that may be neither verifiable nor falsifiable.

*A group as such.* Even if we were to agree about the sorts of groups vulnerable to genocide, do we know what it means to target a group *as such*? On the individual level, it means that one is attacked by virtue of one's (perceived) belonging to the group. The target of genocidal violence is something less than the whole individual and also something more. The victim suffers on behalf of his purported kind. He is selected because of an element of his being—his Jewishness, his being Armenian—and this makes the attack on him an attack on all Jews, all Armenians. Because genocidal violence takes aim at the group, the individual is attacked not because of the particular person he is, not because of *who* he is, but because of *what* he is regarded as being.

It does not matter whether the one attacked claims the identification, has known nothing of it, or actively rejects it. Some of us, in some contexts, are permitted to think of identity in the spirit of democratic multitudes, speaking now as a Buddhist, now as a gay activist, now enacting who I am as a teacher, performing my role as a tourist, a daughter, a voter. Some of us are allowed to be playful, ironic, even provocative and moralistic, permitted to put on a shirt that says "I am Troy Davis."[44] Such freedom is granted by a self-assured but also policed and secured public space, and it is granted selectively.[45] After all, if those around me marked me as Black, it would not matter if I woke up on any given morning feeling quite white. Inge Deutschkron describes how, at the age of eleven in Berlin in 1933, she was told for the first time that she was as Jew.[46] Indeed, when the knock comes on the door, identity and the processes of identification are in no way one's own. When one is interpellated "You filthy ___," it does not matter how one would choose to fill in the blank. It is not that the situation risks violence or that violence might erupt at any moment; the circumstances have become saturated with violence to the extent that the interpellation makes its victim speechless, taking from him the possibility of any gesture toward *who* he is.

*Destruction.* Yet a group can be destroyed *as such* by violence that does not aim at the physical death of its members but rather dismantles the relationships that constitute them to the point of inflicting social death. Indeed, the point may be to keep individuals' bodies alive even as the bonds that connect us to a larger human world and to a close human community are destroyed. Mass killing would have defeated the exploitative purpose of chattel slavery in America, but the practice of slavery dismantled communities, disrupted language groups, and destroyed generations using rape, pointed deployments of violence, the constant threat of violence, and the unrelenting threat of separation. Mattie J. Jackson tells the story of a family enslaved in Missouri in the 1850s: "[Mr. Adams and his wife] had a number of children and Capt. Tirrell sold them down South. This cruel blow, assisted by severe flogging and other ill treatment rendered the mother insane, and finally caused her death."[47]

Indeed, some forms of violence produce their genocidal effects most efficiently by ensuring that the victim does *not* die. Darfuri women raped by Janjaweed militias were cut before they were allowed to return to their camps, ensuring that the fact that they had been raped would be made public there. The rape had harmed them; they were harmed again by the responses of their communities; their specific relationships were damaged; the women's violated bodies in turn made them instruments in perpetrating the social disintegration of their shattered, displaced communities. Sarah Miller writes: "Rapists use individual women and girls as channels through which to destroy the identities and meanings of a group. . . . Surely this is not something raped women and girls themselves will, but rather it is the despicable expression of the will of those who raped them functioning through them."[48] I will return to the story of Darfuri women in Chapter 4.

*Intention.* In order for the Convention to satisfy the expectations of criminal law, genocide had to be specified in terms of the intention to destroy the target group.[49] Yet acts of large-scale violence require a mass of perpetrators who participate with varying, sometimes vague, often conflicting intentions. In the summer of 1942, the members of Reserve Police Battalion 101 of Hamburg were constituted as an *Einsatzgruppe* in Poland, and, in July, this group of middle-aged policemen shot 1,500 Jewish women, children, and elderly people in the village of Józéfów. Yet, on the basis of hundreds of interviews conducted in the 1960s with 125 of the men who perpetrated the massacre, the historian Christopher Brown concluded in *Ordinary Men* that very many committed unspeakable violence with no genocidal intention.[50] His conclusion may merely mean that we must look for genocidal intention elsewhere—in the minds of higher functionaries in the Nazi system or in the structure of the agencies of Nazi governance—but already the relation of intention and action on which the Genocide Convention relies has begun to unravel.[51] The genocidal agent acts on behalf of all his kind; he enacts *his* agency, certainly, but as the agent of the racial, national, or state structure that made it possible, even necessary, for him to inflict cruelty on his victims. When we accuse such perpetrators using the language of autonomy, personal accountability, and personal sovereignty, their attempts at exculpation rebound with an atrocious coherence. As it happens, they *were* following orders; they *were* doing their jobs; what they did *was* legal then. Without a better way of thinking about the displaced and dispersed agency of genocidal perpetrators, we who accuse them struggle to achieve such coherence.[52]

*Insult.* Yet genocidal violence does not just happen, and our horror is fueled by the knowledge that its harm is not incidental or natural but the result of human cruelty. We suffer in our bodies, on our skin, and in our flesh and bones, but there is no insult in the pain that *happens to me*— from a fall or a lightning strike—and I experience it differently from the pain *inflicted on* me. By the same token, I respond differently to witnessing the pain of another to witnessing the exercise of cruelty on another. In Brian Keenan's description of being tortured as a hostage in Lebanon, injury is one thing—"hard on my shoulders, driving into my chest. Then along my thighs, banging into my knees"—but the detail of his torturer's preparation for the beating shows it also to be something else—"Said began by taking deep breaths, deeper and deeper, faster and faster . . . I sat and listened to him exciting himself into violence." Keenan puts it painfully aptly: "Every part of my body was being insulted."[53] We, our bodies, our selves, are not insulted by a rockslide. What insults Keenan in every way is Said's obsessive, self-conscious *action*. James Hatley writes:

> Even worse than the extinction of the human race through a cosmological cataclysm would be the annihilation of the *aeons*, of the crossing-overs in time of the responsibility of one generation to and for another. This latter crossing-out of time occurs only through the efforts of human beings themselves. Only humans can conspire to repress, to destroy the future of a human *genos as a genos*.[54]

The violence may be fueled by passion and the injuries inflicted may be accompanied by hatred, but disdain, disrespect, and disregard are also gathered under the heading of *insult*. Meanwhile, it is not a matter of *real* injury being accompanied by *mere* insult. Rather, insult compounds injury, changing, deepening, and expanding it to the point where, in genocidal violence, it becomes the destruction of a world. I am attacked as a representative of those like me; all my kind, as interpellated by my attacker, are subject to the attack that is borne by my body. When suffering is inflicted on me as a token of a type, an instance of a *genos*, my very substitutability makes my suffering the suffering of all the group.

*Structural violence.* Elsewhere, I have argued, along with Martin Shuster, that shifting attention away from genocides understood as historical events with a beginning, middle, and end and toward the structures that produce genocidal violence allows us to better attend to what Adorno calls the need to give voice to suffering.[55] It attunes us to what Elizabeth Povinelli describes as "crushing if at times imperceptible harms."[56] It reveals the destruction of communities brought about by what Rob Nixon calls slow violence, which proceeds by daily deprivations, perpetrating its effect over lifetimes and generations. I will return to this argument in Chapters 3 and 4, but I note here that the structures of statehood, nationhood, criminality, borders, settlement, rationality, imperialism, and modernity have all been implicated in their distinctive ways in the perpetration of genocidal violence while—with the notable exception of Michael

Mann's work in *The Dark Side of Democracy*—democracy has largely evaded the charge. Indeed, it has often arrived as part of the solution: We need less nationalism and more democracy, weaker state institutions and more democratic control, the end of empire and the rise of democratic self-determination.[57] Accordingly, the real failures of democracies when it comes to genocidal violence might have been averted by *more*. This may be true. As I've pointed out, if we thought in terms of *demos* above all, there would be no stake in genocidal violence. But, as I've also pointed out, democracy has been unable to extricate itself from *genos*-thinking insofar as it continues to rely on *genos* as the principle of its continuation over time; as a result, the *demos* is always in danger of taking on an identity as a naturalized *genos*, for example, *citizens of the German democracy* becoming synonymous with *the German people*. It will not help to have more of that sort of democracy, the version where the *demos* is distinct from *genos* in name only. But nor do we need the self-assertive, self-exporting version that ignores the problem of democratic time and the persistence of *genos* and is blind to what I call the genocide paradox. There is hope for an antigenocidal democracy but only if it can become the place where we give voice to suffering, see harms that otherwise go unnoticed, and bear witness to even the violence that proceeds in small, slow steps, even when it is violence, harm, and suffering produced by democratic structures themselves.

## Ontology and Judgment—On Method

The philosopher Larry May has written of the "near-obsession with genocide in the twentieth and twenty-first centuries."[58] This may refer to a general concern with the Holocaust across the cultures of North America and Western Europe that began to gather pace in the 1970s: *Holocaust* on television, *The Diary of Anne Frank* in school curriculums, *Shoah* and *Schindler's List* in cinemas, public commemoration in Germany, Holocaust and Genocide Studies programs in universities, the establishment of the United States Holocaust Memorial Museum.[59] Yet public attention ebbed and flowed, and I don't agree that it was in danger of becoming a widespread public obsession. Perhaps the claim could refer to the thought devoted to the Holocaust by German Jewish thinkers who wrote in its aftermath, many of them refugees from Nazism: Adorno, Horkheimer, Arendt, Jonas, Anders, and others. In their cases—their number is relatively small—how could it *not* be an obsession? The philosopher's claim could also refer to the intensity with which they and others wrote about the Holocaust and the scope of the claims they made about the world "after Auschwitz," in which case the observation is surely apt. One doesn't come across much tepid writing about genocide.[60] Yet a concern with the Holocaust is not yet a concern with genocide more broadly understood, and indeed the popular, academic, and philosophical focus on the Holocaust has also been blamed for a *lack* of attention to other genocidal incidents and other forms of genocidal violence and, indeed, has constituted a block to broader understanding. May could also be referring to the heated debates that are sparked in international politics by the attempt to designate any given event *genocide*. Significantly, though, it surely cannot refer to an intense widespread interest among philosophers. There has been little such interest, though it has grown in the twenty-first century; rather, the fact of genocidal violence has had almost no impact on the development of the discipline.[61]

There is no debate on the question "Is genocide wrong?" Instead, all controversy is displaced onto the question "Does this count as genocide?" The effort of interpreting the definition given in the Convention is a legal, historical, and philosophical endeavor. Definitions are deployed in the world, in courts of law, and in political debates over sanctions and intervention. The US State Department under President Clinton went to great lengths in 1993 to avoid defining the violence in Rwanda as genocidal, fearing that it would produce a legal obligation to intervene. In 2004, the US Secretary of State Colin Powell *did* describe the violence then raging in Darfur as genocide, but only after being assured by legal advisors that it would entail no legal obligation.[62] The trouble is not that definitions are malleable, subject to debate, and in need of constant redefinition; this is no more than the work of interpretation in action. On the contrary, the trouble lies in our proceeding as if there were such a thing as *the* definition and as if each new contribution to the debate provided that true definition—at last!—or at least provided the closest approximation to date of the ideal form of genocide. The result is that we find ourselves attending to the definition at the expense of the phenomenon.

Bruce Wilshire warns of this distraction: "We shouldn't aim to state definitively the essential features of genocide. The actual phenomenon overflows, to some conceptually ungraspable extent, our powers of conceptualization."[63] If this means that genocide is a matter of exotic evil, necessarily beyond our grasp and guaranteed to defeat any philosophical approach, I don't agree at all. If it means, rather, that philosophical investigation limits itself when its purpose is technical, for example, when its aim is to produce a legally functional definition of genocide or indeed one that is readily actionable in the world of international relations, then it is surely true. I have already indicated some of the problems with the question of intent, suggesting that violence can be genocidal even if not intentionally so.[64] The phenomenon overflows our legal concept and requires a different sort of thinking. The critical attitude requires us to ask *what* we value and *how* we come to value it, in this case the structures of *genos* and generation, not in order to avoid the matter of worldly action but to approach it in other ways. Starting from the phenomenon of judging genocide as the ultimate wrong, I will examine what we value under the heading of *genos* and ask why we cherish it, and with such passion. To be sure, passions arise and judgments are made in historical, epistemological, and existential contexts, which are never independent of the operations of power. Specifically, passions and judgments about the generation and generations of life are always embedded in a biopolitical network.[65] Under such conditions, what can we do to generate an antigenocidal democracy?

That is to say, even as I reach for ontological claims, and even as I treat moral philosophy as a regional ontology not unlike biology or psychology, it is not in order to avoid the problem of norms and normalization. Yet how can an account of the phenomenon compel us? This is a central question for all critical phenomenologies.[66] Specifically, how does phenomenology negotiate the related problems of (1) naturalism and (2) the naturalistic fallacy? Hannah Arendt's approach, setting the problem in the context of political existence, is my example here. She takes appearance as central: To understand political existence, we must begin with what appears to us and, with our appearing together, to one another. That is to say, politics is not a matter of actualizing what already exists elsewhere, or making concrete what is already complete in another form, or moving this world toward its *telos*, or, for that matter, straining toward a regulative ideal. It is, rather, seeing what appears and creating its meaning; insofar as we are what appears, it is a matter of *being* its meaning. To that extent, it is an existential approach; it is for us to give existence its essence, to *be* the essence of existence. What distinguishes it as a *political* approach is that we are constantly reminded that the operations of appearing, seeing, and creating meaning are all plural, in all ways. We are plural, through and through.

When we make such ontological claims, they *look like* statements of fact rather than opinions about the world, and the natural attitude is ready to take them up as scientific assertions. When I declare plurality a predicate of the sort of being we are, it has the same form as a declaration predicating roundness of oranges. When I say we are plural or generational or sexual, it sounds as if I am laying claim to this sort of scientific truth. If phenomenological, ontological claims do indeed reach for this sort of truth, they are doomed to succumb to the naturalistic fallacy. It was Hume who identified this habit of slipping from descriptions of how the world *is* to prescriptions about how it *ought* to be, as though "ought statements" could be derived from "is statements." G. E. Moore codified what Hume observed, identifying it as a flaw in moral reasoning, and this in turn produced a habit in moral philosophy of rejecting *any* connection between what is and what ought to be, between all claims about the sort of beings we are and the ways we should comport ourselves.[67]

Yet Husserl, turning to the world and to the things themselves, makes clear that his phenomenology is not a turn to nature; phenomenological claims cannot be naturalized as familiar empirical *is*-claims, because phenomenology can never lose sight of the conditions of its own possibility as the *logos* of the phenomena, *logos* of appearing.[68] It does not produce claims about the world that are completely (or merely) objective or that are merely (or completely) subjective. Appearance is always appearance *to*; seeing is always a seeing *of*. From the point of view of naturalism, subjectivity is never expunged from phenomenological observation, so its claims cannot escape the shadow of relativism, and facts cannot be extricated from values. Yet the fact/value distinction does not disappear; it remains, and remains in question.

What, then, can follow from the claim "We are generationally" or "We are plural"? What is the status of the claims I might make about political existence on that basis? Arendt shows what a political phenomenology might look like, and *The Human Condition*, *The Origins of Totalitarianism*, *On Revolution*, and the *Lectures on Kant's Political Philosophy*, as well as certain essays, together make up a foundation of sorts. Contemporary thinkers—Jean-Luc Nancy, Judith Butler, Matthias Fritsch, and others—work according to a version of her method.[69] Early in *The Human Condition* she states that, when we each were born, the world had seen nobody quite like us before. That is to say, the fact of my birth *signals* the human condition of natality, and the fact that we are all born under that same condition *signals* the human condition of plurality. The condition is not *derived* from the fact but is *signaled* by it. In the same way, death signals the condition of mortality.

But what is required of us by this? Birth, life-among-others, and death are general facts about existence, and, initially, it is not so much that we are *required* to do anything with or about them but rather that we can't help grasping them and creating meaning for them and out of them—plurally. This is a condition for the possibility of knowledge, and it is a hermeneutic enterprise. As Dermot Moran writes:

Naturalists assume that [the scientific view from nowhere] can be supplemented—with ever increasing detail (e.g. Google's "street-view")—such that it can be made comprehensively objective. Phenomenology, on the other hand, wants to point out that each perspective—including the "street-view"—occupies a particular (and uninterrogated, often undisclosed) point of view which must be assessed and evaluated in its own terms. It is this attention to perspective that pushed post-Husserlian phenomenology in a hermeneutic direction.[70]

As we embark on a phenomenological, hermeneutic investigation of plurality, we find ourselves traveling around the hermeneutic circle together, investigating the condition of plurality plurally. This does not derive moral norms of the sort Moore might wish for, but it does permit the emergence of principles of judgment that differ without being arbitrary, that are more or less meaningful, more or less coherent, and, above all, available for contestation among and between us. The operation of that contestation remains to be seen, though for now it is important to note that principles of judgment are immanent, subject to historical pressures and changing technologies of knowledge, and never safe from the operation of critique.[71] They are constantly required to perform their own justification.

Interpretation is meaning creation, and making meaning together—making sense, or being sense, as Jean-Luc Nancy puts it—is a political activity.[72] Phenomenology is concerned with what appears, and hermeneutics is concerned with a way of questioning the phenomenon that in turn brings the questioner into question. This worldly hermeneutic in turn opens the possibility for a critical phenomenology. The phenomena emerge in the context of the lifeworld, and we are both phenomena and knowers in that world. Classical phenomenology from Husserl to Merleau-Ponty treats this joint meaning-making in terms of intersubjectivity, but we still find ourselves using the first-person singular and resorting to the sovereignty of the singular subject. The givenness of the subject offers itself as the point of departure for the hermeneutic adventure. And yet I—this I in particular, or any given "I"—could very easily never have come to be; any given fact about the world could easily have been otherwise; any given act could easily have gone unperformed.[73] As Silenus pronounced in the Midas story, we are children of chance; as Nietzsche points out when he tells Silenus's story in *The Birth of Tragedy*, this struck horror into the Greek soul and continues to disturb us now in existential ways. As Leibniz's vertigo-inducing question suggests, there may indeed be no reason why there is something rather than nothing, why I came to be rather than some other I, who would not be me. It is a question embedded in our generational being and in the invention of democracy.[74]

The two chapters following this Introduction make up an investigation of *genos*. It is a subject spread across different domains in different eras and encountered in different regional ontologies.[75] Genera are historical, contested, and contingent without being arbitrary, given in and by the world and also having no existence other than in our being the sense of the world. That is to say, the world is not something we stumble upon and then have to *make* sense of. Nor is it a matter of the world constituting us, or of our constituting the world, but instead a matter of our instituting and at the same time being instituted in relation to the world.[76] *Genos* is how relation institutes itself in time among us as generational beings. We experience it in certain clusters of related phenomena: (1) existential anxiety in the face of mess and disarray and the desire for the pleasures and predictability of order; (2) the fantasy of completeness, which is accompanied by unease with gaps and open ends; (3) the thrust toward perpetuation and the hope of redemption, despite the uncertainty of salvation; (4) the need to belong (at the very least as infants) and the joy of belonging, as well as the oppression that comes with possession and the dangers of exile; and (5) the risk and promise of those to come. In this work, *genos* emerges in three forms in three related contexts: in the order of logic as the category; in the order of life as the biological categories of species, family, and clade; and in the order of human life as the genealogical category of kinship. Understanding the *genos* of *genocide* means considering all three as they prepare the emergence of race-thinking.

In Chapter 1, "*Genos*," I study our existential desire for order, completeness, and perpetuation in terms of Aristotle's categories, Linnaeus's sexualist taxonomy, and Darwin's mechanism of descent and inheritance. Porphyry turned the Aristotelian categories into the medieval tree of logic, which was meant to account for everything we might want to categorize. The *genos* that is for him a logical operation becomes for Linnaeus a system for categorizing life, a system capacious enough to organize what we know and also what we don't yet know, that is, the flora of his Swedish farm as well as the unheard-of living beings of the New World. Darwinians took up the descent of species as a description of the necessary arrangement of life in categories that are distinct and remain coherent over time, offering a layer of scientism to race theory and social Darwinism, even while Darwin himself insisted that the boundaries of the groups we call species are far less distinct and more elastic than race theorists would wish. All of this was crucial in the eventual emergence of biology as a discipline in the nineteenth century, which made life an object of study and interpretation and susceptible to biopolitical order. When families or clades become the organizing principle for the study of life and the Assembling the Tree of Life project takes shape as an attempt to plot the relation of all living things, we lose sight of the violence of such epistemic projects, both the violence of extracting an exhaustive order from the world and the additional, compounding violence of enforcing a single, naturalized order of things.

Chapter 2, "How Much Kin Does a Person Need?" concerns the experience of belonging and the complex and delicate relations we maintain with those who *were* and those who *are not yet*. We acquire a model of absolute belonging from the phenomenon of blood relation, even though blood soon shows itself to be a malleable figure that has been deployed in the service of patriarchy, paternity, and religious purity. While contemporary genealogies are built on three sources of knowledge—family lore, the historical archive, and DNA comparison—the discussion of family trees and pedigrees continues to sidestep the arbitrariness of the choices it insists upon and to ignore certain branches and certain people, whose existence is allowed to fall away. Afraid of becoming unmoored, haunted by the indistinct figure of genetic bewilderment, we look for clues as to who we are in the identities of those from whom we came. We quickly find ourselves genealogically disoriented by the array of knowledges available to us. After all, how much kin *does* a person need? Enough, I will argue, to sustain her world by sustaining and renewing the various practices of generation, education, mourning, and world making.

Ethics or moral philosophy provides us with principles and mechanisms for deciding what is and is not permissible in our relations with one another, but it is not clear how well can it respond to the world-destroying power of genocidal violence. This is why Chapter 3 asks the excruciating question: "What's wrong with genocide?" Ethics already has ways to account for the harm of murder, rape, expropriation, and displacement, but the peculiar wrongness of these forms of violence when they are perpetrated as genocidal violence is harder to grasp. Neither utilitarian calculations of suffering nor the rationalist rules for discerning our duty are adequate. The emphasis in virtue ethics on character does go some way toward helping us understand the harm inflicted by those situations where the only choice is among evils—Will I betray this neighbor or that one? Will I save my son or my daughter or neither?—and right action is impossible. Indeed, the thought of *ethos* may suggest ways to understand how such contexts come to be. Yet none is equipped to address the harm done when such conditions prevail, specifically, the harm done to the world as the structure of meaning that holds us in place together and the harm to us all as worldly beings. This is the most fundamental concern of political thinking, which is why genocide is above all a political problem.

Specifically, it is a problem for *democratic* politics, or politics as democracy.[77] We value the *genos* as the group to which we belong, generationally, and abhor genocide as an attack on our generational being. Yet it is the value we place on the specifics of our generational being that leads us to genocidal violence. In contrast, what we value in democracy is the rule of those who belong *democratically* and who need not belong in any other way. This is the argument of Chapter 4. Democracy displaces the naturalized, self-perpetuating *genos* in favor of the unstable, questionable *demos*. But the *demos* is inevitably also made up of young and old together, and belonging together democratically does not evade the need to figure out how to belong together generationally; democracy gives itself the *problem* of past and future. A democratic politics must make a definitive distinction between the *genos* and the *demos*, but it must also sustain itself through generations and satisfy its own need to perpetuate itself. If we understand politics as the work of sustaining the plural world in the absence of a naturalized structure for that work, then this is the paradigmatic problem for politics. Political being is not a matter of programmatic change or making real what has been imagined but of holding open the space where we can continue to work out what it is to live together well.

That openness is the condition for the possibility of imagining and building an antigenocidal democracy. We have seen how Kleisthenes's democratic interruption quickly lapsed into the temporality of generational life, leaving us to assume that the only properly democratic time was the time of disruption, innovation, and revolution. Yet hidden by the drama of insurrection is the mundane time of maintenance (*Who will feed the children? Who will clean up?*), the deferred time of promise and expectation (*Are we the people yet?*), the predictable time of privilege (*Soon, we promise!*), the stalled time of trauma (*This suffering!*), and more, all of them underwritten by the movements of generational time. We live according to many temporalities, and democracy is the place for their expression.[78]

Our judgment of the wrongness of genocide is the acknowledgment of our generational being, and it shows that what we fear above all—even above death in any general sense—is the loss of generational being. This book is an investigation of that judgment and the ontological structures of *genos* and generational being that it brings to light. It is also an investigation of the generational time of democratic life. It is not a complete study; indeed, completeness could not be the aim, given the role that the striving for totality, wholeness, perfection, and purity has had in genocidal thinking.[79] Philosophy helps us think well, or think better, but that is not to be confused with the project of providing the definitive schema, exhausting the entire problem, or having the last word. Rather, at its best, philosophizing makes us accustomed to existing in conditions of uncertainty and discerning meaning in the face of contingency. As Lauren Berlant puts it, genocidal thinking can't stand the mess.[80] Violence has many sources, among them the struggle to endure conditions of uncertainty, an inability to live in a disordered world, the conviction that subjectivity requires subjection, dependence on a sense that everything—more perniciously, every*one*—has a place, and anxiety that some—*those* people—are out of place, refuse to stay in their place, are unplaceable, must be displaced, replaced, erased. I want to think about violence that has roots in a horror of the confusion and uncertainty of social relations. Part of what political philosophy can help us relearn as it takes up the problem of genocide is how to live with the mess.

## A Note on *Genos*

Throughout this volume, I will use *genos* and *genera* to refer to groups who commit and who suffer genocide and to groups regarded as the temporal embodiment of their own principle. This is inconsistent (*genos* is Greek, *genera* Latin), and it will sometimes lead to clumsy formulations (I will often discuss genealogy as the *logos* of the *genos*) and confusions (in Chapter 2, *genos* will refer to both biological genus and biological species), but I hope the reader will bear with me. Lemkin was explicit in his choice of the Greek phoneme. He acknowledged its similarity to a Roman and Sanskrit root but preferred to emphasize that *genocide* should be thought of as a Greek-Latin hybrid.[81] He also approved of the broad *O*, which he felt emphasized the expanse of the destruction it named. I am happy to take on all the accumulations of its *etymos* that made *genos* appealing to Lemkin, along with all that has happened to it since it joined forces with -*cide* and became part of the global lexicon. Used in this way—transliterated, unpacked from its portmanteau—it will help us approach the phenomenon.

# 1 /   *Genos*

*The* genos *is both the unit against which the crime is directed and the unit from which it originates.*
— RAPHAEL LEMKIN, *Totally Unofficial: The Autobiography*

*Our categories are important. We cannot organize a social life, a political movement, or our individual identities and desires without them.*
— GAYLE RUBIN, "Of Catamites and Kings: Reflections on Butch, Gender, and Boundaries"

## Introduction

When Raphael Lemkin coined a new word to describe what he saw under attack in Nazi-occupied Europe, he invoked *genus*—sort, type, kind—but also wanted to make sure that his audience understood something more specific, that is, race or tribe. If they understood it in terms of logical kinds, he wanted to leave no doubt that he was dealing with real existing Poles, Jews, and Czechs whose "personal security, liberty, health, dignity and even lives" were being destroyed.[1] If they wanted his new term *genocide* to refer as narrowly as possible, he argued persistently for understanding it broadly against the violence to come. Though trained in philology, he was campaigning for legal and political change and so was less interested in the deepest historical origins of *genos* than the effective profligacy of the Greek. He did not urge his audience back to the Sanskrit *janás* or the Aryan root *gen*—to beget, produce, to be born—but hovered instead at a term that had gathered connotations from Homer to Aristotle before passing into Latin and into the Aristotelian philosophy of medieval Europe.[2] The result is a morass of meaning.[3]

What do we value when we value the *genos*? Lemkin could have chosen to root his term in nationhood, and, indeed, he often resorts to "the nation" and "national group as an entity," situating his term, for all its newness, in a familiar nineteenth-century political tradition.[4] Yet *genos* takes us behind and beyond the nation, first into the seventeenth century where, as *genus*, it addresses a craving for order in burgeoning natural worlds and sustains a modern fantasy of a complete order. Existential anxieties take shape in particular worlds: if the silence of infinite space terrified Pascal, it was the teeming life of America that silenced Hernán Cortés a hundred years earlier. In 1520, Cortés reported to Charles V that he could not describe the things he saw in the New World because he did not know the words by which they all were known.[5] Already, European taxonomists were at work on his problem. Cesalpino in Italy, Ray in England, Buffon in France, and eventually Linnaeus in Sweden sought out the words and grammar that could allow us to make sense of the living world, indefinitely and completely. Completion would mean having a place for us, that is, a class for the classifiers, and Linnaeus was the first to fit humans into his biological scheme. His genera gave us a way to understand the expanding world and also *a* single *genos* to which to belong, nested within the natural order of things. He was also among the first to try to divide us into races.[6]

Yet if what we can know is what appears to us, how will we ever keep pace with a changing, living world? How can we have full knowledge of what is, when what is and what we are is always disrupted by time and change? We experience its coming to be and passing away constantly and minutely as metabolism, which is redeemed in development and growth. But we also experience it as human natality and mortality and the attendant hope that they too will be redeemed in generation. By the nineteenth century the *genos* was above all a generated group, sustaining itself beyond the life of any of its members according to a generational pattern. We hope that something—something of us, or something of this to which we belong, a way of being or a world that we would recognize as ours—will outlive us, and perhaps, at some point, suffering, defeat, injustice, and death—indeed, the very contingency of the generations gone—will be redeemed in a way we may not be able to imagine, by some others we don't know. They are unknowable in principle, whether distant future generations or the adult selves of our children, and the risk and promise of those to come is central to what we value most of all in the *genos*. This will be my argument here and in the next chapter.

Although what follows in this chapter proceeds chronologically—Porphyry, Linnaeus, Darwin—I do not mean to suggest that the desire for order represented by Porphyry is replaced by a Linnaean fantasy of a complete system, only to be replaced in turn by a hope inspired by Darwin for an evolving, ascending future. These hopes and desires all remained at work in the evolving structures of modern European empires, and they continue their work in the post- and decolonial world. Also, although I will examine *genos* first in logic, then biology, anthropology, genealogy, and finally, in Chapter 4, in politics, this is not a straight line of historical descent and certainly not a line of logical derivation. Finally, although the thought of *genos* can be traced *from* biology *to* politics, biology is not left behind, and politics is not a culmination or destination.[7] Canguilhem, Jacob, and Foucault made as much clear long ago.[8] *Genos* functions as a deep-seated, still largely unthought ordering principle for our political existence.

Everything in the world, all together, is too much for us. The onrush of sensation is overwhelming; the manifold of sensibility is a jumble; nature appears in a dazzling array of forms; new sorts of life burst upon us. We share the earth with more than eight billion others—counting only humans—but we cannot possibly imagine what it would be like to meet eight billion individuals. We need order, or orders, or at least a capacity for ordering. Foucault describes the experience of an aphasiac trying to arrange one small collection of skeins of wool:

> The sick mind continues to infinity, creating groups then dispersing them again, heaping up diverse similarities, destroying those that seem clearest, splitting up things that are identical, superimposing different criteria, frenziedly beginning all over again, becoming more and more disturbed and teetering finally on the brink of anxiety.[9]

It is an anxiety that haunts us in the form of a fear of not being able to establish groups and of not being able to give up trying. We cling to our categories even when there are more exceptions than cases that follow the rule, when the system of classification produces more violence than it deflects, produces more zones of speechlessness than adequate description, more silence and death than speech and life.

Encountering far fewer than eight billion individuals—individual spiders, leaves, stars, microbes, people, objects, others, ways of doing something, anything—we develop taxonomies. This is empirically demonstrable and also epistemologically necessary, but what interests me here, thinking in terms of ontological structures, is its emergence as a response to an existential anxiety. How can we discern anything about Being in general, or Being as such, when our only access is in beings and when those beings show themselves to us differently and, moreover, keep appearing in new ways all the time? How can we discern anything about our mode of Being when we keep appearing to ourselves and to and with one another in new and different ways, constantly?[10] How does anything become distinct against—as Foucault puts it—the confused, undefined, faceless, and indifferent background of differences?[11]

A mode of ordering pulls us back from the brink of two anxieties, one brought on by the vertiginous display of difference, the other rising in the face of unrelieved universality.[12] On the one hand is Cortés, struggling to find words to account for the experience of America, or Foucault's aphasiac fretting over colored threads; on the other is Pascal made fearful by the vastnesses of space or any of us aghast at the Genesis figure of the "tohu-bohu," the "deserted and empty universe crushed under the spirit of God."[13] We generate categories, species, taxa, orders, groups, and genera as a way to gain access to beings, and we need a system that sets them in relation to one another so that we can make sense not only of what is in front of us but also what we have yet to see, whatever that might be. Aristotle's *Categories* respond to that need, as do Porphyry's work of inheriting the categories and bequeathing them and the dynamic figure of the *genos* through medieval philosophy. The impulse to order is no less and no more than the impulse to make sense of the world, but it does not happen in a power vacuum, and it is not separate from the impulse to domination. Taxonomies shield us from that dual anxiety but, at the same time, open us to other dangers when they pass from the *array* of difference to *hierarchies* of difference: complex and simple, advanced and primitive, civilized and savage, doomed and saved, disposable and cherished. The invention of race, the history of imperialism, the domination that culminates in genocidal violence—all are unthinkable without the thought of *genos*.

## The Tree of Porphyry: The Pleasure of Order

*Katagoria* are predications. Insofar as Aristotle's *Categories* is about an action or process, it is about predication, and it aims to determine what can be said of what. This is why it is classed among his works of logic. While it begins with the naming of things, it immediately leaves behind those equivocal names that name just one case alone (1a), since what propels the work is predication applied to many cases and the many predicates that are applied to any one case. That is to say, what is predicated of the individual can be predicated of other individuals, and no single predicate exhausts what can be said of an individual. Things are categorized with others and with various others. Plato is a man, and so are Socrates and Alcibiades; all are classed together under the species "man"; Plato is also an animal, as is this cat and that horse, not to mention Alcibiades, and all are classed under the *genos* "animal."[14]

Encountering any particular person standing before us in the marketplace, there are many things I might want to say about him, but, for Aristotle, there is a finite number of *sorts* of things that can be said. I can pose very many questions as I try to categorize this person, but they will all be versions of ten basic questions that yield ten sorts of knowledge. Aristotle lists them:

> What (or Substance), how large (that is, quantity), what sort of thing (that is, quality), related to what (or relation), where (that is, place), when (that is, Time), in what attitude (posture, position), how circumstanced (state or condition), how active, what doing (or Action), how passive, what suffering (affection).[15]

Is this a matter of words or objects? When Aristotle asserts what can be *said*, is he also asserting what *is*? The answer is not clear, and we need not settle the matter now. Porphyry, a student of Plotinus and author of the *Introduction*, or *Isagoge*, that served throughout the Middle Ages as an introduction to the *Categories* and also as the introductory handbook for logic, simply sidesteps the question, declining to discuss such deep matters, which, he points out, would need a larger investigation.[16] Simplicius reports that Porphyry did investigate their intermediate role between words and things, but in the *Introduction* he takes his task to be simply "showing you how the old masters . . . treated, from a logical point of view, genera and species and the items before us."[17] From his logical point of view, *genos* is part of an order, certainly, but one that is driven by difference, that shows how an item can be ordered under different genera, and, finally, that reaches its fullest expression in us. At the root of Porphyry's tree is a man.

In his *Introduction*, Porphyry entertains some of the senses of *genos* that have been alive since Homer, bringing them to the fore only to then let them recede. There are three ways to be a *genos*, he explains. (1) A *genos* is an assembly of people who are somehow related to some one item and to one another, for example, the Heraclids, who make up the plurality of people taking their name from their affinity with Hercules. (2) It is the order of one's birth, meaning that the items within the *genos* are gathered there by virtue of the one who generated them (father) or the place of their birth (fatherland). Thus, Orestes has his *genos* by virtue of his relation to Tantalus, while Odysseus is from Ithaca "by *genos*." (3) *Genos* is a way of answering the question "What is it?" when the items asked about are of different species, for example, the *genos* animal.[18] This last is his topic here, and he delineates the term rather than defining it, finally completing its outline by distinguishing it from what it is not, that is, from predicates that refer to just one thing, from those that refer to items that belong to just one species, and from accidents and differences that cannot answer the question "What?"[19]

In a central passage, Porphyry sets out the relations that will eventually be displayed graphically by later interpreters as the Tree of Porphyry. It begins with substance and ends with a particular human:

> What I mean should become clear in the case of a single type of predication. Substance is itself a genus. Under it is body, and under body animate body, under which is animal; under animal is rational animal, under which is man; under man are Socrates and Plato and particular men. Of these items, substance is the most general and is only a genus, while man is the most special and is only a species. Body is a species of substance and genus of animate body. Animate body is a species of body and a genus of animal. Again, animal is a species of animate body and a genus of rational animal. Rational animal is a species of animal and a genus of man. Man is a species of rational animal, but not a genus of particular men—only a species.[20]

Importantly, the *genos* is not a stable or absolute category, as it would become for Linnaeus.[21] Rather, between the most general category—the *summum genus*—and the most specific—the *infima species*—all the categories are *genos* from one point of view and species from another. Animal is a genus insofar as it is divided into species, but it is a species insofar as it belongs, along with the class of plants, to the genus of living things.

It is also important that the categories are related by difference.[22] As Ockham explains, *category* refers to any set of predicates ordered into a genus, distinguished from others by some difference or other, a differentium. For example, the category of substance is differentiated into corporeal and incorporeal. In this case, the differentium *divides* the members of the *genos* into species and, at the same time, *constitutes* the various species as themselves genera. Thus, corporeal is in turn differentiated into living and dead, the living into animal and plant, animal into rational and nonrational, rational animals into this one and that one, and rational animals are finally individualized and this one is named—Plato. At each step, a differentium—e.g., living—is brought to bear on a genus—e.g., corporeal substance—specifying it as living body. This in turn becomes a genus, ready to be specified by a new differentia—animation—into plant and animal, and so on.[23]

Porphyry himself made no use of a tree. The earliest diagrams for these relations date from manuscript copies of Boethius's translation from the ninth to twelfth centuries, and they consist simply of shapes related by lines. In the thirteenth century, Peter of Spain for the first time explicitly called the diagram a tree, and thereafter the lines became trunks and branches and the elliptical labels leaf shapes. By the fourteenth century, they were laden with what appear to be heavy fruit.[24] By the time of Ramon Llull's "*Arbor naturalis, arbor logicalis*," it has become a mature, espaliered fruit tree presenting relations as logical and natural at the same time.[25]

But what, in all this differentiation, is the *genos* for? It is a crucial part of a mechanism for answering the question "What?" W. D. Ross argues that the point of Aristotle's *Categories* and its concept of *genos* is to discern what any given item is *at bottom*.[26] However, it also shows along the way the number and variety of ways in which any given thing can be categorized. *Category*, as well as referring to any set of predicates that are gathered into a *genos*, refers specifically to Aristotle's ten highest genera: substance, quantity, and so on. The person standing in front of me shares the whereness of being in the marketplace with everything there, he shares the posture of standing with all standing things, he shares the condition of wearing clothes with every clothed thing, and so on.[27] For Ross, the broadest category is the essential one; Plato is, at bottom, a substance. Yet why ten *genera*? Why these ten? Ockham argued that there were grounds for only two categories; Scotus maintained that there were indeed ten but that there was no proof that there could not be more; Suarez was also committed to there being ten, nine of them accidental and substance alone essential. Kant, however, averred that Aristotle did not have any grounds for his division at all.[28]

I think this is right, in a certain respect. When we understand them as metaphysical categories, we are unable to find metaphysical grounds for them, and likewise, as categories for use in logic, they are not grounded by logic. Picking up the thread from Scotus, Umberto Eco makes the same point:

> A genus is no more than a cluster of differentiae. Genera and species are linguistic ghosts that cover the real nature of the tree and the universe it represents: a world of pure differentiae. . . . The classical Porphyrian tree . . . *is no longer a hierarchical and ordered structure.* It does not provide any guarantee of being finite.[29]

The tree "blows up in a dust of differentiae," and all those Porphyrian trees, down to Llull's rigorously pruned pear, turn out to have been ways of insisting on order where there was none. Eco's interpretation delivers us back to the brink of the aphasiac's anxiety.

Yet the number of categories is not merely arbitrary, and their coherence is not merely hermetic. There is something haunting about them, but it is hauntingly familiar.[30] Remember that, while the *Categories* is an attempt to gather under its headings everything that can be asked and answered about any item, the only item to which all ten apply will be a human individual.[31] The example explained in Porphyry's Tree is *the* example. The categories cannot be grounded to the satisfaction of metaphysics, but they can be traced to our mode of being as *Homo taxonimus*, and in that context they make a rigorous, if inevitably incomplete, existential sense.[32] Just as the being that structures Heidegger's existential analytic is each time mine, the being who fulfills the Aristotelian system of predication is the sort of being we are. From the point of view of existence and existential anxiety in the face of fear and emptiness, ten is all right—plenty, enough, not too many—and these ten are likely, offering a reassuring suggestion—though no promise—of completeness, remaining enigmatic and brilliant enough to guide our knowing while respecting our anxiety, neither dismissing nor succumbing to it but letting it be such that we can bear it.

## Linnaeus: The Sane Systematizer

Otherwise, we might go mad. As a student in 1720s Uppsala, Carl Linnaeus learned the history of taxonomy in its still largely Aristotelian form, though now overgrown with new and, to his mind, maddening systems that proliferated complexity and instability at every turn.[33] In one sense, he sees that the fault lies with nature. Robert Morison and John Ray before him had both attempted to find a system for botany, but they made the mistake of looking for it *in* nature; without the Ariadne's thread of system, they got lost in its meanders. In another sense, Linnaeus sees the problem as being with the passions we bring to our encounters with nature. The lovers of flowers, for instance, have vast experience and elaborate ways of discussing their subject but, Linnaeus warns, "no sane botanist would enter their ranks."[34] In yet another sense it is a problem of language—"no sane person" would indulge the temptation to introduce barbarous or primitive names into the orderly naming of plants.[35] What madness might ensue if not just specimens of plant life but also specimens of language started coming back from America?[36]

He first produced his own *Systema Naturae* in 1735, and from the beginning it was a practical and economic endeavor. The section on minerals promised to make it "easy to learn minerology in a few hours";[37] the use of Cochineal in the dyeing industry and bees in the food industry justify the general study of insects; the proliferation of principles in contemporary taxonomy had to be stopped, since it was getting in the way of scientific progress.[38] Yet there is something holy about the task too. Surely, he speculates, we are put on the earth's globe to observe what is in front of us and praise its Maker.[39] He writes:

As there are no new species (1); as like always gives birth to like (2); as one in each species was at the beginning of the progeny (3), it is necessary to attribute this progenitorial unity to some Omnipotent and Omniscient Being, namely *God*, whose work is called *Creation*. This is confirmed by the mechanism, the laws, principles, constitutions and sensations in every living individual.[40]

In the century before Darwin, a biologist could assert that nature was complete and could be confident that procreation, "the secret working plan of the Creator," would continue to produce more of the same. We already knew a lot about it and had names for many things, but the desire Linnaeus was working to satisfy would never be satisfied by the accumulation of information; compilers can do the work of enumerating classes in a catalogue, thereby adding to our knowledge of nature, but true systematic authors use a system that of itself indicates what is omitted.[41] Linnaeus wanted a system that would let us know what we didn't know.

The compilers' habit of naming species after saints might be pious, but Linnaeus suggests that the more pious attitude is the scientific one that would eventually match human knowledge with the completeness of God's work. There were systems already available—Crespalino's, Ray's, Tournefort's, and too many others—but none was systematic enough. For instance, among those trying to give a comprehensive account of plants alone, he lists alphabetists, root-choppers, students of the shape of leaves, dealers in unguents, chronologists, those who favored the criterion of indigenous location, and empirics, who were interested in medicine.[42] Rejecting all these, he turns to the orthodox systematists, those who arrange the genera (of plants) according to some part of the fruit-body. In his taxonomy of taxonomers, this is where he places himself, specifically among the "sexualists," since he has "worked out a sexual system according to the number, relative size, and position of the stamens, together with the pistils."[43] This really is a system, on his own terms, since it allows us to point out things that are present, and "then those that are absent make themselves obvious."[44]

He writes: "The absence of things not yet discovered has acted as a cause of the deficiencies of the natural method; but the acquisition of knowledge of more things will make it perfect; for nature does not make leaps."[45] Not even in India or the New World, apparently. For all its teeming growth and global expanse, nature is a whole for Linnaeus, and the task of the classifier is to make it intelligible by naming everything in sight and establishing criteria for naming what has yet to be seen. Naming had to be taken from the hands of the root-choppers and dealers in unguents, from the compilers and the failed systematizers who got lost in the meanders of botany, and from the folk who called their local plants by the names their parents taught them. This scientific system could give a Cortés words for things seen in America but unheard of in Europe, words coined in an artificial European language.[46] Indeed, observation had to be carefully controlled too, since "very few people are lightly to be trusted, as far as observations go."[47] While he insists that the student of his system needs no prior knowledge of plants—in fact, the ideal student will be "unlearned"—he himself embarks on his work equipped with his knowledge of Swedish flora, already ordered according to one and another of the unstable systems he will displace. His system has five divisions—class, order, genus, species, and variety—and any plant will be completely named once it is allotted to a generic and a specific name.[48]

Genus and species are now fixed categories. So long as we followed Porphyry, differentiation was a movement repeated from branch to branch of the tree; now differentiation happens once into genus and from there, a second time, into species. Since, for Linnaeus, all species have existed since Creation, species could be differentiated, once and for all, by virtue of the one essential feature that sets it apart from all others in the genus, and the mechanism of procreation could be relied upon to sustain the specific difference over time. Difference differentiates *and* defines. Eco argued that, on Porphyry's model, differentiation could never become a reliable (dictionary) definition. For Linnaeus, only reliable definition will do. The name for a species must distinguish the plant from *all* those of the same genus; it ought to be derived from the parts of the plant *that do not vary*.[49] He adds:

> An essential specific name shows a feature of difference that is particular, or peculiar only to its own species. . . . When we have identified stable genera, and species by means of essential differences, we have attained the highest point in botany. If botanists were to arrive eventually at the position in which they could identify all species by essential names, there would be no possibility of further progress.[50]

Moreover, this system of names is not merely linguistic. Each specific name "contains the *differentia* that is contained within the plant itself."[51] Linnaeus can embark on a project of naming all genera and species because he already thinks of nature as a continuous whole, made up of discrete, contiguous parts.

*Systema Naturae* appeared in its first edition in 1735. It reached its complete canonical form in the tenth edition in 1751, and between these two dates the category of *Paradoxa*—in Greek, "the unexpected"—disappeared.[52] A complete taxonomy has no place for the unexpected. In the first edition, this section was populated by a collection of mythical creatures, hoaxes and beings described only in untrustworthy reports: the hydra, satyr, barnacle goose, pelican, Scythian lamb, frog-fish, dragon, phoenix, unicorn, and death watch beetle. In the second edition (1740), four more were added: manticore, antilope, lamia, and siren. Why incorporate such contradictory and unexpected creatures in the new taxonomy? Gunnar Broberg understands it as, in part, an effort to tackle superstition, extending the range of scientific explanation to the mythical animals of an earlier time, with the hydra turning out to be "fraud and artifice," the phoenix "in reality the date palm," the unicorn "a figment of painters," and so on. Linnaeus saw himself as tidying up nature after the barbarisms and darkness of the Middle Ages.[53] Yet Broberg suggests that it is also, in part, an indication of a deeper, more ambiguous tendency to want his system's categories to function efficiently and discretely while also preserving the continuity of nature. Perhaps Linnaeus, like Aristotle, is endowed with what Lovejoy describes in *The Great Chain of Being* as the two mental habits:

> There are not many differences in mental habit other than that between the habit of thinking in discrete, well-defined class concepts and that of thinking in terms of continuity, of infinitely delicate shadings-off of everything into something else, of the overlapping of essences so that the whole notion of species comes to seem an artifice of thought and not truly applicable to the fluency, the, so to say, universal overlappingness of the real world.[54]

Both habits serve the fantasy of completeness, though only the former needs the category of *Paradoxa* to keep the dream intact. If the taxa were allowed to overlap, the frog-fish or the plant-sheep would pose no systematic problem. When differentiation is harnessed to the production of definition, and when definition defines our expectations (δόξᾰ), then the unexpected (παρα-δόξᾰ) must also be defined and must have a category of its own.

The complete system of nature must include humankind, and, while the frog-fish might be a vague curiosity, the woman-fish is the object of obsessive erotic fascination.[55] The mermaid eventually loses her place in the *System*, either quietly absorbed into the species white dolphin, *Delphinus leucas*, or consigned to a footnote at the end of the classification of marine mammals.[56] While the category of *Paradoxa* vanishes definitively with the sixth edition of *Systema Naturae* in 1748, confusion persists and intensifies around the question of our place in the system. Immediately after introducing the genus name *Homo*, Linnaeus adds the subtitle "*Nosce te ipsum*"—"Know thyself." Note that he does this *before* designating the species *sapiens*. As a result, we who are exhorted to self-knowledge may be humans (*H. sapiens*) but could also include cave people (*H. troglodytes*), certain long-limbed people (*H. lar*), or people with tails (*H. caudatus*). Yet even if we, the addressees, are *H. sapiens*, we may be of the Wild variety, or else American, European, Asiatic, or African. We may, finally, be Monstrosus. The certainty that characterized the system, and which Linnaeus so desired, slips now, when most is at stake, and he struggles to make sense of the reports he hears of wolf children and pale cave dwellers, indolent Patagonians and flat-headed Canadians. He is unsure whether to note them as particulars or develop for each one a new category on one side or the other—or now on one side, now on the other—of the dividing line between the genera *Homo* and *Simia*, between the human and the nonhuman animal.

On one level, the uncertainty is just an empirical matter. Surely if Linnaeus had met the alleged troglodyte girl who was put on display in London in 1758, or if he had traveled beyond Europe, he could have gathered the evidence he needed to settle the matter.[57] Yet he reminds us often that to be led by nature is insane, so how do we know which phenomena merely need to be examined more closely and which need to be moved to another category or granted a category of their own? As it happened, those long-limbed people first classed as *Homo lar* were reclassed as gibbons (*Simia lar*), and *Homo troglodytes* was decided to be the chimpanzee (*Simia troglodytes*). As Jami Weinstein notes, the result was that *sapiens* found himself alone, taxonomically speaking, the only species of the genus *Homo* to survive the reorganization.[58] (Indeed, *sapiens* are the only *Homos* to have survived at all. In Darwinian biology, the genus *Homo* was taken up as consisting of one living species plus a void, which the archeological record would gradually fill with hominids and missing links.) The system had a place for us, alone at its summit.

If the system could be adjusted, what would it take to make a sane systematizer rethink the particular distinction between European, Americans, Asiatic, African, and Monstrous humans? What would it take to reconsider the need and warrant for such a distinction? As we know, centuries on, it would take a great deal, more than we have yet been able to muster. The disappearance of the category of *Paradoxa*, together with the arrangement of humans on an isolated summit, suggests a particular hubris. The system that now emerges is committed not just to working toward ordering the maddening variety of nature but toward complete order. The law of the orders, that is, the *nomos* of the *taxa*, requires that there be a place for everything; natural science succumbs to the model not just of physics but of metaphysics. In the *Critique of Judgment*, Kant writes that accomplishing "a system of pure philosophy, under the general title of metaphysics . . . quite completely is both possible and of the utmost importance for our use of reason in all contexts."[59] Yet there is a gulf between pure philosophy and a pure understanding of nature. Ernst Cassirer asks:

> What justifies us in seeing nature as a whole that assumes the form of a logical system and is capable of being treated as such? Whence comes this harmony between natural forms and logical forms, and upon what is it based?[60]

Kant agrees that the understanding, by which we grasp nature, is prone to its own hubris. Since it has access to the a priori conditions for the possibility of everything it can cognize, it runs beyond itself and claims to have thereby given a full account of everything possible. While he dismisses this as the arrogance of the understanding, its workings are nonetheless redeemed precisely by a principle of completeness provided by reason and not by nature. The understanding will never attain complete knowledge, but cognition, when it contemplates nature, will be guided in the right way by using the principle of completeness as a regulative idea.[61] This is essential for Kant, and in the *Critique of Pure Reason* he observes that, even if the taxonomers do not describe it in such terms, it is clearly how reason is at work in their classifications.[62] Regulative ideas bring unity into particular cognitions *as far as possible*. So, when we approach nature with the idea of completeness, we find ourselves studying the parts or elements of nature—e.g., water, earth, air—*as if* they also existed or could exist in complete or pure form.[63] Kant writes:

> The logical principle of genera therefore presupposes a transcendental one if it is to be applied to nature. . . . According to that principle, sameness of kind is necessarily presupposed in the manifold of a possible experience (even though we cannot determine its degree a priori) because without it no empirical concepts and hence no experience would be possible.[64]

What makes it possible to know nature at all is also what exposes us to the danger of misconstruing experience; we risk forgetting the *as if*. Faced with the need to presuppose the purity of the ideas of reason, we transform it—mistakenly, disastrously—into a necessary purity of natural kinds. Kant returns to the problem repeatedly, emphasizing that this thought of complete purity has its origin in reason alone and that principles in general have their source in reason and are not objective.[65] Thus he imagines observing a conflict between two insightful people regarding the particular character of peoples. (Like Porphyry's "Plato," it is an example that is more than an example.) One interlocutor assumes that certain characteristics are based on hereditary distinctions between families and races, while the other assumes that differences are based on external contingencies. (Significantly, neither doubts the coherence of the category "people.") Kant continues:

> There is nothing here but the twofold interest of reason, where each party takes to heart one interest or the other, or affects to do so, hence either the maxim of the manifoldness of nature or that of the unity of nature; these maxims can of course be united, but as long as they are held to be objective insights, they occasion not only conflict but also hindrances that delay the discovery of the truth, until a means is found of uniting the disputed interests and satisfying reason about them.[66]

It is not clear that the interests can indeed be unified, and I take their unity to be itself a regulative idea. The value of Kant's scheme lies in the prospect of having logical and natural forms coincide in the thought of natural purpose and purposiveness. If Kant can be described as the logician of the Linnaean system, it is because, in a line of thinking that stretches from early essays and lectures through his writings on race and culminates in the *Critique of Judgment*, he displaced a scholastic logic founded on a set of categories whose number was fixed according to no principle in favor of a principle of formal purposiveness. This was the solution to the problem that lay hidden at the heart of Linnaeus's work.[67] As Jennifer Mensch argues, a key to this achievement is his advancing it initially as an *idea*, meant for *academic* instruction, aimed at *pragmatic* knowledge, even though it was essentially a philosophical speculation in the hitherto forbidden territory of biological origins.[68] Compelled by Buffon's rule, whereby interfertility is the basis for a natural division of nature into species, Kant acknowledged this as a "natural system for the understanding" but regarded it as falling short, as Linnaeus's principles did, of a dynamic principle of natural history.[69] Buffon's efforts remained too reliant on empirical grounds, with the result that, at a crucial point in the development of his theory, he became entangled in the search for fertile mules in an effort to explain one of the *paradoxa* produced by his rule.[70] As Linnaeus would have put it, he became lost in one of the meanders of nature. At this point, Kant posits a germ (*Keim*) that would unify nature and reason. Mensch writes:

The ends of nature and humanity could be connected, even identified . . . once the grounds for their unity could be located outside the
push and pull of empirical experience. Nature had provided mankind
with a germ of reason and with dispositions intended for the gradual
perfection of the species as a whole.[71]

In Kant's early writings, God was the only figure that could provide a
logical basis for the unity of nature; in 1775, it was a germ of reason; in
the *Critique of Pure Reason*, it was the idea of completeness occupying the
place of a regulative idea; in the *Critique of Practical Reason*, it was the
regulative idea of the perfectly good will and our human aptitude for
purposes, though the generation of those purposes remains a task for us
as free beings.[72] In the *Critique of Judgment*, it takes the form of purposiveness as a principle of reflective judgment. We must suppose that nature organizes itself and that its original organization "uses mechanism
either to produce other organized forms or to develop the thing's own
organized form into new shapes."[73] Reason imposes certain constraints.
It would be absurd, Kant writes in a remarkable passage, to suppose that
crude, unorganized matter would generate an organism but reasonable to
suppose that an organism generates its like, a supposition supported by
our empirical experience. Experience in turn imposes other constraints;
reason, in adventurous mode, might allow us to suppose that an organism could produce something unlike itself, for example, that an aquatic
animal could produce a marsh animal and, after several generations, a
land animal, but "experience does not show an example of this."[74] Not yet.

For now, the presumption of purposiveness is borne out most thoroughly in humankind but also in different ways and to different degrees
in all genera of animals and plants, down to polyps, mosses, lichens, and
even crystals. The genera are narrowly separated—they approach one another gradually, as Kant puts it—and we must be free to think of them as a
family of creatures if the "thoroughly coherent kinship among them is to
have a basis."[75] Reason does not dictate. Rather, we must make judgments
about how to approach the world. Cassirer writes that for Kant: "We find
that nature 'favors' the effort of our faculty of judgment to discover a systematic order among her separate forms, and, so to speak, meets it half
way."[76] As it happens, all Kant's efforts to insist on the role of the subjective, heuristic, regulative use of reason's principles will be almost entirely
lost on his philosophical and scientific contemporaries.[77] I will come back
to this, both in the discussion of Darwin that follows, and in the discussion of attempts to develop a political theory of reflective judgment in
Chapter 4. For now, what Kant contributes with the thought of natural

purpose is the structure of a self-generating *genos*, one whose principle is understood to be embedded in its origin. The affinity among the individuals who belong to the *genos* is accounted for by their shared origin, so he can present the work of the naturalist—"the archaeologist of nature"—not as discerning the boundaries between genera but as discovering empirical evidence of the organic origin of each *genos*, which reason has already allowed us to suppose. This is fundamental to Kant's thinking of race.[78]

## Darwin: Heredity and the Temporal Order

When Linnaeus rejected the practice of naming species after saints or famous men, he made one exception: "Generic names that have been formed to perpetuate the memory of a botanist who has done excellent service should be religiously preserved. This, the only and pre-eminent reward for such labor, should be religiously preserved and fairly awarded." Granting it to all and sundry would be an abuse.[79] It is a revealing admission. We want to extend ourselves, and we hope that our work may persist in some way when we have gone. Perhaps something of us will continue modestly, as one of the myriad anonymous contributions that will have sustained the world, or perhaps famously, my own work marked with my own name: the tree of Porphyry, Linnaean classification, Darwinian evolution. Linnaeus was the father of modern taxonomy, the progenitor of a body of scientific writing, the intellectual father of a group of students whom he taught and then dispatched on scientific missions, and he was the father of seven children.[80] His name has indeed been reverently preserved by the scientific community, even though it disappeared as the name of a family within a generation.[81]

Of course, the practice of drawing family trees existed long before Linnaeus, and it was entirely possible to speak of resemblances between parents and children, to deploy the criterion of *consanguinitas*, and to organize kinship and social structures according to lines of inheritance, despite the fact that there existed no systematic theory of heredity. Yet, as François Jacob writes:

> Until [the late eighteenth century] living beings did not reproduce; they were engendered. . . . The generation of every plant and every animal was, to some degree, a unique, isolated event, independent of any other creation, rather like the production of a work of art by man.[82]

Groups related by common descent tend to share traits, so it is not surprising that phylogenetically related groups were long recognized *as* groups, even though their relation was not yet expressed in terms of a system of descent and modification.[83] Though himself a sexualist, for whom the sex parts of plants were the key to their classification, Linnaeus was not interested in their sexual and reproductive *lives*.[84] After all, if each species was preformed and if all its members descended without embellishment from the pair of ancestors created by God, parentage was a trivial element in the classification of living beings. Linnaeus has no tree of life.[85] Rather, it was Buffon who developed the theory of reproduction that would eventually prepare the way for Darwin, who would in turn insist that the only figure that could capture the process of diversification over time was a genealogical tree.[86] He writes:

> As buds give rise by growth to fresh buds, and these, if vigorous, branch and overtop on all sides many a feebler branch, so by generation I believe it has been with the great Tree of Life, which fills with its dead and broken branches the crust of the earth, and covers the surface with its ever branching and beautiful ramifications.[87]

The scene of the young Darwin aboard the HMS *Beagle* is a microcosm of the forces of nineteenth-century biopolitics: illness and health, trade and profit, madness and civilization, empire and race, surveillance and calculation, order and contingency. The son and grandson of physicians, supported by fortunes made in China and in the English canal works of the Industrial Revolution, Darwin belonged to a distinctively nineteenth-century British professional class. His training at the University of Edinburgh involved studying minerology and colonial botany alongside young men destined for careers in the East India Company. Unlike most of those around him, he was raised in Unitarianism, but he was exposed to the thinking and the institutional power of the established Anglican church at Cambridge, where science in the 1820s rested on the authority of Reverend William Paley's *Natural Theology*, an exposition of the teleological argument closely allied with Ray's 1691 *Wisdom of God Manifested in the Works of Creation*. In Cambridge in that era, the position of religious Dissenters was not always secure.

The invitation to join the voyage reached him through a set of academic, familial, naval, and social networks originating with Captain Robert FitzRoy, an aristocrat and dabbler in geography, art, science, imperial government, and missionary projects; he would go on to be governor of New Zealand for two years in the 1840s. The *Beagle* was a Royal Navy brig-sloop designed for war and equipped with ten guns; it spent most of its existence being used to survey the coasts of South America and Australia with the purpose of creating trade routes and new markets for the products of British industry. FitzRoy first became its commander after the suicide of its previous captain; he himself was sometimes concerned for his sanity in the course of a long voyage in bleak conditions. For the second voyage, he assembled a group that would extend the mission of the *Beagle* beyond the mandate to measure land and coast. He recruited an artist (Augustus Earle) and Darwin, the naturalist, whose company he valued. Yet, on at least two occasions, the two men argued over slavery, which Darwin found intolerable, once disagreeing so seriously that Darwin threatened to quit the voyage. Also on board were three natives of Tierra del Fuego whom FitzRoy had taken hostage on the earlier voyage. Their story is its own account of the distinctive madness of mission and empire. FitzRoy had named them Fuegia Basket, Jemmy Button, and York Minister; a fourth, named Boat Memory, had died of smallpox in England. While in England, they had received some education in English, religion, and gardening (in Tierra del Fuego people lived as hunters and gatherers) and were now being transported back in the company of a young English missionary in order to establish Anglicanism among the people of Tierra del Fuego. The mission failed almost immediately; the way of living of the Fuegians disappeared within decades, the Fuegians dead, dispersed, or assimilated.[88] FitzRoy died by suicide in 1865.

The voyage marked a vast expansion of the geographical horizon of observation, just as the growing fossil record would expand the geological horizon; together, these two formed the horizon of interpretation within which Darwin would construct the theory of evolution.[89] *On the Origin of Species* was published in 1859, and, while Darwinism is deeply implicated in all the efforts to arrange life and death that followed, from Social Darwinism to eugenics, we should note what Darwin's own work did and did not do in that process. In the first part of this chapter, I argued that *genos* had its place in a logical order, its members distinguished by *differentia*; in the second part, *genos* acquired content in the form of living things, and its *logos* required us to choose both a system by which individuals were identified as members of the *genos* and a structure by which the *genos* would sustain itself. In this part, that *logos* is a temporal order. This invokes two desires, or two aspects of the same desire. One is scientistic, a desire for a true system that could be read off nature, making biological taxonomy systematic on the model of physics; the other is now explicitly historical, a desire for generation as a system that can set us in relation to past and future and encompass the predictability and contingency of life over time. From one point of view, what is important is that the *genos* is real; if we can regard it is a temporal, historical structure, then we can regard history as scientific.[90] From the other, what is important is that the *genos* extends itself over time; in this way, science can turn out to be historical.[91] The scientistic approach regards its values—not least the value of clarity—as self-evident, and the great risk it runs is that we will allow an evident, scientific commitment to the search for clear *epistemological* taxa to collapse into a dangerous preoccupation with *ontologically* pure genera. A beautiful system of classification is nothing less—but also no more—than a technology of knowledge. The historical approach acknowledges contingency, thereby courting instability, and it compounds the threat of instability by returning often to the question of value. For both, the line of descent is essential to the *genos*, giving the scientistic response a mechanism for accounting for change and the historical response a way to address continuity. With *On the Origin of Species*, heredity took center stage, and both empirical research and the *logos* of *bios* entered a new, historical phase.[92] In the process, Darwin shifted the biological gaze from the individual organism to large populations; this is where the history of natural groups would be seen.[93]

Darwin acknowledges the usefulness and ingenuity of the Linnaean system, which gathered beings according to their resemblances, but rejects the thought that such classification adds anything to our knowledge.[94] To observe *that* there are resemblances falls far short of explaining *why* there are resemblances. Darwin adds two transformative elements. First is the insight that what lies behind resemblance is propinquity of descent. Observing resemblance in nature and classifying living beings according to their shared characteristics certainly prepares us for a principled explanation, but classification alone cannot demonstrate the plan of the Creator or the truth of any other general proposition. Only tracing descent through a common ancestor can show the cause of similarity among organic beings.[95] That is to say, Darwin's theory, developed inductively over the course of twenty years of empirical research, claims for itself the truth it denies the taxonomers. Second, its general principle involves descent with modification. Proceeding empirically, naturalists note similarities in the midst of difference, affinities shared across otherwise diverse groups, and find the explanation for "true affinities" in the fact of a common ancestor. Darwin writes:

> [Thus] all true classification is genealogical . . . community of descent is the hidden bond which naturalists have been unconsciously seeking, and not some unknown plan of creation, or the enunciation of general propositions, and the mere putting together and separating objects more or less.[96]

For Darwin's early scientific supporters, this was indeed the truth of things. Connections that had been merely postulated were now replaced by a thoroughly naturalized relationship of real blood; final cause was definitively displaced by an accomplished system of proximate causes; scholastic categories and the persistent anxiety that there may be infinitely many of them had been banished in favor of a principle that emerges as a *fact* of inductive research.[97] *Phylogeny* was the "magic word" destined to solve all the problems of biology.[98] That specific hope may have waned, but the view persists that the ongoing success of scientific thinking is grounded in the idea that nature is objective and that only in the systematic conjunction of logic and empirical experience can we find true knowledge.[99] (Indeed, the thought of a simple idea worked out in a coherent scientific practice and leading to complete knowledge has unrelenting biopolitical force and persistent popular appeal.) At the end of the nineteenth century, biology's new disciplinary structures could be made to coincide with a broad social and cultural conviction that it would soon give answers to the central questions of our existence, and moreover, as Müller-Wille and Rheinberger put it, "that these solutions would be the ultimate ones to be desired."[100] More recently, the Human Genome Project saw an outbreak of claims that its completion would be the completion of all we needed to know about our species, and the current Assembling the Tree of Life (ATOL) and Genealogy of Life (GoLife) projects are the subjects of similar claims.[101]

But can all this be laid at Darwin's feet? Note that final cause persists in Darwin's theory in the (Kantian) concept of purposiveness, specifically in the purposive concepts of "fitness," "selection," "struggle for existence," and "survival of the fittest," and evolutionary causality is difficult to fit into the structure of proximate cause. Note also that the source of Darwinian principles is a matter for debate.[102] Julian Sachs, a biologist and historian of biology writing in the 1870s, celebrated the emergence of the principle of developmental history out of observation, while the philosopher and historian of philosophy Kuno Fischer would understand Darwin's contribution as the completion of Hegel's teleological doctrine of historical world development. What Hegel had achieved in thought, Darwin fulfilled in the realm of empirical research, so that world history and natural history could be understood as completing each other at last.[103] That is to say, with Darwin, the *genos* can become historical. Cassirer writes:

> The historical, barely tolerated previously, was not actually to supplant the rational, for there is no rational explanation of the organic world save that which shows its origins. The laws of real nature are

historical laws, and only through their discovery is it possible to escape a bare logical schematism and get back to the actual causes of the phenomena.[104]

Thus, the laws that govern the naturalized *genos* arise in distinct temporal contexts, and they are meant to show how continuity and contingency, or, in Darwin's terms, descent and modification, are held together. After all, descent is a matter of offspring, not clones, and despite Buffon, every act of reproduction is also an act of generation that brings a new being into being. Each newcomer is an instance of the line of descent from which it springs, but we do not know which of the new ones bring genetic mutations or which mutations will produce adaptations, and we cannot possibly know which of these will turn out to be evolutionary adaptations. The occurrence of the mutation has no causal relation to the environmental condition that will be the occasion of its being naturally selected.[105] Any given mutation is contingent, and it is by chance that the environment changes in such a way as to select the characteristic produced by that mutation. (Some variations never meet their environmental match and, in a phenomenon known as random genetic drift, may happen to persist in the population without propelling any evolutionary development.)[106] The internal change that happens on the level of the gene and an external change in the environment meet in the organism. This is the essential structure of Darwinian (as opposed to Lamarckian) evolution. From close up, we experience every birth as a miracle of individuation; from a middle distance, if not every birth, then every splitting event (a misnomer, given the causally complex and protracted process I have just outlined) that produces a branch on the evolutionary tree is a natural miracle of speciation; from the furthest point of view, it is all natural history.

As far as taxonomy is concerned, descent with modification does nothing to resolve the tension Lovejoy described between the desire for sharply distinguished classes and a continuity between all beings. If anything, it intensifies it. For Darwin, there is a finely graduated continuity in the living world; the distinctions between species that *appear* obvious to us are a result of extinctions that opened gaps in the continuum. He writes:

> Extinction has only separated groups: it has by no means made them; for if every form which has ever lived on this earth were suddenly to reappear, though it would be quite impossible to give definitions by which each group would be distinguished from other groups, as all would blend together by steps as fine as those between the finest existing varieties, nevertheless a natural classification, or at least a natural arrangement, would be possible.[107]

All true classification may be genealogical, but, with all of life available to us, how would the classes be discerned, and how would we be sure there are not infinitely many of them?[108] It would not be a matter of *defining* groups, Darwin admits, but of picking out types that give an *idea* of the differences between groups, a practice of picking that suggests taxonomy as judgment and art.[109]

Yet what place could there be for art and judgment after the advent of genetic *science*? Darwin relied on morphology and could not himself satisfy the desire for self-evident self-identity, but note that this did not prevent others, beginning with Francis Galton, from using evolutionary theory to claim just that: self-evident races, racial hierarchy, and white supremacy. Meanwhile, Mendel's successors in classical genetics looked forward to finally drawing clear lines of descent and thus clear boundaries between genera.[110] Doing so would be the key to establishing the authority of the new science. They would go on to draw those lines, but only by means of a series of decisions that took up two particular experimental practices of purification and anointed them as foundational. First, when Mendel undertook his experiments with hybridization, which would come to be regarded as the birth of genetics (he published his results in 1865), he began by selecting a variety of pea whose purity had to be established in the course of several years of cultivation under carefully monitored conditions.[111] Second, when his experiments were rediscovered at the turn of the twentieth century and genetics began to emerge as a scientific discipline, it was in the context of a biopolitical deployment of the idea of purity across social and economic fields: animal breeding, the production of food and medicine, eugenics. Wilhelm Johannsen, the Danish scientist who coined the term *gene*, worked for a time in the research laboratory of the Carlsberg brewery, where brewers needed a pure line of yeast to control and make predictable the quality of beer. Johannsen understood his contribution to experimental basis of the new discipline of genetics to be the production of pure lines that could then by hybridized. As Müller-Wille and Rheinberger point out, purity functioned as an instrument of control in all realms. The productivity of work processes could be measured in relation to the input of *pure* materials. Products made with *pure* ingredients could be fixed and made predictable, recognizable in any place at any time. Indeed patents, trademarks, and seals of quality were developed specifically to underwrite marketing claims of purity.[112]

By the early twentieth century, Darwinian heredity had been received as the structure for understanding the generation of difference and genetics as the science of generation. Later, using mathematical models and statistical analysis, on the one hand, and practices of purification, on the other, the science of genetics produces numerical and apparently precise results.[113] Its results *look like* certainty, but a science of generation is a science of history and constantly finds itself having to account for impurities, contingencies, idiosyncrasies, the unexpected, the paradoxical, that is, the essential uncertainty of its temporal subject. It must concern itself with the relation of generation and time. Thus, Linnaeus's taxa could not account for all knowledge, and post-Darwinian, post-Mendelian heredity cannot give us self-certain, self-identical genera. "Community of descent" indicates a structure by which the generations of a group are related, but it does not confer fixed specific boundaries. This is why the revolutionary theory that began with *On the Origin of Species* continues to confront the question of speciation.[114]

After all, plasticity, or the capacity of a phenotype to respond to its environment, means that the relation between an organism's genetic constitution and its phenotype is not a straightforward causal relation but complex in every case and on every level.[115] At the molecular level, there are translations and edits—that is, contingencies—at each step from DNA to RNA to specific proteins. At the level of the organism and its life, a gene does not always make its presence felt in the morphology of the organism and does not always serve a function given the organism's particular environment. Since the relation of genotype and phenotype is plastic and since one genotype can produce more than one phenotype when exposed to different environments, it is impossible to read off the present genetic state of affairs from the study of forms—or even forms and functions—of the present population.[116] A gene may be present in the population but produce no observable phenotypic effect.[117] A member of a new generation may exhibit an atavism, or, in the case of taxic atavism, a whole population may revert to an earlier form.[118] The genetic material of an extinct species, for example, the cave bear, which died out about 24,000 years ago, can turn out to be present in the bodies of brown bears living today.[119] The genetic material of Neanderthals remains present in the bodies of twenty-first-century non-African humans. This plasticity and the gap it opens between the genetic material present at any given moment in the persistence of a *genos* and the character of the individual members of the *genos* mean we can think of an ever-present reservoir of genetic material available for selection, untapped potentialities hidden in the genome.[120]

Johannson introduced the term *gene* in 1911; Aleksandr Sergeevich developed the thought of *genofond*, or gene fund, in Russia in the 1920s; the American geneticist Sewall Wright introduced *genetic drift* in the 1930s, and the expression *gene pool* emerged in English in 1941. The term invokes a stream of genetic material that has gathered in a place isolated to some degree from the great genetic current of life in general or, more commonly, from the broad current of the species—hence the Russian *genofond*, for example, or the gene pool of influenza viruses in seabirds. In 1949, there emerged the term *genetic load* to describe genes that effect phenotype in ways that hamper evolutionary fitness in a changed environment.[121] The content of the pool is not determined, nor is it determinative. It will be fed by genetic flow from other populations, and certain mutations will slowly disappear from it. At any given moment, only some of the available genes will be manifest in living bodies, while others are passed, quietly, into the future. This is the gene's mode of being in time.

Discussions of time and evolution emphasize above all the long scale of evolutionary time compared to the span of a human life: life appeared on the planet 650 million years ago; the dinosaurs came and went over the span of 250 million years; humanoid animals have been here for 23 million years. The *genos* comes to be by virtue of persisting over many generations; the *genos is* by virtue of being past and future; it is the structure that makes this present the inheritance of all the ancestral pasts and, at the same time, the source of all that is to come, the crux of a self-generating order of inheritance and bequest. What counts as present in this generational sense is everything that has come to be the case. We think of this in terms of individuals and the cohort of those of us alive here now; genetics allows us to think of it also in terms of the genetic material that is present here now. It is not a matter of deciding whether it is all in our genes or all about individuals. Rather, when we make genes our focus, the temporality of the *genos* takes shape around the thought of the gene pool, underwritten by the phenomenon of genetic plasticity; when individuals are our focus, the temporality of the *genos* is experienced in the group of individuals and their relations and accessed through our experience of belonging to and with those who have gone and those who will come. The two temporalities—the time of the gene and the time of the individual—are not mutually exclusive.

Those implications become clear in the phenomenon of mourning. Genetics knows nothing of mourning; the generational flow of genetic material presents no occasion and no need for it. Mutation and modification occur constantly, and while some combinations persist and others disappear, neither the deaths of individuals nor the extinction of species appears as a loss on the level of the gene. The pool is the figure of continuity as slow-moving, nonlinear change. In contrast, the experience of the death of a singular, irreplaceable individual is the experience of an utter loss, and it is as individuals within a generational structure that we learn how to mourn, that is, how to undergo the loss of someone as a matter of both loss and continuity. Insofar as we experience loss in its completeness, melancholy and despair are no more than appropriate responses. Genetic time deflects the melancholy that would overtake individual time. Genetic thinking offers a basso continuo of reassurance that we cannot know that any such loss is irredeemable, and it authorizes the hope that something remains. Instead of melancholy and despair or forgetfulness and heedlessness, they together provide the possibilities of mourning and hope.

## The Unstable Clade and the Naturalization of Generational Being

Through the eighteenth and nineteenth centuries, knowledge of life shaped itself into a science, configuring the very concept of life, accruing the authority to describe it and simultaneously arrange and naturalize it.[122] As Foucault notes: "The sciences always carry within themselves the project, however remote it may be, of an exhaustive ordering of the world."[123] The earlier systematizers of the eighteenth century were at times unabashed as they acknowledged that their systems were inventions. Buffon writes: "There are only individuals in nature, and genera, orders and classes exist only in our imagination."[124] At other moments they are at pains to insist that their work was aimed at *discovering* what was essential to beings amid the array of accidental characteristics. Under the theory of preformation, a species was identified by the essential elements inherited from the original ancestor; the essence put in place at Creation was preserved by nature, and the struggle of the systematizer was to discern the essential in the least arbitrary way possible. In this way, the order in which living beings were arranged could be understood as dictated by nature and not by human reason.[125] The struggle continues. By the early nineteenth century, the search for order among beings was joined and then dominated by the search for order in the internal arrangements of beings; the organs of various living bodies and their functional roles seemed to point to function as the ordering principle that had remained mysterious until then.[126] In the course of the century, the source of the principle dropped to the level of the cell and, by the time of Johannson's contribution in the early twentieth century, to that of the gene. Each shift was a move toward smaller and simpler units of study and toward descriptions that depended less on the demands of system and more on demonstration by observation.[127] More significantly, each suggested a shift from a systematic ordering principle to an empirical ordering mechanism.

The disciplined *logos* of life was, for Foucault, both a product of bio-power and a mechanism by which power would control, optimize, and organize life forces in the name of life as such. Biology would facilitate harnessing the powers of the human body in global systems, on the one hand, and managing the species body by examination and control of the natality, living, sickness, and mortality of populations, on the other. He points to disastrous results: "It is as managers of life and survival, of bodies and the race, that so many regimes have been able to wage so many wars, causing so many men to be killed."[128] In the next chapter, I consider some of the successes that have reinforced the broad authority of genetics, but those triumphs cannot be divorced from the fact that imperial regimes colonized territory and settled land, traded in humans, and extracted re-sources in ways that worked bodies to death and caused so many *peoples* to be killed. Utterly central to the study of life as it struggled to discipline itself was the relentlessness of biological change that is experienced as the ongoing explosion of difference: This is why classification proves so essential and so difficult, why Linnaeus insisted that a taxonomy be agile enough to encompass unknown unknowns, why Darwin understood the problem of variation as a problem of time, and why Mendel's discovery of the mechanism of change over time brought on the emergence of the new field of genetics.

With the advent of a functionalist, mechanized biology, where—thanks to Mendel—the secrets of generation took on the transparency and rigor of mathematics, biology could take its place among the natural sciences and stake out life as its proper domain.[129] Biology could be *scientized*, shedding the suspicion of arbitrariness displacing it onto the human sciences; life could be *biologized*, and biological description empowered to naturalize its objects. Foucault, from *The Order of Things* through the late lectures on biopolitics, committed himself to complicating the scientistic narrative and showing that (on the archeological level) the knowledge of life bears a far closer relation to economics and philology, its appearance of transparency and self-evidence a glamour granted by its relation to other forms of knowledge.[130] Undermining the naturalness of generation would be the focus of his book on heredity, a work he sketched in 1969 but never published. He wrote:

> [Knowledge of heredity] developed throughout the nineteenth
> century, starting from breeding techniques, on through attempts to
> improve species, experiments with intensive cultivation, efforts to
> combat animal and plant epidemics, and culminating in the estab-
> lishment of genetics whose birth date can be placed at the beginning

of the twentieth century. On the one hand, this knowledge responded
to quite particular economic needs and historic conditions. . . . On
the other hand, this knowledge was receptive to new developments
in sciences such as chemistry or plant and animal physiology. . . . But
this dual dependence does not deprive it of its characteristics and its
internal regulation.[131]

Jacob's *The Logic of Life*, which was published in 1970, does this work,
with the distinction that where Foucault would have taken power as the
organizing concept of his investigation, Jacob took interpretation. The
approaches are not incompatible, but what Jacob makes possible is an
understanding of the struggle of interpretation, for example, the struggle
between an attitude of discovery and one of invention, as inherent in the
discourse of genetics. By the mid-nineteenth century, generation was established as the temporal hinge in biological description, the key to discerning patterns of change in the phenomenon of life. Heredity became
the order of biological order; the logic of generation is what united all levels of biological organization from the cell to large population groups.[132]
Moreover, since human life was now understood within the continuity
of life as such, generation was the naturalized pattern of our lives. This
would continue even after the expressions *life as such* or *life itself* fell out
of favor as too mystical and too closely tied to vitalism, giving way to a focus on the function, history, and structure of living systems. The study of
generation would continue as a hermeneutics of generational life.[133] Jacob
writes: "Evolution is the result of a struggle between what was and what is
to be, between the conservative and the revolutionary, between the sameness of reproduction and the newness of variation."[134] The struggle tends
toward increased interactions between organism and environment and,
at the same time, toward increased "openness," that is, ever greater potential for variation in how what is encoded in the genotype is expressed in
a given environment.[135]

When we study genotypes in molecular detail, classification becomes
a matter of arranging individuals by relations of descent, subordinating
one grouping to another according to grades of difference. That is to say,
members of a species have more in common with one another than members of a genus have with one another, who have more in common than
members of a family, order, phylum, and so on. Genes come to be understood as determining *genos*. In this way, the *genos* takes the form of the
clade, and, in the mid-twentieth century, cladistics emerges as the dominant mode of taxonomy. As Stephen Jay Gould describes it, cladistics is
"the science of ordering by genealogical connection *and nothing else*."[136]

A clade is the group of organisms descended from a common ancestor. Whether any given organism belongs in the clade is decided by appeal to information embedded within the organism, which can be matched with the information from the ancestor and all its descendants, including descendants yet to come. Shared identity is encoded, unambiguously and persistently, and, once a species' genome has been mapped, we can read that identity off in unambiguous terms.

Which identity? That is to say, which ancestor? Which clade? Gould's "*and nothing else*" is misleading.[137] As he notes, proper taxonomy requires two sorts of insight: the selection of the relevant phenomenon for study and the decision about which method for sorting the information will produce categories that indicate cause and process.[138] This does not mean that there is a propriety inherent in taxonomy as such or that proper taxonomy is universal in the Linnaean sense of providing a way to classify all that there might be but, rather, that any given taxonomy will serve its proper biopolitical purpose. After all, the causal relations of natural selection are essentially obscure, as we know, and the method for best allowing them to reveal themselves is by no means evident. If descent is the relevant phenomenon, each one of us can draw a (conceptual) family tree and come up with more than a million ancestors to choose from within a span of five hundred years (assuming that we descended from each ancestor by just one line).[139] A family tree is not the Tree of Life—we can't know of any evolutionary event within a five-hundred-year span—but in both cases, telling a million possible stories of descent tells nothing; belonging to a million possible clades is, from the point of view of taxonomy, as good as belonging to none. The arbitrariness that the eighteenth-century systematizers tried to minimize cannot be eradicated, with the result that we have to make judgments.

Genetics goads the desire for a true system, suggesting that study will yield more detail, fill in more gaps in our knowledge, and let us complete our genetic map. It lets us hope that the process will reveal true groups, endogenous, self-generating groups that can be shown to be more or less pure, groups that manifest the criteria for their own identity. But descent cannot itself provide the answers to the question of how much in common will count as enough in common at any given level or for any given grouping. Enough for what? Enough for whom? Enough for now? As Carol Kaesuk Yoon discovers in *Naming Nature*: "The ordering and naming of life was and always has been, at its heart, something much more democratic, subversive to the dominion of science."[140]

Yet if the taxa are not self-evident, they are also not arbitrary. Even as the scientistic desire is frustrated, the historical desire, far from hostile to evidence and method, is drawn along by the hermeneutic challenge of change and continuity. DNA counts as evidence, to be sure, and the logic of descent gives the narrative its structure of origin and development, but once *self-evident* has been replaced with *not arbitrary*, the question of value crops up everywhere. What is the arbitrating principle? What is this taxonomy *for*?[141] We saw Linnaeus explicitly offer his human taxonomies as devices for self-knowledge, folding them into the great biopolitical project of systematization as an aid to human industry and agriculture. In 1775 (and again in 1795), Johann Friedrich Blumenbach described himself as serving the purpose of human self-knowledge, arguing for the unity of humankind even as he—fatally—classified humans into five races. Kant saw himself as intervening in order to clear up some conceptual confusions.[142] Gobineau, meanwhile, simply made it explicit that *the* purpose of taxonomy was to demonstrate natural racial inequality and naturalize white supremacy.

A version of Blumenbach's classification remained the organizing principle for human biology and geography until as recently as 1972. Only in that year did biology devise a study to respond to the question: "How much of human diversity between populations is accounted for by more or less conventional racial classification?" R. C. Lewontin's answer in "The Apportionment of Human Diversity": 6.3 percent. He does not hesitate to spell out the moral:

> Human racial classification is of no social value and is positively destructive of social and human relations. Since such racial classification is now seen to be of virtually no genetic or taxonomic significance either, no justification can be offered for its continuance.[143]

Luigi Cavalli-Sforza made the point again with a substantial study published in 1994. In 1996, the American Anthropological Association made a statement on "Race," appealing to the same evidence.[144] But answers that are current among professed, disciplined biologists do not always surface in public or popular or folk biology. When Siddhartha Mukherjee published the bestselling *The Gene: An Intimate History* in 2016, his repetition of Lewontin's argument—now over forty years old—still attracted comment.[145] At the same time, to the dismay of many geneticists whose work he used, Nicholas Wade's *A Troublesome Inheritance: Genes, Race, and Human History* repeated old theories of biological determinism, and it too became a bestseller.[146] Georg Forster's statement from 1789 remains disastrously pertinent: "Most of the old divisions of the human species have long been rejected anyhow. Noah's sons, the four parts of the world, the four colours, white, black, yellow, copper red—who still thinks of these outdated fashions today?"[147] Who, indeed?

Lewontin's is an argument against *that* classification, not classification as such. Darwin sought the origin of species, and his observations revealed the relations among many of them, but the massive work of deciding where each being belongs continues. Lewontin reminds us that taxonomy is not basic science. That is to say, it is not the sort of elemental scientific activity that proceeds without hypotheses, the activity Wernher von Braun described as "what I am doing when I don't know what I am doing."[148] Basic science offers itself as its own justification; biological taxa, in contrast, find their value and justification in the macro- and micro-management of life.[149] The Assembling the Tree of Life (ATOL)[150] project (funded by the US National Science Foundation since 2009) is a self-conscious effort to do the basic work of completing what Darwin began, but it also acknowledges its instrumental value in the arrangement of life:

> Darwin's theory of evolution explained that millions of species are related, and dealt biologists and paleontologists the enormous challenge of discovering the branching pattern of the Tree of Life. Work on this great challenge is producing a map of species-relatedness through Earth history, and answering questions such as "what is the closest relative of a species?" and "what species make important products?"[151]

Important for whom, or to what end?

In 1830, Goethe wrote: "Nature and art are too sublime to aim at purposes, nor need they; for relationships are everywhere present, and relationships are life."[152] Relationships *are* everywhere, and making sense of life means choosing a set of relationships that will arrange life into taxa that are orderly and lively enough, scientific and historical enough, sufficiently capable of making life predictable in the face of contingency, even as that contingency inhabits the taxa themselves. Nature may not aim at a goal, but we encounter life in the organism, a being that is a nexus of relations with the form of purposiveness. The organism extends itself into its world and its future. Darwin chose relationships of descent. Cladistics chooses descent from a single ancestor. Any given attempt to draw a distinct branch on the Tree of Life means choosing a particular ancestor and attending to the lines of descent from that individual.

Like the Tree of Life, the family tree—for example, *my* family tree—is a figure of organic coherence. For Eco, medieval logical schemata were ghostly trees covering the real nature of things. Yet more haunting by far is the apparition of the complete tree, the one that would depict the nature of things completely. This tree—let's call it the Borgesian tree, since it is analogous to the famously complete map in Borges's "Of Exactitude in Science"—is the only figure that could present the mass of differentiated individuals, a tree of completion and distinctness, the tree of all relationships, a figure extending through all of life, each individual branch and twig unbearably distinct and ready to grow on and on or simply to stop, who knows which. All of life is there, just as all the territory is there in Borges's map. This is exactitude in life science. As the figure for the descent of species, the Tree of Life does the inexact sense-making work of plotting branching lines through the mass of historical data, discerning the nodes of the tree. Those nodes are the species-making changes that happen within individuals and populations and can only *turn out to have been* evolutionary events.[153] The Tree of Life does not show itself as it grows. We discern it as we study living and dead things, as we invent new modes of classification, and as we develop a capacity for making the judgment of what goes where. In this way, generational being is naturalized.

A family tree is either a pedigree or an ancestral chart. A pedigree is a figure that includes all who descended from a single ancestor or a single pair of ancestors; the ancestral chart is the inversion of this figure, showing my descent from—2, 4, 8, 16, 32, how many?—ancestors. Each tree would eventually encompass a large number of relatives, but the organizing element in each instance was an individual: The former is a tree-shaped graph naming ancestors of a particular individual, and the latter an inverted tree shape naming the descendants of a particular person.[154] In both cases, it is a process of tracing a linear pattern through a mass of individuals, ignoring collateral relatives, passing over the dark matter of unknown great great-grandparents, irrelevant cousins, bastard children, the children who didn't live long enough, the bachelor uncles and maiden aunts, the infertile, the exes, steps, and halfs, the ones who were adopted, the ones who did not receive the name or who got it and did not or could not pass it on. Who goes with whom? Who belongs with whom? With whom do I belong? It takes the Borgesian tree to show us that all belong to all. It haunts the figures we draw as answers to such questions, just as the possible infinity of categories haunts Aristotle's ten categories. Why *this* number? Why *this* tree? Why *this* family? Put another way, the self-evident, self-identical, endogenous *genos* remains the fantasy that gives shape to our longing to belong to past and future; it is also a fantasy of dispatching ghosts and guiltlessly consigning the untold dead to oblivion. The name for it, central to anthropology, the logos of humankind, is *kinship*.

# 2 / How Much Kin Does a Person Need?

> *The idea of belonging creates and undoes us, both.*
> —PADRÁIG Ó TUAMA, *In the Shelter: Finding a Home in the World*

> *The fact that man is by nature a social being means at the same time that, from the perspective of this distinctive human origin, he is familiar with the world both by nature and by historical generation.*
> —HANNAH ARENDT, *Love and Saint Augustine*

> *The tragedy of the man is that he was once a child.*
> —FRANTZ FANON, *Black Skin, White Masks*

## Introduction

In the previous chapter I asked how and why we valued the *genos*, and discovered a substantial obstacle to the investigation in the refusal of the *genos* to be a thing. That chapter began the approach to the phenomenon of genocide by examining *genos* in terms of the blend of pleasure, fantasy, joy, and security that it promises, but, far from a thing, *genos* turns out to be the way of generational relation, and far from satisfying the desire for those pleasures, it turns out both to provoke and frustrate it. Belonging to a *genos* is a mode of belonging to those who came before and those who will come after, and the *genos* sustains itself—though neither an *it* nor a *self*—by generation. Generation is the self-sustaining activity of reproduction and modification. Linnaeus found a place for *Homo sapiens* in the order of nature, but what does it take for us to then occupy *our* place in a taxon determined by heredity? When we entered the completed system of nature, the system entered us. Having found our place, we internalized it; having disciplined the living world into taxa, we disciplined ourselves.[1] For Kant, the truth of a taxon would be uncovered in the natural purpose embedded in the ancestor organism; therefore, belonging would involve finding that same purpose, or a derived version of it, embedded in me and my descendants.[2] The knowledge we then desired was knowledge of how *we* once were and how we came to be in our present state. That is to say, questions of identity would be answered by taxonomy, specifically by a historical taxonomy. This was the eighteenth-century fantasy of the *genos*.

How relevant can this be, now that we're all twenty-first-century hybrids? If the choice is between what Zygmunt Bauman called the dream of purity on the one hand and the celebration of hybridity on the other, or between the clean lines of racial hygiene on the one hand and the mess of sexual mixing on the other, of course we will celebrate the mix. Yet hybridity is not yet a solution. As Nicholas Thomas puts it, hybridity is "almost a good idea."[3] It has done the necessary work of demoting purity as a social end, but it has also affirmed its position as a taxonomical condition, efficiently obscuring the question of whether a pure line of descent is a matter of a natural kind or another epistemological *techne*. As we will see, the starting point—the desire to know where we belong—becomes intensified as a desire for absolute knowing and absolute belonging and then confused with a desire to belong to an absolute *genos*.

There is never *a* taxon, only taxa. We may belong to several at once, and what we experience—or long to experience—as belonging to a self-evident, self-generating group requires us to generate and police boundaries: this and not that, this because not that, us because not them. We must establish the distinction between groups before we can have them overlap; we must establish purity in order to give sense to hybridity. The anthropologist Stephan Palmié describes the process: "[Genera] are in no way mere reflections of empirically ascertainable, objective 'occurrences.' . . . They are the results of the work of situationally authoritative technologies of discernment and discrimination and their specific 'rules of recognition.'" The problem is that our taxonomic artifacts are taken as ontological givens, and the patterns of classification that are responsible for "hybridity effects"—in this case, blurring effects— are rarely if ever opened to scrutiny.[4] What Lewontin's 1972 paper might have been expected to do for the conversation within biology and beyond, Palmié's treatment of hybridity aimed to do for anthropology forty years later.

And still the fantasy of the *genos* has not gone away. If it manifested itself only and simply in violence, there would be no genocide paradox and indeed no special category of violence called *genocide*. As it is, the thought of *genos* drives genocidal attacks *and* conditions our cherished ways of being together as kin. We like the experience of belonging, but we all also need to belong with an intimate and inescapable need. We are at stake, which is to say that the approach to the problem is necessarily hermeneutic.

*Belonging* and *propriety* both speak of ownership, but propriety is derived from the Latin *proprius*, what is one's own, special, particular, or peculiar. Appropriation is rooted in *ad-* (to) and *propriare* (take as one's own).[5] In contrast, the Germanic *belonging* in its earliest sense means to go along with, to be proper accompaniment to, to be appropriate to. In

English, the verb *to long* at first meant both *to long for* in the familiar sense of desiring or pining after and also to belong with, thus incorporating both desire and necessary separation. Meanwhile, the archaic adjective *belong* has its roots in equality: The primary notion appears to have been "equally long, corresponding in length," whence "running alongside of, parallel to, going along with, accompanying as a property or attribute."[6] Thus, when *belonging* and *propriety* coincide, it is in companionship and suitability rather than ownership and appropriation.

The German *Zugehörigkeit* (belonging) suggests accompaniment, affiliation, and membership, but embedded in the word is *hören*, to hear. Hearing initiates belonging. For Gadamer, the knowing subject *belongs to* the object of knowledge.[7] We belong to the world—specifically, the tradition—that addresses us, and it is not insignificant that hearing is a passive sense. We cannot hear away as we can look away, and we cannot choose which address we hear. To use another of Gadamer's figures:

> The way the interpreter belongs to his text is like the way the point from which we are to view a picture belongs to its perspective. It is not a matter of looking for this viewpoint and adopting it as one's standpoint. The interpreter similarly finds his point of view already given, and does not choose it arbitrarily.[8]

The subject of the classic version of modern scientific method must approach the world as though from elsewhere or from nowhere, as if, extracted and abstracted from the world, it can choose its relation to the world. Acknowledging givenness and belonging turns us away from that familiar epistemology of nonbelonging.

The study of belonging is, then, a privileged hermeneutic reflection on world. We come to be in a context that we have no choice but to experience as *the* world, as world-as-such. It is our world—though we don't yet know to call it that—because its address provokes us to understanding. It conditions us as knowers. The world calls us, lays claim to us, puts us on the spot, and gives us what we need to begin to understand its signs, and we belong to it before it belongs to us. It is not required that I do indeed understand all the signs—complete transparency is not the criterion—but we find ourselves in the hermeneutic situation where belonging means having been introduced into the language and sign system as a passive and then also active participant in the activity of making sense.

We come to be by virtue of our passive initiation into the world and then our passive and active engagements in various worlds. The plural is significant. It only occurs to us to claim the world as *our* world in that moment when we realize that there are others, that is, the moment when we are addressed in languages and by signs we have to struggle with in a new way. The world that had been right there in the most intimate way suddenly addresses the infant across an appalling distance, and she develops the game of *Fort-Da*; the schoolchild is set upon in the schoolyard in ways he never experienced at home; the music lover catches glimpses of other worlds; the student encounters the world of molecular biology; the newlywed tries to understand his in-laws; the migrant scrambles to learn a new language; the patient tries to decipher the sign system of the medical-pharmaceutical complex. We encounter worlds, each with a history and tradition, each one addressing us. We will come to belong to some, but not all at once and not all in the same way, and we will not belong to them all.

If the subject of scientific knowledge studies the world from the condition of not belonging, so the subject of liberal politics is understood as choosing her relation to the world as though from an original position of not belonging. For Gadamer, it is the privilege granted to not belonging that most needs to be dismantled for the sake of the renovation of epistemology. More recently, Shannon Hoff makes the same argument for the renovation of political philosophy.[9] That is to say, an examination of belonging is needed for the sake of nothing less than truth and justice. When I turn here to an examination of belonging and not belonging, it is in the context of the tradition of thought that now includes these two as dominant positions. Gadamer writes: "Belonging is the element of tradition in our historical-hermeneutic activity, and is fulfilled in the commonality of fundamental, enabling prejudices."[10] These are the common, enabling prejudices I rely on here: that truth and justice emerge in the belonging-together of the knower and known, self and others, passivity and activity.

The title of this chapter is derived from Jean Améry's essay "How Much Home Does a Person Need?" At the end of a series of reflections on how he lost his home when the Nazis arrived in Austria in 1938, Amery concludes, simply, devastatingly: "It is not good to have no home." His essay takes a *via negativa*, expanding on the thought and experience of home-*less*ness rather than defining some thing that goes by the name *home*. Yet how can he describe his loss when the terms available to him, even *home* itself, had become so drenched in the Nazi imperialist ideology of blood, soil, *Heimat*, and fatherland? He rejects the cosmopolitan alternative and instead returns to those very terms: "Home ceases to be home as soon as it is not at the same time also *fatherland*."[11] As we will see in the case of family, our belief in what it should be survives many terrible experiences of what it is. What Améry lost in 1938 was the sense of being at home, as well as the protections that *should* be offered by home-as-fatherland. Also, on a level deeper than either, he lost his existential rootedness in the world.[12]

In the same way, *kinship* has been the name for patriarchal, sexist, Eurocentric, genetically determined structures toward which we may be deeply ambivalent, but it is not good to have no kin. I take this as axiomatic. *Kinship* names the structure of our generational being, our being between past and future, the exercise of nurture and mourning, our initial belonging to a world and the possibility that the world might continue (as ours) after our time. It is a vital part of the language we use to describe the injustice and the harm of generational violence. Yet how much kin does a person need? For survival? For solidarity? For identity? For flourishing? For now?

## Absolute Belonging: *Atavus* and Beyond

Long a political preoccupation for aristocratic and religious dynasties, genealogy became an obsession with blood in sixteenth-century Spain, a middle-class hobby throughout Europe and North America starting in the mid-nineteenth century, and a popular television phenomenon in the twenty-first century.[13] In 2004, the creators of a BBC celebrity genealogy series named their program *Who Do You Think You Are?* Each episode has the shape of a hermeneutic exercise, in most cases a more or less failed one. The specific initial question varies—Where were my grandparents born? What became of my errant great-grandmother? Am I related to somebody famous?—but they share the character of being the distinctive questions of a historical person. So far so good. Yet asking them under the supervision of that oddly accusatory question—Who do you *think* you are?—means that when we begin, we are already being invited to think in terms of the gap between the sense of ourselves we accumulate in a lifetime of acting, speaking, and being with others, on the one hand, and the truth of who we *really* are, on the other. We embark on any hermeneutic quest in the expectation of being changed—anything else would be a disappointment—but the difference is that we do not presume that there will be a truth of who I *really* am. A hermeneutic begins by putting us in question, but it fails if it concludes by putting us beyond question.[14]

Celebrity genealogy offers the exercise as spectacle. Its appeal implicates us in the pleasures of grand historical narratives and small human stories, schadenfreude and the celebration of diversity, the thrill of discovery and the horror of recognition. Public people attract our attention not least because they appear to have committed the constitutive Oedipal sin of acting as if they know who they are. As a result, we enjoy hearing about their families because the stories they cherish make explicit what they value about themselves, and a distinct pleasure of the spectacle is the possibility of a revelation that will dismantle the public persona and show who it is we're really dealing with. Each episode is crafted along a narrative arc that brings us to a nugget of truth—if not *the* truth—of *who* the subject is. In one of the early episodes of the US version, Sarah Jessica Parker finds out that she had an ancestor who died in the California Gold Rush and another who was accused in the Salem Witch Trials. "Wow," she says on camera. "It's changed everything about who I thought I was. Everything." These are the moments the show is made for. It introduces itself in just such terms: "Because to know who you are, you have to know where you came from."

Medieval genealogies took as their subject a group of relatives—a *truncus* or *stirp*—with the terms for individuals—*ipse* or *ego*—entering only in the eleventh century. Now the subject is—and must be—me, that is, you, me, a celebrity, or any one of us already guilty of Oedipal hubris. After all, we each act as if we are singular, self-conscious beings who can claim our actions as *our* actions, that is, who in acting can answer to ourselves the question "Who am I?" Genealogy asks "Where did I come from?" and reinserts those singular selves into a network of historical and geographical relations, expanding self-consciousness by deepening generational consciousness. The word *where* captures an atavistic ambiguity between people and places. Location and descent became empirically widely separated when colonialism settled large populations of Europeans in Africa and America and transported enslaved Africans to the Americas—even as it transplanted plant specimens from the soil of all continents into the imperial botanic gardens of Europe.

The formal distinction between who? and where from? followed, to atrocious effect. Kant observed in 1785, "The Negro Creoles in North America and the Dutch on Java remain true to their race."[15] That people could be transplanted to a new continent and have children with the same skin color as their parents rather than their neighbors was evidence for Kant of the racial germ. Now, in the continuing struggle with race thinking, location and descent bear down again in the question of belonging. If the starting point of the genealogical pursuit is me, the question that sets the hermeneutic under way is the question of where and to whom I belong. The desire to belong marks the *genos* as an affective order.

We belong *no matter what* to those from whom we descended, whoever they were. In this sense, genealogy TV programs are on to something. Such absolute and passive belonging is an ontological status, and to experience it without content is to experience it as though religiously, in the broadest sense of the term. "I belong, absolutely" is a statement as incomprehensible as Wittgenstein's example from the "Lecture on Ethics": "I am safe, nothing can injure me whatever happens."[16] Belonging "come what may" has the same affective appeal as Freud's "oceanic feeling."[17] (Wittgenstein regarded his example as worthy of deep respect; Freud had no respect at all for his.) Featured on another genealogy show, Deepak Chopra discovers more information about his forebears than he had thought possible and describes the experience as finding an opening onto the universe.[18] Yet rather than transcendent, it is an earthly belonging, born of the planetary fact that we came from and belong to the earth. Genealogical research is how we give discriminatory content to the feeling of belonging. It is not accidental that Chopra glimpses the universe through his family line: "Chopras all the way."

In one sense, we all belong to the same earth in the same way; that element of our being does not require a real or imagined other against whom to construe our belonging. In another, we each belong differently to our different parents. We share the condition of being somebody's child, but the fate of being the eldest daughter of my mother and father, born where and when I was born, is different from the fate even of my older brothers or my younger sister, different from the fate of all you sons and daughters of all the other parents. What needs to be thought through here, in the crux of the genocide paradox, is that in the existential gray area between being an earthling and being our parents' child, each of us could belong in many lineages, most of which we know nothing of. In terms of inheritance, we each occupy an intersection of ignorances. We will never know all the places we came from or all those people from whom we came, and identifying with one line of descent happens at the expense of the others that are disavowed, forgotten, or never known.

How we belong to our forebears shifts at specific generational removes: I am my parents' daughter in a different way than I am my great-great-grandmothers' great-great-granddaughter and in a different way than I am the descendent of a million distant ancestors. I merely know *that* there were such millions and can acknowledge them as conditions for the possibility of my coming to be; I may know the names of my eight great-great-grandmothers without having known any one of them; I knew my parents as closely as I have known anyone. Yet I belong to them all with that absolute, helpless, irrevocable belonging. There is nothing possessive about it. It is, rather, a matter of belonging to the past that brought us into

being and that we cannot appropriate, in the sense that there is no decision or action of ours that would bring it under our control or subject it
to our mastery. Actions cannot be undone; injustice cannot be made not
to have happened; the defeated cannot have their suffering and humiliation erased; the dead will remain dead forever, and I cannot not have
been born.

The ancestors belong to me as absolutely as I belong to them, but our
existential reciprocity ends there. Our helplessness takes different forms.
I could never have done anything about all the begettings and bearings
that eventually turned out to have been the empirical conditions for my
being born, but those ancestral begetters and bearers could have decided
to avoid procreation or to have had different children with different people. Yet they were helpless too. However deliberate they had it in their
power to be, however much control they had over their fertility, however
much freedom or thought went into their choice of partners, they could
not have known whom they would bring into the world. My great-great-
grandmothers may have imagined descendants, but none of them could
have known there would be me. My parents may have chosen to have a
child, but not even they could have known that that child would be me.
And yet, for all that—because of that—we each belong. Hoff writes:

> The individual lives inside broad worlds and structures of signifi-
> cance, and she is able to live a more or less meaningful and compe-
> tent individual life because of the various forms of involvement she
> has with these worlds and structures—the involvement of belong-
> ing, participating, enacting, mattering, and so on. She develops the
> capacity for meaningful activity as a consequence of being passive
> both to their formation and cultivation of her as well as to their
> meaningfulness.[19]

We did not choose to be or how or with whom we would come to be. Yet
we arrived configured for meaning into a world that is already meaningful and that was reconfigured by our arrival.[20]

Put in a way that acknowledges the passivity and activity of our existence as social beings and that anticipates the discussion of political
forms in Chapter 4, I might say that we are instituted, not constituted.
Adam Blair writes:

> We do not *constitute* the sense which we find in the world, but, in-
> stead, our structures of perception are *instituted* within the world, as
> general horizons that open onto being, which then develop imma-
> nently in concert with our environment. This immanent development

allows us to acknowledge the import of learning and upbringing—consciousness is not spontaneous ex nihilo—while also admitting to a degree of control and self-cultivation as we grow and learn.[21]

What do we think we know about the past that institutes us—*our* past? It is significant that in Athens by the mid-fourth century BCE, *genos* referred specifically to the three generations issuing from a single ancestor.[22] Even without knowing how that single ancestor was to be selected, this understanding of *genos* specifies a limited set of relatives I might know or have known and whose names and identities could be preserved in living, spoken tradition. This was not a clan or tribe but a group of people linked through a great-grandparent. The Romans identified a comparable break but set it further back. For them, the great-grandparents of my grandparents—the generation of the *atavus* and the *atavia*—lay definitively beyond reach. This marks a certain reality. Somewhere between my grandparents and their great-grandparents, living memory of the ancestors gives out, so that the *atavus* marks a point by which oral family history has generally failed.[23] What had been clear lines of descent reaching back from one person to the next now become branches fading in the direction of unnamed nodes. At this point, "To whom do you belong?" cannot be so easily answered with named, storied men and women, with the result that *my people*, plural, which used to refer to the many particular people from whom I came, becomes *my people*, singular, *a* people.[24] No longer able to answer the question "Who are my people?" we slip toward "What is my people?" as if these were the same question.[25] The diachronous project of filling in my ancestral tree cannot determine such a thing; beginning with me, the tree branches infinitely into the past and provides no criterion that will fend off infinitude.[26] We have to draw a criterion from somewhere else, and the ghosts of all the lineages not chosen and the ancestors still unknown haunt every selection.[27]

In contrast, the synchronous project of drawing a pedigree seems to banish ghosts from the start. That inverted tree grows from a single ancestor, identifying all his or her living descendants, and secures a place for me among them. Documenting the rhythm of generation and the geometrical increase in the number of descendants, the pedigree branches out but has its own limiting structure: To belong among these cousins I need only show that I belong to that ancestor. It is an elegant figure and a perilous one. Once the contingent, sovereign decision—this ancestor, not that one, him, not her—is made, once *a* family tree or a clade stands out against the Borgesian tree, the fact that it was a decision at all must be forgotten. This group, decisively delineated and consisting of those held together by the naturalized bonds of procreation, becomes both a natural group and the occasion of my experience of belonging absolutely. This is where we indulge the fantasy that the *genos—my genos—*is the embodiment of its own principle. The desire to know those to whom we belong absolutely is confounded with a desire to belong to some*thing* absolute, an absolute *genos*. It is a tragic longing, at best. At worst it is the pernicious conviction of the reality and exclusivity of race. There is nothing inherent in the thought of *genos* that can reliably intervene in the slip from best to worst. *This is why democracy had to be invented.*

## The Life of Blood

*Kinship* is the name for the object of our longing when we long to belong absolutely; it is the essentially generational structure that takes as its central element the relation of parents and children. *Kin* are those to whom we belong, and *kinship group* is the name anthropology used to identify the natural, self-generating *genos*.[28] Since it is a universal fact that children are born of parents, this would seem to be the natural, readily legible substructure to which all the varieties of human families and generational communities can be traced. Anthropology assumed so for 150 years; in 1969 Claude Lévi-Strauss could still refer casually to the "natural links of kinship."[29] But already in 1984 David Schneider demonstrated in his *Critique of the Study of Kinship* that "the way in which kinship has been studied does not make good sense."[30] Yet the tenacity and the social power of blood-thinking are exceptional. We remain committed to "our own flesh and blood" and understand a set of significant values when we are told that "blood is thicker than water," and we know what the television genealogists are getting at when they claim that "to know who we are we must know where we come from." It is also true that the language of blood remains a way of articulating the experience of a specific, genocidal injustice. We can call into question the status of kinship, blood, and nature as ways of knowing, but it's still wrong to steal people's children and kill people because of who their parents were, and the name for that is *genocidal violence.*

The conflation of blood and birth seems to come naturally, having been normalized and naturalized to such an extent that it is now difficult to trace the identification in historical terms.[31] Can we get a clear view of what a "tie of 'blood'" is independently of form and law? Blood runs through all of us, cold-blooded and warm-blooded, red- and blue-blooded, full- and half-bloods, and all men are brothers, but is there a natural phenomenon that is the foundation of any of these ways of speaking? Or is it a matter of what Claude Meillassoux calls the *ideology* of consanguinity?[32] The difficulty in unraveling these relations is not just that the conflation happened long ago (though only accomplished in the late Middle Ages) but that it happened in stages, lurchingly, inconsistently, and it keeps happening. Moreover, as Gil Anidjar argues in his theologico-political history *Blood: A Critique of Christianity*, it happens on several levels at once, in ways that sometimes reinforce one another and sometimes do the opposite but that always demand examination from several points of view, at the very least, according to Anidjar, "as *material* or physiologic substance, as a *symbolic* repository into which social energies are merely poured, [and] as a *metaphorical* marker that inherently structures the understanding."[33]

How do we experience blood? How does blood appear? (1) For a child it is a matter of the first blood that beads on her skinned knee, a fascinating new fluid emerging from her own body; when she turns to someone for help with the shock and pain of the scrape, she also wants to share the discovery. This is *her* blood. Before long, the association is made between any spilled blood—hers or others'—and that combination of distress and fascination; she goes to stare when another child falls and returns often to the scene in the film where the witch is struck by a spear and bleeds. Blood appears in being shed. This also holds for the blood that appears in Genesis, though the blood shed is brother blood, the blood of Abel spilled by Cain on the ground, from where it cries to God. There is no suggestion of a relation or identity between the brothers' bloods; instead blood is the mark of violence and death rather than kinship.

(2) Yet if, as Augustine reminds us, we are born between urine and feces, we are born *in* blood. Before the word *experience* has sense for us, the first ones to behold us see us bathed in blood that appears at first as the blood of our mothers. Only when we are wiped clean and the afterbirth has been delivered can the sources of all these bloods be traced: our mother's torn flesh, our own bodies, and the placenta and cord that joined them. Birth blood turns out to be three bloods: mine, hers, ours. Significantly, we do not appear as made *of* blood. Aristotle, who thought of the quickening of a fetus as the coagulation of menstrual blood by semen, acknowledged the difference between that monthly blood and the blood that is spilled when our skin is pierced. In Genesis, it is not blood but flesh, bone, and semen that are the stuff of generation.[34]

Even if we are not *made up of* mother blood, it is what surrounded us as we came to be, preserving, warming, and feeding, though not precisely touching us. Our mothers experienced our quickening, and the beat of her heart reverberated through us. We "heard" the roar of her blood flow before we had ears. It did not flow through us as through an organ or a tumor in her body but brought to the placenta the nourishment out of which our cells were assembled and on which we grew. The placenta is the site of an exchange in which the two bloods remain distinct even as material passes out of the maternal body into the internal amniotic space, out of the maternal bloodstream and into the blood of the fetus. This boundary makes it possible for the maternal body and the fetus to exist in the same place and yet be of different blood. The bloods are tied in an asymmetrical relation, one absorbing what is passed over the placenta by the other, one blood tied to the other as the necessary condition of its existence, one quantity (250 milliliters) accumulated out of the greater quantity (five liters) of the other. All of this happens in the body of the *gestational* mother, who may not be the genetically related mother; it is experienced and can be understood without recourse to what will later be understood as a genetic relation.

Maternal blood finally touches us as we come to light, covering our skin and getting into our eyes and mouth, meeting our blood wherever our skin is broken. Blood appears in the separation of the bodies. *It* does not establish a bloodline. We are washed so the world can get a proper look at us, meaning, on the one hand, that doctors or midwives who know about such norms can identify problems, abnormalities, or deformities and set in motion the process of intervention and rectification and, on the other, that the relatives can peer at us and decide if we look like our father or have our grandfather's nose. (Let us call these "grandfather's nose" conversations.) Out of those bloods and out of the ritual of washing them away comes the opportunity to be recognized by my father and his family and, simultaneously, the start of my being gathered, fashioned, and cultivated.[35]

(3) Does the blood of the father ever appear? Howard Eilberg-Schwarz argues that the appearance of blood does indeed mark the genealogies of the Hebrew patriarchs, but it takes the form of the blood spilled at circumcision: "[One] is brought into the covenant when his own male blood is spilled. His blood is clean, unifying, and symbolic of God's covenant."[36] Like begetting and bearing, it is something unchosen by the one who undergoes it. In one case, birth brings the child into the world; in the other, the father's decision ushers the male child into the covenant. Yet this blood is not the blood of his father. The act may be a repetition of the ritual induction experienced by his father, but what is replicated here is the spilling, not the blood. Neither the mother blood that appears at birth nor the father blood of ritual circumcision establishes or relies on genetic connection. After all, the conditions of the covenant with Abraham were that all boys born *in his household* must be circumcised, both those

he begat and those he bought. Circumcision is symbolic as the mark on the body of the boy that testifies to the father and master's commitment to the covenant. A boy becomes attached to the group by virtue of that choice, but the cut does not make the covenant the boy's inheritance. Nor does the blood of circumcision complete the account of bloods that remained unfinished when the mother's, child's, and placental bloods of birth were seen and wiped away. That accounting is still waiting for the blood of the father.[37]

The appearance of that blood is the central event of Freud's primal scene, manifesting the paternal claim and setting the family drama in motion.[38] Killing their father, the brothers complete the array of bloods that account for the blood of the generation of brothers. As well as a fantasy of possession—specifically, the sexual possession of the mother—it is a fantasy of completeness. My blood can be known once the blood of my mother and now also my father has been displayed. But what makes this victim a father? How does his paternity appear other than in his access to the mother, his assertion of the fantasy of exclusive control of her, and in his being murdered? His blood becomes father blood only in the act of its being spilled by the brothers.

In fact, the blood of the father historically exists first as a legal form. The Roman legal title of *consanguinitas* identifies the father's blood with the blood of the child. Under this law, we need not await the father's blood because it has already appeared at birth with the appearance of the child's blood, which in this schema is understood not as a new mixture of maternal and paternal but as identical to the father's. Here, for the first time, is a bloodline, and it is solely paternal. Maternal blood has no legal existence, and there is no recognition of the bloods of parturition as establishing a kinship relation.[39] Only in the late Middle Ages, at the moment when the notions of aristocratic and royal blood begin to emerge, does Christian canon law develop a doctrine according to which mother and father contribute to the blood of the child. This happens at the same time that the church begins to develop liturgies for marriage ceremonies, and it happens *before* shared blood becomes part of the medical account of generation. If we find this a shocking inversion of the order of things, it is because of modern science's success in establishing its own order, according to which inheritance is a natural category.

By this point, Christianity has developed the cult of blood sacrifice and has invented itself as the community of blood, a community that thinks of itself as held together by a substance. The blood of the Eucharist is shared daily; the blood of the Crucifixion is depicted constantly; bloody relics are cherished, bought, and sold. Babies continue to be born bloody, but this has no generational significance, since law has superseded appearance, and maternal blood is now recognized as a mark of kinship only on the model of the invisible, legal consanguinity of the father and child.

Once the bloods of generation have been identified juridically, they no longer need to appear. Indeed, they should not appear. If the line of paternal inheritance is legally described as a bloodline, it must be protected from the appearance of any blood that would threaten to confuse the issue by asserting its independent claim in the form of the maternal claim of birth. Mother and father are consanguineous with their offspring, but legally, invisibly so. I pointed out earlier that circumcision does not involve the appearance of the father's blood, yet supervising the circumcision of his sons is a blood ritual of mastery and fatherhood. One effect, if not cause, of the abandonment of the ritual by Christianity is that the question of blood is foreclosed once again. Since the law of consanguinity is now in place, sustaining or establishing a paternal blood ritual would be to protest too much; it would give expression to the anxiety brought on by the persistent appearance of that female blood, which serves as the sign of a privileged maternal claim and a reminder of the relative uncertainty of the paternal one. The question and the questionable character of paternity should rather be repressed at every turn and paternal anxiety displaced onto the elaborately repressive structure of the purity and honor of women. Father blood still does not appear; the female blood of the maidenhead is offered in its place.

## The Evidence of DNA

Blood is slippery, and it's everywhere, and we won't ever be finished with it. We will continue to talk of bloodlines, but insofar as blood came to be understood as our access to the biological specifics of generational being, it has been decisively overtaken by DNA. If I have my DNA tested and compared, I can establish, according to the *logos* of the *bios*, the relations of descent that blood was supposed to testify to. But how did DNA accrue the social authority of *evidence*? Evelyn Fox Keller describes the twentieth century as the century of the gene, beginning with the revival of Mendelian genetics in 1900 and Johannsen's devising of the term *gene* in 1906, followed by the identification in 1943 of the role of deoxyribonucleic acid (DNA) as the bearer of biological specificity, the 1953 discovery by Watson, Crick, Wilkins, and Franklin of the double-helix structure of DNA, the development of recombinant technology in the 1970s, and culminating in the Human Genome Project that ran from 1990 to its completion in 2003.[40] Genetic predispositions became discernable, for example, the mutations in *BRCA1* and *BRCA2* that indicate increased risk of breast cancer. Women who know their inheritance of the mutation can intervene in the pattern of heredity, specifically resisting the gene's determinative force by having preventative surgery, prolonging their lives, holding open their own potential for sustaining generational life. As Keller puts it, genes have had a glorious run, and the science of genetics made possible such impressive expansions of understanding and such exciting agricultural, medical, and reproductive technologies that its scientific developments were quickly translated into the language of business, nutrition, therapy, family, science fiction, and popular culture. Fox Keller has urged that this success should be the moment when glory gives way to humility and genetics recognizes the need for new and different ontologies.[41] The opposite has happened.

The case of DNA forensic evidence is crucial. So long as genetics was the language in which scientists and science writers were telling the story of life itself, and so long as it was grasped as the knowledge that drove biotechnology, the question of evidence could remain a technical matter for scientists and philosophers of science. In 1986, DNA entered law courts in the United States. The first exoneration on the basis of DNA evidence came in 1989; from that point the chemical structure of our cells was a matter for forensics, and the question of evidence was a highly public question. In the case of Gary Dotson, convicted of rape in suburban Chicago in 1979, virtually every source of evidence used in his trial turned out to be unreliable.[42] The victim had invented her story to protect herself from scandal, the state police forensic scientist presented garbled evidence of a match of body fluids based on blood antigens, the prosecutor had overstated hair "matches," the defense attorney had not offered the defendant's own unscathed body as refutation of the victim's claim that she had scratched him, the judge overruled the objections the defense attorney made regarding the matching hair evidence, the *Chicago Tribune* printed leaks from the prosecutor's office aimed at spreading disinformation, Dotson's own alibis mangled their stories because one of them had been driving on a suspended license, and so on. Even the promise of genetic evidence initially failed because the samples of body fluid had deteriorated over time. When a new test and comparison eventually showed that Dotson could not have committed the crime, the structures of the criminal justice system worked to prevent the evidence doing its forensic work. The prison review board failed to recognize the test result as requiring action of them; the governor of the state did not act because he reportedly wanted assurance that the evidence was evident enough; prosecutors vowed to resist the petition for a new trial. Finally, the Cook County Circuit Court judge declared: "It's my belief that had this evidence been available at the original trial, the outcome would have been different." The charges were dropped. Dotson had served ten years in prison.

Out of a forensic quagmire, DNA evidence emerged into popular consciousness as decisively evident.[43] Dotson's case was by no means unique: In the United States between 1989 and 2018, 353 convicts were exonerated thanks to DNA evidence. In a movement Alondra Nelson describes as trans-scientific, DNA moved beyond the traditional bailiwick of science and acquired a complicated scientific and social authority; it came to mean truth, justice for individuals, and racial justice.[44] After all, 219 of the 353 were African American, and against the backdrop of a criminal justice system with deep roots in slavery, racism, and the Thirteenth Amendment to the US Constitution, which ended slavery except as punishment, this put genetics on the right side of history.[45] If DNA could fight injustice and be evidence of what really happened, if it could show the innocent and the guilty, what else could it make evident? Could it tell us where we came from? Could it tell us who we really were?

Luigi Cavalli-Sforza asks the question with the whole of humankind in view: "Can the history of humankind be reconstructed on the basis of today's genetic situation?"[46] If I submit my DNA for genealogical analysis, the result is a chart that addresses me in particular but is articulate only as a comparison with the DNA of very many others. (The database of 23andme.com now contains the genetic information of over 10 million people, and the number is growing.) The more DNA samples analyzed, the more there are to compare, the more detailed an individual's chart will be, the more complete we can make our map of the human earth, and the more we will know about the history of humanity. This is how DNA appears on the level of earthly humanity. As biogeography—once again, the questions of who? and where from?—genetics describes the DNA of people living around the world, plotting genetic information onto place, and for Cavalli-Sforza, this in turn yields a history of the great human migrations.[47] DNA appears in the plotting of timelines, the color coding of world maps, and the arrangement of cladistics charts.[48]

Cavalli-Sforza has made a point of arguing against racist deployments of population genetics and against efforts to make racist claims in the language of genetic science. He argued early and often against the authors of *The Bell Curve* (1995). He also acknowledges the uncertainty built into his field of research thanks to the propensity of scientists to make mistakes and the impossibility of repeating history as though the world were a laboratory and history an experiment. He stresses the need for a multidisciplinary approach to his motivating question and effectively dismisses the thought of a pure race by carrying it to its "uninviting," incestuous conclusion.[49] But, in the face of the effort to map the human genome (*the* human genome) he poses his biopolitical question: "How many people do we have to analyze before we have done the job properly?"[50] It would be impossible to test everyone and prohibitive to test even a large number, so how could science capture most of the significant variations among humans? How can we get a good, detailed picture of today's genetic situation? The real question turns out not to be *how many people*? but *which people*? His colleague on the Human Genome Diversity Program, Allan Wilson, favored a simple geographic sampling: We should lay a grid over the globe and sample by transect.[51] But Cavalli-Sforza argued that the greatest variation would be found in populations that appeared to have been isolated for a long time. The clues to their isolation include their remote homeplaces, their distinctive languages and cultural practices, and their exotic bodies. By collecting blood from them—the San, Pygmies, Basques, and Yanomamo—we could look into our human past.

Indigenous groups disagreed. Cavalli-Sforza describes (what he experienced as) a successful journey in the 1980s to collect blood samples from Pygmies he knew in central Africa. But in the 1990s and the early twenty-first century, groups began to protest at being made objects of historical interest rather than living human communities and at being examined by researchers who were more interested in excavating their genetic past than ensuring the survival of the community. In 1993, the World Council of Indigenous Peoples labeled it "The Vampire Project."[52] After all, who would own the information? Who would profit from patents? Who would decide on medical research priorities? Who would decide on the fate of immortalized genetic strains? Would the results be used to challenge historical and cultural claims to territory?[53] At the same time, the project was criticized for relying on the antiquated notions of racial purity that its proponents were working to undermine. "Recent, urban" populations were taken to be a genetic muddle that could yield little information, whereas "isolated, indigenous," less mixed populations would provide more information. The project tried to avoid such questions, partly by positioning itself as pure science removed from the politics of populations. The anthropologist Jonathan Marks writes:

> These well-intentioned geneticists went to bed with the idea of a genetic repository of the human species—a nice idea, and one that has been proceeding on a small scale for decades—and they woke up on the cutting edge of anthropological ethics and bioethics—having to

account publicly for the apparent exploitation of the bodies of indigenous peoples in an ostensibly postcolonial world.[54]

The project was abandoned. It was replaced in 2005 by the Genographic Project, which pursues similar data collection but with two important differences: It does not claim to do so in the interests of medical research, and it is privately funded by the National Geographic Society, IBM, and the Waitt Family Foundation.[55] The stated commitments are optimistic and antiracist. Project Director Spencer Wells, who also serves as the project's public explainer, states: "We are all much [more] closely related than we ever expected. Racism is not only socially divisive, but also scientifically incorrect. We are all descendants of people who lived in Africa recently. We are all Africans under the skin."[56]

Yet, as Kim TallBear points out, it means little to say that all our ancestors came from a place we now call *Africa*, a name freighted by a colonial history that cannot be bypassed on the way back along the genetic line of human descent.[57] Also, the thought that science can show the incorrectness of racism misses the point that racists also appeal to science; they just tend not to be concerned with its correctness. Even as the disciplines of population genetics and physical anthropology strive to challenge racism, they remain entangled in the structures of *genos* that undergird race thinking. Even as they celebrate the blurring of lines that were thought to separate us and make a theme of our genetic relatedness, geneticists and DNA genealogists find themselves simultaneously seeking out disparity and discreteness.[58]

## Genealogical Thinking

In this way, DNA takes on the authority of absolute knowledge that suggests absolute belonging, though we appeal to it in differing and contingent ways. Sometimes it responds to the question "Belonging to whom?" and sometimes to the question "Belonging to what?"—and the difference is profound. To slip from one to the other is to slip from ancestry to race. Why the two questions stand within slipping distance and why the slip happens so frequently are not easily accounted for and are worth examining here in the experiences that show varieties of genealogical thinking: (1) genealogical curiosity; (2) genealogical bewilderment, as it appears in the testimony of those separated from their biological parents and as it features in the debate over anonymous gamete donation; (3) genealogical orientation and reorientation; and (4) genealogical disinterest and exhaustion.

## Genealogical Curiosity

*Finding Your Roots*, the US public television series hosted by Henry Louis Gates Jr., represents a new generation of celebrity genealogy programming. Here, guests investigate their family histories first through family lore, then in the historical archive, and finally (unlike *Who Do You Think You Are?*) by offering up a cheek swab and having their DNA analyzed and compared. The premise is made explicit: "By decoding our DNA and revealing the diversity that is hidden in the branches of our family trees, we'll discover just how blurred the lines that divide us really are."[59] Each guest is presented with a DNA pie chart, which is then discussed as a picture of who she is: "You are 12 percent Native American, 28 percent sub-Saharan African," etc. The designators marking the pieces of pie are all geographic, usually referring simply to continents, but occasionally they are made to refer to more specific groups: Ashkenazi, British, Iberian, Ibo. Each chart does indeed show a diversity of genetic origins, and each one is offered as further evidence of blurred boundaries.

I fear that the premise perpetuates the problem. Imagine the most satisfying of surprises in such a show: An antisemite is presented with a chart showing that she has Jewish ancestors, or a white supremacist turns out to be descended from Black forebears. The racist is convinced of the ontological claim that where you come from *is* who you are, but this is also the unspoken premise of the show's epistemological-ontological claim that to know who you are, you have to know where you come from. The racist declares that the divisions between the races are *real*; for Gates, DNA analysis shows that the blurriness of those divisions is *real*. Both reinforce the expectation that by showing us what is in our cells, science can tell us where we *really* come from, set us straight about who we *really* are and where we *really* belong.

We speak of blood as the *material* substance of kinship, though it doesn't appear as such. We speak of DNA as the material code of our relations and must consider how *it* appears. Blood spills without anyone asking it to; DNA shows itself only in answer to a question that, very often, has been an encoded expression of the anxiety that permeates patrilineal societies: "Who's the father?" The opinions traded casually and ritualistically about whom the child looks like—the grandfather's nose comments—are translated when necessary into the probability-tending-to-certainty of the genetic paternity test. In these tests, DNA appears in the form of a table of figures arrayed in three columns, each one displaying the codes for a set of genetic markers in the cells of the child, the genetic mother, and the alleged genetic father. Paternity appears in the relation of all three columns: what genetic identifiers the child did not receive from her mother, she must have had from her father; the information in the paternal column must fill the gaps left after the comparison of the DNA from mother and child. Thus, genetic truth emerges. The data appears in figures and columns, but it acquires its meanings in the conversation between a woman and a man, in a law court, or in the spectacle of reality television, all of which happen within a kinship structure still shaped by biologically construed norms.

On the level of kin, it is a matter of asking "Who were my forebears?" and submitting my DNA for comparison to a large—but selective—pool of data. Genetic code identifies relationships, and *Finding Your Roots* sometimes uncovers genetic evidence that fills a specific gap in the historical record. For people whose enslaved ancestors were not named in the US Census before 1870, this can mean an explosion of information and an incomparable satisfaction.[60] Deval Patrick, the first Black governor of Massachusetts, had his Y chromosome compared to the Y chromosomes of descendants of the family that enslaved his ancestors. CeCe Moore, the show's genetics expert, writes: "It was very clear that Deval carries the Y-chromosome of the original Wetmore immigrant, Thomas Wetmore of Middletown, Connecticut who was born about 1615 in England. We even identified a candidate who was extremely likely to have been the father of Deval's direct paternal enslaved ancestor, supported by DNA matches to one of his [named] descendants as well as others with shared ancestry."[61] This was possible because the Whitmore/Wetmores of New England had archives and family lore to support a dynastic sense of themselves, enough to lead them to set up and sustain an active DNA project to which family members—those who bear the name and/or already have a place in the family tree—had contributed their genetic information. For Patrick, DNA directs him back into the historical record and the world of narrative, adding a name where there had been an empty place in his own family tree. For the Whitmore/Wetmore family tree, it meant that an unacknowledged scion could now be recognized.

The moments of recognition are not always simple or easy. When the education reformer and author Geoffrey Canada traced his lineage to enslaved ancestors in Franklin County, Virginia, genealogists identified the slaveowner who was probably Canada's ancestor and also identified the white descendants of that owner. They declined to submit DNA or participate in the show. Canada responds on camera:

> I've always hated slavery and always felt "Thank God I had nothing to do with it." And [now] maybe my ancestors were very much

part of this system so, in some sense, I have to claim both sides of this equation. You can't push this off on one group without assuming some responsibility, I think, ourselves, and that's what makes this so complicated. That's what makes, I think, being an American so complicated.[62]

Notoriously, in an incident that led to the show being suspended temporarily in 2015, the actor Ben Affleck successfully lobbied Gates to leave out the fact that one of his ancestors was a slaveowner. Once the incident became public, Affleck wrote:

I didn't want any television show about my family to include a guy who owned slaves. I was embarrassed. The very thought left a bad taste in my mouth. . . . I regret my initial thoughts that the issue of slavery not be included in the story. We deserve neither credit nor blame for our ancestors and the degree of interest in this story suggests that we are, as a nation, still grappling with the terrible legacy of slavery.[63]

If DNA shows us new branches of our family tree and leads us to otherwise unknown names and stories, that's surely a good thing. If it gives African American families access to information about their forebears that is otherwise denied them by historical racist practices, that's also a good thing. If it produces a ferment of embarrassment, satisfaction, inspiration, regret, and pride; a bad taste in our mouths; reflections on responsibility, credit, and blame; and grapplings with the legacy of slavery, this is a good and politically necessary thing. But if DNA shows itself in the form of a racial pie chart, what does that show us, other than a racial pie chart? Dorothy Roberts puts the case starkly:

The ideology of race as a natural division between human beings that is written in our genes will have devastating political consequences. It can serve as a linchpin of a new, already emerging biopolitics in which the state's power to control the life and death of populations relies on classifying them by race.[64]

The invention/discovery of the gene in the late nineteenth and early twentieth century gave us a path for thinking about the causes of family resemblances in terms of the material structures of our bodies. It was an era dominated by the ideology of purity. Roberts argues that biological race and genetic determinism are two powerful ideologies that have been ascendant in America since that time and that have a large and—more troublingly—growing influence on public policy and public understanding. Even if the scientists who frame the Human Genome Diversity Project and the Genographic Project are insistently opposed to genetic determinism, and even if one of the leaders of the Human Genome project can state that nothing was learned from the endeavor, the producers and consumers of folk biology remain eager to accept genetic explanations for social relationships and behaviors because they believe that race is inherited biology.[65] Roberts writes: "These race-gene claims simultaneously confirm the myths that races exist in genes and that genes can tell us everything about ourselves. Together, they support a biological explanation for the widening racial chasm in health, incarceration, and social welfare."[66]

## Genealogical Bewilderment

We need enough kin to support and feed us and keep us socially alive here and now, for the time being, to be sure, but we also appear to need kin to anchor us in the past and orient us for a future. We need ties to others who are here with us but also to those who are not here, no longer here, and not yet here, and the persistent figure for this has been the bloodline and the genetic relation. We may not dismiss genealogical curiosity as idle curiosity. The number of viewers of television genealogy shows, the amount of writing and reflection on the theme, and, most of all, the vast number of people who have submitted their genetic material for analysis mean that it is a phenomenon to be reckoned with. After all, if some—the poor, the enslaved, nonwhites, migrants, indigenous people—have left little trace in the archive and have lost the social resources for transmitting lore, that is, if they have fewer avenues for satisfying their genealogical curiosity, DNA analysis is of particular value.

Hoff's phenomenology of belonging identifies our need, at the most general level, for a set of kin a generation older who beget and conceive us, bring us into the world, and sustain us here. These need not be the same people. It is not insignificant that they very often are, but, just as the roles of begetting, conceiving, gestating, delivering, feeding, and caring are conceptually and functionally distinct, so the individuals who perform those roles are empirically separable. Each term indicates a mode of being tied to a world, materially. Each of these specific actions ties the actor to a new being and to their shared world and draws the newcomer into relation, that is, draws her into the world. Hoff writes:

> First, there is an organized material reality in relation to which we
> develop the basic bodily engagement that lies at the root of our

development, which I will call "intermateriality." To be a person is to be passive to a specific material reality and a specific set of material conditions out of a relationship to which I emerge as the specific individual I am; to be a person is to be defined by "intermateriality."[67]

Modes of material relation indicate different relations to experience. The existence of our genetic parents is a material condition for the very possibility of experience, but the question of our experience *of* them can be postponed—indeed, postponed indefinitely.[68] Our initial intermaterial experiences are of being held, touched, and fed, and the attachment of carer and the one cared for is more relevant than a genetic connection that is inaccessible to experience.[69] In Hoff's terms, we come to be *intersubjectively* in relation to "specific people whose attachment to us cultivates us as beings capable of action," and in a *context* that eventually makes specific actions available to us. The intermaterial genetic connection may dispose our parents to care for us, but it cannot by itself institute the *experience* of heredity for the newcomer; rather, we must be introduced *to* the social structures of generation and ancestry even as we are introduced *into* them.

The groundwork is laid as soon as someone peers into your newborn face and begins the "grandfather's nose" conversation. For sociobiologists, this phenomenon grounds social belonging in genetic belonging. R. I. M. Dunbar writes:

> Evolutionary biologists have been inclined to insist that . . . a relationship [between biological kinship and cultural kinship classifications] does exist, mainly on the grounds that cultural kinship classifications are never entirely arbitrary with respect to biological kinship. . . . The fact that humans sometimes make some kinship assignations that have no basis in biological kinship does not, in itself, invalidate this claim.[70]

Yet for social anthropologists, the emphasis is reversed. Alan Barnard points out that biology is one *logos* among many, and human groups have understood the relation between generations, and the connection between sex and birth, in various ways. Barnard writes:

> "Kinship," as defined in the human context, depends on the existence of [culturally articulated] rules, which in turn are understood by ordinary human beings in relation to culturally specific sets of linguistic and extralinguistic categories. The notion that kinship has a biological foundation is really dependent on the cultural definition of "biology." Even in Western societies [which emphasize biological

relation], "biological" kinship is often as much a metaphor for social relations as a statement of relevant biological fact.[71]

How does *genetic* kinship enter our experience? We cannot remember the first time that conversation was carried on over our cribs. These observations are by no means universal, but they are ritualized in patrilineal, Western cultures, and, if we grew up in such a culture, their repetition was a key element of the process by which we were inculcated into our familiar world. It is a process that institutes the *genos* as a norm and simultaneously gives us the expectation of a *genos* to love.

The concept of genealogical bewilderment was introduced into the language of psychological counseling in 1952 and has received renewed attention in the era of conception by sperm or egg donation.[72] In an article—"Children without Genealogy: A Problem for Adoption"—Erich Wellisch argued that adopted children who have little or no knowledge of their "natural parents" (that is, birth parents) suffer because of their ignorance.[73] (This interpretation has had a new lease on life in contemporary debates over whether to permit anonymous sperm and egg donation.) In 1967, his colleague H. J. Sants offered the observation that not knowing can become a focus of anxiety and obsession for adopted and fostered children.[74] He quotes an eight-year-old boy in foster care: "I do not know nearly enough about my Daddy. I'd like to find out some day where he is. I'd like to know his address and send him a letter."[75] The boy's distress is heartbreaking. The *genos* is far from his mind; he wants to know the *one* to whom he belongs. In Hoff's terms, the longing for the unknown father may be the form the boy gives to the inchoate longing for an enduring, specific attachment that would allow him to come into his own. It is not irrelevant that he speaks from an experience of life in the temporary condition of foster care. However, Sants claims that not only adoptees and foster children are susceptible:

> Genealogical bewilderment may be found in any family where one or both of the natural parents is missing. Thus step-children and foster-children may show this condition, as well as those reared by one natural parent in the absence of the other, most commonly the illegitimate children of unmarried mothers.[76]

In a society (postwar Britain) and a profession (clinical psychology) committed to the principle of normality, the figure of the normal family—father, mother, their biological children—is the enabling hermeneutic prejudice. For Wellisch and Sants, normal psychological development requires knowing those to whom we belong biologically because only

"natural parents" can provide the right love and care and because the biologically related family is the mechanism for the transmission of genealogical knowledge.

Kim Leighton points out the gaps between the evident pain of the
eight-year-old fostered child and the conclusion that his abnormal family
is its cause.[77] As Sants himself notes, bewilderment is not universal among
those growing up without one or both birth parents. Meanwhile, people
living with substitute parents are not the only ones who feel estranged
from the people who raise them; children growing up with the very ones
who engender them are known to hope and wish for the moment when
they discover their different, better, "real" parents, what Freud dramatizes
as the family romance.[78] Indeed, a developmental period of detachment
from the people most attached to us has a better claim to universality. In
this context, Sants's argument stands out as making a seamless transition from parenting to ancestor veneration, from forebears to a people.
He writes:

> In adolescence, when the normally maturing child is satisfactorily
> weaning himself from his parents through displacement of tender
> feelings on to wider groups such as clan or family, it could be argued
> that the genealogically deprived child is handicapped by not know-
> ing which clan or family he belongs to. . . . The disturbance ensuing
> when it is not possible to identify and incorporate [oneself into a line
> of ancestors] suggests that some incorporation of ancestors into the
> self-image does normally take place.[79]

The order of inference is confused: The norm must be *assumed* before "the
disturbance" mentioned can be discerned as such. In this vision of normality, the ones whose genes we carry, the ones who sustain us, the ones
whose care cultivates agency in us, and the communal context that offers
specific possibilities of action for us, the ones whose deaths we mourn,
these are all assumed to be identical, and our identity is formed in seeing
ourselves in those people and their context. The operations of generating
offspring, nurturing children, and transmitting a culture collapses into a
single naturalized operation of generational family life. Ignorance of one's
more distant ancestors is presented as part of the harm suffered by the
genealogically bewildered. For Sants, it is not a separate argument; the
problems that spring from the lack of one or both one's birth parents are
of a piece with the problems that spring from not knowing one's grandparents, one's *atavus*, and one's race.

The appeal of this figure—and its danger—lies in the promise of self-
identity that it holds. One adoptee, in a letter to the Canadian ethicist

Margaret Somerville on the question of anonymous gamete donation, protests the practice in terms of a genealogical distress Sants would recognize: "You are not only encouraging people to intentionally separate people from their families, you are going to be the cause of people who have to question their identity, and no one on this earth should ever have to do that. How dare someone take away someone else's freedom to know themself!"[80]

Yet the figure makes less sense when we approach it from the point of view of experience. We are not born knowing who or what we are, and any knowledge of ancestors that we later acquire does not close the circle of our being, confirming what we already knew all along. All the "grandfather's nose" conversations, the childhood stories of dead forebears, the patterns of given names and family names, the legal and genetic laws of inheritance, the genealogical research, even the cheek swabs, go to hide the fact that our *experience* of heredity is not obvious and that we cannot count on it to yield certain belonging. Leighton writes:

> Genealogical bewilderment thus comes from the fundamental uncertainty of becoming a kind in the context of heredity. If our (imagined) heredities seem to be like the (imagined) heredities of the people who provide us loving care as children, we will be recognized as real members of their clan. If our (imagined) heredities don't seem to be like the (imagined) heredities of the people who provide us loving care as children, then the question of our clan membership becomes a problem. The problem is how to prove membership in something the reality of which is itself uncertain. Without evidence of family membership that is beyond doubt, the family to which we belong could seem arbitrary, and the knowledge claim that our family is our real family, becomes unverifiable.[81]

What Sants presents as a cycle of reassurance and recognition in the face of such uncertainty cannot provide the experience of absolute belonging, and what it does offer comes at a cost. When the bonds of genetic inheritance are wound so tightly, other bonds strain and break; when we counter uncertainty with an insistence on blood-belonging, we narrow our possibilities, not least the possibility of belonging to more than one family, of having more than one identity, of there being more than one kind of kin.

The ones who beget and bear us may not be the ones who nurture us, but we cannot separate the experience of coming to be and the experience of inheritance. It is never a matter of first being born, having our basic needs for food and protection met, and only then beginning the process of being inculcated into the world. We come to be by being attended to by people who had in their time been fed and tended by those of the generation before them, and all of the ways in which this is done is a matter of culture. There is never a moment when we merely *are*, individually or singularly. We *are* singularly plurally generational. Transmitting the logos of a *genos* is an integral element of what it is to be a parent or caregiver, because to tend the new generation is to be a conduit between the new and the old, the ones who are coming and the ones who have gone. Sants gets this right; the mistake is in thinking this is only understandable, or even best understood, as a set of genetic relations that commits us, beyond the *atavus*, to a logic of race. Unless we understand it instead as a practice of cultivation—that is, of tending what arrives, sheltering what is given, making claims and answering them, remembering the dead—that is, of culture and world creation or context creation, we cannot spring the trap of race thinking.

## Genealogical Aspiration, Orientation, and Disorientation

We embark on a genetic genealogical search in the hope of evidence that is beyond doubt. Few African Americans have as much success as Deval Patrick in tracing a line of inheritance beyond or even up to the *atavus* and *atavia*. Even for him, the earliest named ancestor is an Englishman; his African ancestors remain unknown, and for almost all, the Middle Passage is a definitive break that not only shapes tragic longing but also injustice. It may also be the source of an aspiration for Africa, the desire for a connection with an ancestral place that was home to one's people then and whose present population is in some sense one's people now. Called upon to do so, DNA addresses that break. On its own, it has no authority to lodge a person in a dynastic history, but it points to *possible* inheritances. The evidence will be categorical but not precise.[82] Will it be beyond doubt? This depends on whose doubt, and when.

The African American actor Isaiah Washington was spurred to submit a DNA sample for comparison to AfricanAncestry.com because of a "feeling of being adopted," which he experienced as a need to find a connection with people he could acknowledge as *his* people in Africa. AfricanAncestry's database at that point contained genetic information from two hundred different ethnic African groups; Washington's test showed that he had genetic similarities with present populations in Sierra Leone (a mitochondrial DNA match, which tracks inheritance in the female line) and in Angola (through shared Y-chromosome, or patrilineal, DNA). He responds to the information: "All the external things that I thought I needed to connect me to Africa were now unnecessary. Africa had been inside me all along."[83] Yet, whatever is inside, however we and Washington understand that, we perform ourselves, and the categorical knowledge of what had been there all along was, at the same time, imprecise for his purposes. It gave him *two* peoples to whom to belong; a larger database for comparison might have given him more. After all, AfricanAncestry's sampling of two hundred African groups seems extensive until we know that 250 ethnic groups are identified in Nigeria alone. He chose to belong among the people of Sierra Leone, where he attended a homecoming ceremony; established a foundation to support schools and hospitals; was ceremonially inducted into the Mende community; and received his Mende name.

If Washington embarked on his genealogical research out of bewilderment, others do so with an existing orientation. Alondra Nelson describes the experience of a genealogy researcher who identifies as Hottentot on the basis for family lore and who did not feel immediately compelled to give up that identification once a mitochondrial DNA test placed her forebears among the Akan of Ghana. Her response from AfricanAncestry.com included a certificate saying she was Akan, but this was in no way decisive for her. She was committed to the reliability of DNA information—"I've seen people let off jail sentences based on DNA ... I'm not questioning about DNA"—but in fact took it upon herself to decide what her results meant and to do so in her own time. She talked to her genealogy group, struck up a friendship with a Ghanaian neighbor, and attended cultural events, challenging not DNA but those who thought to interpret it on her behalf. DNA evidence is always underdetermined for genealogical purposes; those who produce it offer knowledge that is far from specific and always ahistorical, generating what Nelson calls the paradox of imprecise pedigree.[84]

Nelson argues, with some optimism, for openness to the techniques of the digital and genomic age not as decisive interventions but as tools for various political and social efforts.[85] Genealogical searchers like Washington use their genetic results to open up new avenues of social interaction and engagement. Through such negotiations, Nelson writes, contemporary racial politics have begun to move into the terra nova, if not the terra firma, of genetic genealogy. Yet it is a tentative optimism. In the pleasure and relief of finding a place in the world, we can forget the violence in each genetic claim that takes the form "I am Ibo" or "I am Welsh" or even the fractioned or percentaged "I am half-Greek" or "10 percent Icelandic," the violence that blocks out all the other branches of one's pedigree. Also, while the movement from ancestry to race is not a simple or inevitable shift, it is a slip along a path greased by the nostrums of popular science. The problem is not that the same sort of evidence that now produces affirming stories of returned lost sons and daughters of the group is the sort of evidence that was once used to produce justifications of slavery and is still heard in apologies for white supremacy. The problem is the extent to which the evidence of our bodies, the truth in our genes, is regarded as obvious, natural, and incontestable.

## Genealogical Exhaustion as Social Exhaustion

Some who use DNA to answer genealogical questions speak of "genetic kin" or "genetic cousins" in the ancestral homeland or in a diaspora. *Cousin*, like *kin*, is a capacious term that names, creates, nurtures, and perhaps enforces a sort of relatedness that comes to be specified into more particular modes—*cousin on my mother's side, second cousin, cousin in America, distant cousin, Cousin Eddie*, and now *genetic cousin*—depending on the question asked and the kin we need. A genealogical investigation can never get to the end of it, not least because we exhaust ourselves along the way. Jeanette Edwards and Marilyn Strathern's study of the people of Alltown, Lancashire, England, show how a kinship group evades definition in practice.[86] Shifting their focus from social and biological relations to modes of relatedness, they sidestep the anxiety produced by the Borgesian family tree; none of the sets of connections they describe in their study is infinite. All of them peter out, not because of the extinction of genetic lines but thanks to lack of interest or social exhaustion. There in Lancashire, an English population that might be expected to present all the features of the familiar Eurocentric kinship model, turns out to use *own, our own*, and *disown* in ways that include people and exclude them according to a shifting and unpredictable set of criteria. People are directly connected to one another or linked through mediating people who may or may not be relatives. Some people drop off the chain of connections and fall out of the group, whether they are relatives or not. Edwards and Strathern write: "Limits are set by how far one wishes to claim—or own, or own up to—such connection."[87]

Kinship is made up, put together out of what's available in response to what we need. The kinship group may be a self-limiting group after all, but with the limits provided by the contingencies of lack of affection, interest, or time, all of which the authors regard not as external factors that interrupt the endless chain of kin but as internal to the workings of kinship. What is crucial is that the responsibility first felt in the context of familial belonging—in the case of mourning, the desire to keep something of the ones we know and love—passes into the context of kinship as a responsibility to remember a more expansive group of "our dead." But who are they, *our* dead? Whose dead? How far back? There is no principle that answers the question for us. The originary existential responsibility is a practice of *making genos* that reckons with the limits of interest, forgetting, and what we might call memorial and genealogical exhaustion.

## Creating Kin

Frederick Douglass writes in his 1845 *Narrative of an American Slave*:

My mother and I were separated when I was but an infant—before I knew her as my mother. It is a common custom, in the part of Maryland from which I ran away, to part children from their mothers at a very early age. Frequently, before the child has reached its twelfth month, its mother is taken from it, and hired out on some farm a considerable distance off.[88]

His mother was sent to a farm twelve miles away, and on a few occasions she managed to see him, setting out at night to walk to where he was, lying with him as he settled to sleep, and then walking the twelve miles back before sunrise.

I do not recollect of ever seeing my mother by the light of day. . . . I was not allowed to be present during her illness, at her death or burial. . . . For what this separation is done, I do not know, unless it be to hinder development of the child's affection toward its mother, and to blunt and destroy the natural affection of the mother for the child. This is the inevitable result.[89]

Injustice can be said in many ways. Douglass responds in terms of nature, as will Orlando Patterson more than a century later when he names this fate of natal alienation a "natural injustice" and a denial of claims of blood.[90] Douglass's father was a white man, perhaps Aaron Anthony, the owner of the farm and the owner of Douglass and his mother. Douglass belonged to Anthony as an instrument and an object, making impossible the relationship by which he could have belonged to him as a son. In Patterson's analysis, Douglass was alienated from birth and severed from the practices that institute a subject as a person capable of action and to whom a culture may be transmitted. He was alienated from the instant of his birth, which is to say there is no question of agency or responsibility on his part. No one will his own birth. Birth is not an act one performs, so any consequences that rebound on him by birth are not of his doing. The words *bastard* and *slave* attach to us with no reference to anything we have done. Yet so do *son* and *daughter*.

Moreover, Douglass was denied *at birth* the capacity to make the claims *of* birth, and this gives specific shape to Patterson's thought of a natural injustice. Douglass was alienated from his own birth, which would have tied him to past generations and an existing community, would have given him native, local status and allowed him to make a claim on those who brought him into the world. He writes of the natural maternal affection that was destroyed in his mother and the filial affection that was stunted in him by an owner whose sexual and generational violence makes a hideous paradox of the word *father*.[91] Patterson writes:

> It was this alienation of the slave from all formal, legally enforceable ties of "blood" and from any attachment to groups or localities other than those chosen for him by the master, that gave the relation of slavery its peculiar value to the master. The slave was the ultimate tool, as imprintable and disposable as the master wished.[92]

Being able to make a natal claim on our forebears allows us to turn toward the new generation and in turn open ourselves to their claim on us. Because enslavement meant that the enslaved could not make a claim on his parents, he had no natal claim or power to pass on to his children. With *natural* injustice Patterson is not objecting to a contingent, natural distribution of characteristics.[93] Nor is he concerned with a natural unfairness in the distribution of talents or characteristics.[94] Instead, he points to a breach of what he, like Douglass, takes as a natural order that stands beyond the law. It is the language he has available to name the injustice of a law that attacks the relations of mothers, fathers, and children. What word other than *blood* communicates the value that is denied when families are broken up by the practice of selling out? What term other than *kinship* describes the structure that implodes when, as Hortense Spillers describes, one's father is also one's owner and the owner of one's mother, siblings, neighbors, and coworkers, indiscriminately?[95]

Yet, whose nature is this? What kin? Enforceable ties of "blood" existed for landowning whites in the plantation system in the form of legal institutions of marriage, ownership, and inheritance supported by social institutions of the cult of female chastity, the fantasy of dynasty, and the ideology of white supremacy. The child of the white slaveowner and his white wife did not suffer natal alienation; he could grow up protected by (and also subject to) his parents and the law and need never undergo an experience such as that of Mr. Reed, a once enslaved man interviewed by Ophelia Settle Egypt of Fisk University around 1930:

The most barbarous thing I saw with these eyes—I lay on my bed and study about it now—I had a sister, my older sister, she was fooling with a clock and broke it, and my old master taken her and tied a rope around her neck—just enough to keep it from choking her—and tied her up in the back yard and whipped her I don't know how long. There stood mother, there stood father, and there stood all the children and none could come to her rescue.[96]

What was denied to Mr. Reed and his family was something the white family had: the capacity to respond, the ability to protect one another, to be responsible for one another, and to have those responsibilities supported by law.[97] In that case, the injustice can be described by appealing solely to existing legal forms, and the claim to equality can take the form of an appeal for equal treatment under existing law. Justice is a matter of extending protection so that no one may whip a girl without fear of interference from her kin or fear of punishment under the law.

Still the question persists: What kin? Daniel Patrick Moynihan could write in his infamous 1965 report for the US Department of Labor that, although African Americans had achieved legal liberty, they had not yet achieved equality, because of the "pathologies" of family life to which the Negro family fell victim: "divorce, separation, and desertion, female family head, children in broken homes and illegitimacy." He observed that in 1963 nearly one-quarter of Negro births were illegitimate, nearly one-fourth of Negro families are headed by women, and Negro women have "too many children too early," all evidence that the Negro family was disorganized and broken down. While the white family "remains a powerful agency not only for transmitting property from one generation to the next but also for transmitting no less valuable contracts with the world of work and education," the Negro community "has been forced into a matriarchal structure which, because it is too out of line with the rest of the American society, seriously retards the progress of the group as a whole."[98]

Enslaved people called upon the law; the response, when it came, took the form of access to the naturalized rules that had supported the dominance of white men all along. Meanwhile, as Spillers writes:

The captive person developed, time and again, certain ethical and sentimental features that tied her and him, across the landscape to others, often sold from hand to hand, of the same and different blood in a common fabric of memory and inspiration. We might choose to call this connectedness "family," or "support structure," but that is a rather different case from the moves of a dominant symbolic order, pledged to maintain the supremacy of race.[99]

What other nature, then? What other kin? How else to describe what Douglass and his mother, Harriet Bailey, suffered in their separation? "My poor mother," Douglass writes, "like many other slave women, had *many children*, but NO FAMILY."[100] Slavery imposed conditions that undermined enslaved families and communities in order to eliminate kinship as a mode of identification and as a place of resistance to the imposed identity of mere slave, the property of this or that plantation. Claudia Card, drawing on Patterson (though making no claims about "blood"), gives us the language of social death, a condition in which the bonds between people are broken by suppressing the customs that mark our distinctive modes of being, our entry into the human world, our passage through it, and our departure from it.[101]

Yet Bailey's response, in the face of that death threat, was to create a nighttime world where she could put her son to bed. We don't know how she did it—what support she had from the people who would cover for her, the arrangements she made with her own mother, who was permitted to care for the infant Frederick—but we know enough from his testimony to recognize her as a subversive working to create the kin they needed. Meanwhile, who did feed Frederick Douglass after he was separated from mother and then, at six, from his grandmother also? We each come to be within specific structures of significance, and Douglass was shaped by white supremacy and racist exploitation as well as nurture and care; as he grew up, there would be occasions on which all of these would be exercised by the same person. Even as he was treated as instrument and possession in one relation, he came to belong and matter in others. Our capacity for action rests on our initial passive involvement with our world; not only did we not ask to be born, but we did not choose the institutions and structures that would shape our lives or the people who would form us. We were passive as regards their very meaningfulness.[102] Douglass took on the capacity for meaningful activity in spite of and in resistance to a system that cultivated him for enslavement. Self-possession is an achievement we arrive at—not once and for all but repeatedly—in the midst of attentive others.

These others may have no genetic relation to us. Anthropologists used to distinguish between real kin (formed through relations of birth) and fictive kin (formed by adoption), but Janet Carsten and others have argued for a broader language of relatedness.[103] In *After Kinship*, she describes Andean villages in Ecuador where kin are the people with whom you share food and whaling teams in Alaska where kinship relations are established on the basis of the role played in the hunt.[104]

In neither case is it a matter simply of nature or choice but the givenness of circumstance shaped by everyday practices of eating, working, and living together. She writes of Malaysian migrant communities:

> Malay relatedness is created both by ties of procreation and through everyday acts of feeding and living together in the house. Both procreative ties and shared feeding create shared substance or blood in a community largely made up of migrants. Here the small acts of hospitality and feeding, together with longer-term sharing of food and living space which fostering and marriage involve, create kinship where it did not previously exist. Women and houses may be said to be central both to the "domestic" process of creating relatedness inside houses, and to the larger "political" process of integrating newcomers and the establishment and reproduction of whole communities.[105]

In other circumstances, estranged from those to whom we were born, we create other kin. The givenness of our birth and inheritance cannot be undone, but it can be refused.[106] Studying gay communities in 1980s California, Kath Weston described chosen families. She writes:

> Gay or chosen families might incorporate friends, lovers, or children, in any combination. Organized through ideologies of love, choice, and creation, gay families have been defined through a contrast with what many gay men and lesbians in the Bay Area called "straight," "biological," or "blood" family.[107]

On the one hand, choosing to describe this phenomenon in the language of family risks submitting to the heterosexist order all over again; indeed, before long, heteronormativity would join forces with its homonormative foil.[108] On the other, admitting the element of choice more deeply into the structure of kin (where it had always been, though confined to the selection of sexual or marriage partners) meant queering kinship, rejecting its self-presentation as simply the "natural" order. Weston writes: "Denaturalizing the genealogical grid would require that procreation no longer be postulated as kinship's base, ground, or centerpiece."[109]

Leo Bersani takes the thought further, arguing that the sameness or "homo-ness" of homosexuality and the sterility of the homosexual relation give us a way to think of homosexuality as antirelational.[110] Forms of community—kinship most of all—are troublesome "if only because nearly every lesbian or gay remembers being such before entering a collectively identified space, because much of lesbian and gay history has to do with noncommunity, and because dispersal rather than localization continues to be definitive of queer self-understanding."[111] Sometimes, a community of kin might be the last thing a person needs. Sometimes, the time of ancestors and descendants, the temporality of overlapping generations is precisely what a person needs to *shed* in order to make possible forms of queer existence, as Lee Edelman argues in his polemic against hetero-norms, reproductive futurity, and the figure of the Child.[112]

Sometimes. Even as Bersani works to undo the presumption of relation, he acknowledges the privilege granted to white men, gay or straight, that others might not enjoy.[113] In contrast, how much kin do the queer Black girls at Savannah Shange's San Francisco High School need as they confront violence in their homes and high school halls?[114] How much kin does Gloria Anzaldúa need as she navigates her *frontera*?[115] When might any of us discover that it is not good to have no kin? In journals written as he was dying of AIDS, Derek Jarman struggles with fears that he and his generation would be forgotten or remembered in distorted, self-serving ways.[116] Whose responsibility would it be to remember them properly?[117] Gay history is still told as a story of generations—the Stonewall generation, the lesbian-feminist generation, the AIDS generation. Gay activism is marked by attention to "kids coming out now" and to aging queers.[118] The figure of procreation is displaced early and often, but people continue to be born and die, and the overlapping time of generations continues to lap. Edelman proposes a queerness that is "unaware of the passing of generations as stages on the road to a better living. It knows nothing about the 'sacrifice now for the sake of future generations.'"[119] These are queer generations, or generations of queerness, that would be constituted in willful, liberating ignorance of the norms of reproductive futurity, but they would be modes of generational being nonetheless.[120]

## Genocide as Aenocide

In Chapter 1, the *genos*, understood as a matter of genetics, emerged as having a plastic relation to time. It is constituted genetically by the repetition and sharing of genes, and, while a gene does not always find its expression in the phenotype of a given individual or a given generation, it can pass on silently, biding its time until the contingencies of sexual reproduction and environment align to allow it to (re)appear in the world. For genetics, what dies in the death of an individual is the expression of a genotype and a particular configuration in the propagation of the genetic code; genetic material passes on, sometimes addressing the world in the form of a particular trait and sometimes remaining silent.

At the end of that chapter, I noted that the fantasy of the self-identical, self-generating *genos* gives shape to our longing to belong; here I have argued that the structures of kinship belonging do not operate naturally or mechanically but are the product of judgments made by descendants, researchers, kin keepers, sons and daughters, in various states of curiosity, vulnerability, bewilderment, and exhaustion and in response to various contexts. I noted also that the genetic *genos* was a fantasy in which no ghosts stalked the living and in which the dead could dissolve into an oblivion from where they would make no more accusations and demands. After all, the fantasy that makes the *genos* a thing means that we can regard all the possible but unchosen *genera* as nonentities, failures to exist for which no one is called to take responsibility. On this understanding, genealogies are expressions of reality, not patterns of sense making that exist among alternative and intersecting ways of making sense. The patterns of inheritance and passing on that sustain the *genos* thus understood rely on a seamless temporality in which overlapping generations absorb the contingencies of natural and sexual selection, corralling difference while producing the best of all possible descendants. In the logic of *bios*, we embody our ancestors and pass on something of them to the next generations. Indeed, everything we pass on is *of* them. Biological time includes the frenetic temporality of metabolism, the thrum of circulation, the rhythmic time of birth and death, the biopolitical ordering of populations and, on the evolutionary scale, the time of flows, drifts, and pools.

In the logic of the *anthropos*, we inherit the culture of those who have gone before and inhabit it in anticipation of passing it on. The word *culture* cannot be used without specification, not only because it sent Goebbels reaching for his Browning but also because of the favor it has found with nationalist conservatives, who use it as a stand-in for *essence* in general, *race* in particular. We might think about the term in three ways: First, it encompasses the intellectual creations of a cultural elite; second, it is the capacity to discuss and engage with those creations, an ability that marks one as belonging to a cultured class; and third, it is the ways of life of a group.[121] This last is what concerns me: culture anthropologically speaking, which includes norms, stories, images, imaginings, commemorations, and the differentiated *temporalities* of our being together. It encompasses how we are together, not only in terms of the periodic rituals of public life but also the daily practices of work and physical existence. A *culture* is not an object or collection of artifacts, but speaking of culture is a way of speaking of ways of living and how things are done. We are instituted by changing practices developed among us over generations, but what this *over* means and *how* we experience the overlap differs.[122]

Generational time is the overlapping time of ancestors and descendants but also of a world *where* we overlap, that is, a world that endures beyond a lifetime and is inhabited by people of all ages with whom we *find ourselves* and in relation to whom we *become ourselves*. We arrive into a world, a culture that already exists without us; world and culture are given and generational without being biological. We become responsive to and in a specific set of nonreciprocal, asymmetrical relations; we are cultivated as responsive beings, and the relations are relations of responsibility. Generational temporality is the mode of being-in-time of Card's social existence, marked by our entry into a human world where we are surrounded by our elders; our passage through it accompanied by contemporaries, the old, and the young; and our departure from it making way for new generations.[123] The pace and manner of our passage, that is to say, how we pass, will differ historically and culturally. Genealogists resort to a rule of thumb that sets the time of a generation at twenty-five or thirty years, but the pace of generational time is immensely variable, and years are not its proper measure. Arendt invokes the patriarchs of the Hebrew Bible living into peaceful old age enjoying long layers of generational overlap with their children and their children's children. In contrast, Vincent Brown describes the world of the Jamaican sugar plantation of the seventeenth and eighteenth centuries, where atrocious living conditions, paired with the constant influx of new captives from Africa, virtually broke generational time. The birth rate among the enslaved was low, infant mortality high, and many who survived transportation from Africa died soon from starvation, smallpox, dysentery, hurricanes, and overwork. The island's Black population was not sustained by generation but by the import of captives, allowing Jamaican planters to essentially outsource the work of child raising to African villages.[124] With such diminished generational overlap, Brown sees emerge a structure of kinship and mourning that integrates the dead and the unborn into community life. He writes: "In the struggle to shape the future the dead do not necessarily have the last word, but they always have a voice."[125] Their generational relations violently dismantled, the survivors set about creating a depth of generational experience otherwise.

Genocidal violence is not just a matter of mass killing; it may not involve killing at all.[126] Indeed, perpetrators may be driven by the desire to preserve individual lives—of enslaved Africans in the New World, of native children taken and forced into residential schools and white foster families in North America and Australia—even as they destroy intergenerational relations. When all else is threatened by such violence and domination, generation may be the very ground of resistance. Toni Morrison's *Beloved* is a story of ghosts and generations and of mourning despite the odds. Sixo is one of the men enslaved at Sweet Home, and he is named for the generations that separate him from Africa. While the other men on the farm were named by their owner—two are called Paul—Sixo's forebears somehow kept count, and his determination to continue counting is worth more to him than life. He is caught on the night they try to escape, but his Thirty-Mile Woman, pregnant with their child, is waiting for him among the trees and manages to get away. Sixo, tied hand and foot beside his hunters' campfire, laughs and calls out into the darkness, calling to the wife and child-to-be his captors know nothing about: "Seven-O! Seven-O!" He refuses to stop. "They shoot him to shut him up. Have to."[127] Perhaps the hope is for a genetic redemption in the "blossoming seed" she carries, but what would that redemption be, what meaning would it have, without a name? What drives Sixo to keep calling is the ritual of naming and keeping generational count; he insists on it, even though it is the death of him. His suffering, and the suffering of all those forebears, may never be redeemed, but his and their having existed might be preserved, for a while, in the world that holds his son or daughter.

The concept of *genos* has long served the desire to belong and the desire for absolute belonging. Yet it has no internal brake to stop slippage from *genos* terms used to refer to the relation between children and the people who bring them into the world and bring them up, to the set of generational relations that allows us to belong with our people (parents, grandparents, and great-grandparents), to the people (singular) we identify as *our* people and the race we are told is *our* race. Generating is not nothing. Far from it: It keeps the world peopled, links us to past and future, and underwrites whatever sense we have that how things are now is how they may continue, though not how they will always be.[128] Yet generation comes to have meaning only as a condition to which we respond. Kinship is the structure of our responses to generational existence, responses that disrupt the path to race thinking if only by making us decide. Kinship is how we take responsibility for the generations, and which generation counts, or who belongs, is not merely given. In *Suffering Witness: The Quandary of Responsibility after the Irreparable*, James Hatley identifies the generational element of genocide as *aenocide*, the murder of generations: "Generations disappear, time as an articulation of a responsibility collapses, and no-one remains who can carry on that specific line of responsibility."[129]

Thus, the Jewish cemetery in Kazimierz Dolny, Poland, like almost all the Jewish cemeteries of Central and Eastern Europe, was destroyed in the 1940s, the gravestones smashed or taken to be used for other buildings. In the 1980s, some of the broken stones were recovered and incorporated into a memorial wall based on a design by Tadeusz Augustynka. The wall stands along the front of the cemetery but is broken by a jagged opening that cuts through it from top to bottom; the genocide cut through the succession of generations. It broke the rhythm of living and mourning, the pattern of commemoration of a community, the link between generations.

The world in which those stones marked the graves of somebody's grandmother or somebody's child was erased; the generations whose responsibility it would be to mourn that woman or that boy were consigned to oblivion, and those who would mourn the annihilated never came to be. We cannot do their mourning for them. Yet the destruction of that world is a fact of our world, and, as Hatley puts it in response to reading Primo Levi's *Survival in Auschwitz*, the testimony of Levi or the presence of the Kazimierz Dolny wall calls us to an uncanny and disturbing responsibility. We are initiated into a relation with a generation destroyed and a generation that never was and asked to own up to a kinship with them. Taking this on as a responsibility across time (it is irrelevant that these things happened before I was born) is an act of holding time open, a time, as Hatley puts it, that would be again diachronic, that would again allow difference and would open up into the generosity of one generation succeeding another.[130]

It is not a personal inheritance but a worldly one; as I will argue, it is not so much a matter of ethics as it is of worldly existence. Radically democratic politics provides the structure for the openness that allows for the succession of generations, the articulation of multiple temporalities, the existence of many worlds.

# 3 / What's Wrong with Genocide?

*There is a special level of horror, loathing, and disgust that we encounter in genocide: a cringing recoiling at the very possibility of them being in the same world as are we, the genociders.*

—BRUCE WILSHIRE, *Get 'Em All! Kill 'Em!*

## Introduction

"What's wrong with genocide?" looks like a question for ethics, but it lies beyond its limits. It seems disgusting even to ask it. Can there be anything worse than Auschwitz, Ntarama, or Srebrenica? We hear the testimony of Doriane Kurz from Bergen-Belsen: "There was a squadron of people that pulled this wagon around and came into the barracks and took the corpses, and then they would, two of them would take the corpse, one at the feet and one at the hands and they would toss them up to the top of the heap." Speaking almost fifty years later she ends her testimony: "I still have trouble with that. I still have trouble with that."[1] Once we've heard or read the testimony, once we've stood in those places or seen those photographs, what is there to ask about the wrongness of what happened there? What do we hope to find out that we don't already know?[2] We hear the testimony of DD, a witness at the International Criminal Tribunal for the former Yugoslavia describing the day she was separated from her twelve-year-old son: "And he turned around, and then he told me, 'Mommy, please, can you get that bag for me? Could you please get it for me?' . . . That was the last time I heard his voice."[3] We see children in prison stripes behind the barbed wire and small skeletons and skulls in the piles of bones. The deaths those children met can only be wrong. Why then waste time asking questions when we should be making sure it never happens again? And if we do need to ask what exactly is wrong with killing children or with storing people in barracks where they die night after night, isn't ethics already up to the task?

There are those who argue that genocide is just violence and that there is no phenomenon of genocide that demands specific attention independent of our studies of war, torture, and violence generally speaking.[4] Indeed, having spent the two chapters before this attempting to undo the concept of *genos*, I'm sympathetic to this argument. Some of what follows applies to reigns of violence, whether genocidal or not. Yet even as the concepts of *genos* and genocide come undone, we persist in working ourselves into *genera*, understood, minimally, as the network of enduring temporal relations linking us to those (of us) who have gone and to others (of us) who have yet to come. We ignore this phenomenon at our peril, because doing so would leave us unprepared for the theoretical work of understanding the relation of *genos* and violence and disastrously unprepared for the genocidal attackers' knock on the door—if not ours, then our neighbor's or the door of the family across town or across the border. It also leaves us unprepared—not finally but in the first instance—for the reassuring, pernicious appeal of the rhetoric of *them* and *us*.

Alfred van Cleef, an author and journalist who traced the experience of a single family in Yugoslavia in the 1990s, tells the story of how war came to their village. For months the Berberovics had been picking up the increasingly virulent radio broadcasts from Belgrade and Zagreb, but they hadn't paid much attention because where they lived, Serbs, Croats, and Muslims coexisted peacefully.

> Then the war was just two valleys over, but still they didn't worry, and then it was in the very next valley, but, even so, no one could imagine its actually intruding into their quiet lives. But one day a car suddenly careered into the village's central square, seeming to single out a particular house and cornering its occupant, whereupon the leader of the militiamen calmly leveled a gun at the young man and blew him away. The militiamen hustled back into their car and sped off.

Ethical theory would have no difficulty showing what was wrong with the gunman's action in terms of his flawed character, his refusal to see his victim as an end in himself or the suffering his action would produce. Alternatively, or in addition, the mention of the encroaching war would require a discussion of his act in terms of rules of combat and the justice or otherwise of the war. But van Cleef continues the story:

> They left behind them a village almost evenly divided. Those under fifty years of age had been horrified by the seeming randomness of the act, while those over fifty realized, with perhaps even greater horror, that the young man who'd just been killed was the son of a man

who, back during the partisan struggles of the Second World War, happened to have killed the uncle of the kid who'd just done the killing. And the older villagers immediately realized, with absolute clarity, that if this was now possible *everything was going to be possible.*[5]

What did the people in the Berberovics' village experience that day? We can imagine them sharing Arendt's response when she first began to grasp what had been done in the camps. She recalls thinking: "This should not have happened." The villagers had never *quite* imagined something like this happening in their world, in their valley. Yet, when it did happen, all the structures were in place that would give the act its genocidal sense: son, father, us, nephew, Chetnik, uncle, them, Turk, killing, the War, revenge. The *genos* asserted itself, murderously, in broad daylight, and whoever knew the relevant family relations knew that this was the erection of a new genocidal order on the old structure of the *genos*, newly mobilized and weaponized.[6]

We must ask "What's wrong with genocide?" in order to give content to the exhortation "Never again" but also because investigating it will shed light on ethics and, more particularly, on politics.[7] Genocide is best understood—most understood—as a political rather than an ethical problem, and studying it as such in turn forces us to rethink the nature of politics.[8] Ethical thinking, operating in terms of self and other, allows us to identify the killer and the one killed, the act of murder and its wrongness; legal thinking has us identify the perpetrator, his intentions, his crime, his victim, and the harm inflicted; but political thinking has us consider the shared world and the harm done to it and to all of us worldly beings.

The starting point of this train of thought is Arendt's essay "Collective Responsibility," where ethics is centered on the relation of self and other, while politics is concerned with the world.[9] As she writes elsewhere: "Strictly speaking, politics is not so much about human beings as it is about the world that comes into being between them and endures beyond them. To the extent that politics becomes destructive and causes worlds to end, it destroys and annihilates itself."[10] Rather than arranging ethical thinking and political thinking—still less, arranging ethical life and political life—into independent spheres, the distinction indicates a set of entangled relations. (1) Ethics concerns the singular and the relation-between-two, while political life has to do with the plural and relations among many, relations between one and many, between the few and many, between nations, and inevitably, despite Arendt's protests to the contrary, between social groups. (2) Ethics concerns the question of what should happen between us, now, while political thinking broaches the generational question of what should happen in and for the world we have inherited, that will last longer than our lifetimes, and that we will pass on. Ethical thinking *may* extend to our generational condition of plurality and *may* take up questions of how we receive what came before us and our relation to what is to come, but it also may presume to ignore them. Meanwhile, these worldly concerns constitute political thinking.[11] (3) Ethics may reach for a transcendent ground or posit a regulative idea, whereas politics cannot avoid the reality that it has to work out its principles immanently. It is not the job of ethics to provide principles for political life; those principles must come from the context of political relations themselves. The ideal of the Good may rightly reign in ethical life, but in political existence it would be despotic.[12] (4) Finally, ethics is compelled to take on, as a minimum, the structures of subjectivity and agency, while political thinking since Marx not only allows but requires us to interrogate those existential structures.[13]

I do not suggest that traditional ethical thinking becomes irrelevant in genocidal situations. Ethical action is certainly called for in the face of attack, and nothing I say here is meant as suggesting that we avoid moral judgment of those who perpetrate or facilitate genocidal violence. Some people hid Jews from the Nazis; others betrayed them. Some Hutu rejected the instructions of the Interahamwe for as long as they could; others took up machetes without delay.[14] Some people helped men and women escape slavery; others hunted them. The fact that none of us can have any confidence about what we would have done in the circumstances does nothing to obviate those facts. What I will argue is that familiar ethical categories are inadequate for understanding genocidal violence, which demands a different thinking.

Confusingly, elements of the different thinking I'm after are already available under the heading of *worldly ethics, intergenerational justice,* the *democratic ethos,* or *the ethical turn in democratic theory.* Inspired by Foucault, thinkers uncover the modes of cultivation of the complex self; inspired by Levinas, they turn us toward the relation to the Other; responding to the demands of care, they disrupt the presumptions of agency, self, and autonomy; confronted by the threat of climate change, they rethink the relations of self and earth.[15] I will turn to questions of normativity before this chapter ends, but my general worry is that the ethical turn cannot avoid moralizing politics and that ethical thinking cannot grasp what is to be feared from the despotism of the Good. I am concerned that it will not recognize the need for a space for the appearance of difference, contestation, dissensus, and judgment, a space where violence is among the objects of contestation. After all, politics is not essentially the place of contestation without violence. It is where the decision *about* the use of violence is treated as a matter of democratic judgment; it is the frame within which that decision is made.[16] As we will see in Chapter 4, this is not the same as being a place of nonviolence. I am also concerned that thinking in terms of democracy and ethics will ignore democracies' own practices of exclusion and their designation of some lives as disposable and some deaths ungrievable.[17] I fear that, under the heading of consensus, whether real or imagined, particularly on the question of who is included and excluded, who counts and who doesn't, ethics provides cover for reversion to a *genos*-thinking that affirms the utter wrongness of genocide but will never be up to the task of giving an account of that wrongness.

In what follows, I argue that approaching genocide with the tools of calculation used in consequentialist ethical thinking or with the thought of *ethos*, from virtue ethics, carries us to the end of ethics; approaching from with the imperatives and duties of deontology takes us beyond its end.

## Genocide and the End of Ethics

How could we calculate the wrongness of genocide? If wrongness could be quantified or marked on a scale, genocide would be the phenomenon that came last in the list, the worst of harms. Then we could think of what's wrong with genocide as just more of what's wrong with the next worst thing. We could mark it as being as wrong as anything, and then some, so all of our ethical knowledge, theory, and practice would have done its work in getting us to that point and would support us in the assertion that it must not happen again without needing to quantify its wrongness further. Yet it is difficult to make sense of such an accumulation of wrongness in the same way that it is hard to compare the wrongness of events of mass violence. Even if we could grasp a calculation according to which one death is wrong, two deaths twice as wrong, and so on, our calculations would give out in the face of mass murder. We can understand, if not imagine, the difference between 999 murders and one thousand; we can neither imagine nor understand a difference between the *wrongness* of 999 murders and one thousand.[18]

It is not just a matter of number of victims or the quantity of harm. Genocide is, rather, a distinctive type of harm, requiring, if anything, a different sort of comparison. We could, alternatively, devise an ethical scale borrowing a model from criminal justice. The state of New York groups felonies into five classes with minimum and maximum sentences specified for each, driven, we must assume, by an effort to have the punishment fit the crime. Likewise, we might develop an ethics where assault is worse than robbery, rape is worse than assault, and murder is worse than rape. Then we could assign genocide the last position, beyond murder and even beyond mass murder, and, again, we would avoid specifying its wrongness further. But genocide is not a phenomenon that exists independently of specific forms of violence. It is carried out in beatings, expropriations, evictions, rapes, kidnapping, and killings, so we would have to draw a double scale, one track for assault, murder, etc. and another for those same injuries when they are genocidal. Genocide would then mark the worst instance of any particular wrong.

In this case, the category *genocide* remains no more than a placeholder; conventionally, it acquires content in the form of intent. The UN Convention begins its definition with this requirement and specifies definitively the content of the intention: "Genocide means any of the following acts committed with *intent* to destroy, in whole or in part, a national, ethnical, racial or religious group, as such." As we know, "the following acts" are all already bad things—killing people, stealing children, and so on—and the intent to destroy the group that adds to the individual's injury and the seriousness of the harm. Yet, in a situation where a mass of victims is set upon by an organized mass of perpetrators, the ethical structures of agency and intention, action and consequence become stretched and twisted. The one who intends and the one who acts may be widely separated, with intention and act no longer attached to a single ethical subject but institutionalized or spread through a structure of command and circumstance. Hitler, Himmler, and the Nazi elite intended to commit genocide, and their statements to that effect are well documented; of those who did the killing some shared their intention, some did not, while in many cases it is impossible to know.[19] Genocidal consequences may be produced without any genocidal intention, as in the genocidal structure of settler colonialism. Actions on the part of European migrants who established sheep farms in Australia in the nineteenth century propelled the destruction of aboriginal peoples. Their actions included direct violence against indigenous men and women, but more destructive by far was the very introduction of sheep and the appropriation and adaptation of land for farming.[20] In 1970s Bangladesh, members of Jonab Ali Munshi's family registered to participate in a government scheme to settle land then inhabited by Jumma people in the Chittagong Hill Tracts, a scheme that was to have genocidal consequences of which Munshi had no idea. His family had already been deported from India and resettled numerous times in forest land, swamp land, and in a town slum. As another settler put it, "We had to find a new way to survive, which was to move to the Chittagong Hills."[21] As Dirk Moses and Donald Bloxham write: "[Genocides] and the people who enact them, are constantly evolving phenomena, subject to a multiplicity of external influences as well as internal volition. Structure and agency are inextricably entwined."[22]

Can the categories of virtue and character support our thinking where calculation and intention fail? From the theaters of genocide come stories of people faced with atrocious dilemmas. The Tutsi teenager is told he may survive if he kills his parents; if he refuses, all will be murdered. The Jewish mother must decide whether to answer the front door and be arrested by the Gestapo or send her daughter to answer it while she escapes through the back door to alert her husband; not to decide means condemning the whole family. In William Styron's *Sophie's Choice*, Sophie, waiting in line with her two children, is told by the drunk Nazi doctor that she may keep one child. What is Sophie to do? This looks like a question for ethics. Sometimes, in an act that approaches pedagogical sadism, ethics teachers will ask their students to work on the example of Sophie, having them discuss the *consequences* of choosing one child over the other or the *duty* that would compel Sophie to choose one or neither. Deontology, which gives us a rational, universal rule to show us what our duty is each time, will not recognize the dilemma; consequentialism leads us into hideous calculations of the relative value of the life of each child.[23] In the face of a tragic choice, neither theory can guide us, and that machinery of ethical decision-making grinds to a halt.[24]

Virtue ethics initially offers something more promising when it allows us to acknowledge the cost of the resolution. It's not that the dilemmas are irresolvable. The teenager killed; the mother sent the daughter; Sophie chose to keep her son. Yet what is left of Sophie then? She is unrecognizable to herself, incapable, eventually, of living with herself, and this would have been the case no matter which choice she made. "What's wrong with Sophie's decision?" is a horrific question because there is nothing right about the world in which she finds herself. "What's wrong with the Nazi doctor's command?" is also horrific but more revealing because it turns our attention to the world in which he came to be as he was. Character is formed by education and custom, or *ethos*; what *ethos* produced a character who would permit himself such a deed? What world made his action possible? Arendt names it *dictatorship*.[25]

In her analysis, Hitler's dictatorship produced a political system that reached its apotheosis in the camps. She describes the steps by which prisoners were turned into nonpersons, losing first their legal existence, then their moral existence, and then all existence. By the time physical life ended, the several aspects of personhood had been destroyed. The juridical person was eliminated, partly by making the camps the place where criminals, political enemies, those who had committed no crime, and those who had done nothing at all would all be interned together. Arrested on no charge, the noncriminal prisoner could appeal to no authority. There was no court in which he could make his case, no way for somebody to speak on his behalf. A person can still make a moral claim for himself, can still act morally in the absence of law, but the camps destroyed moral personhood too. Arendt writes: "Through the creation of conditions under which conscience ceases to be adequate and to do good becomes utterly impossible, the consciously organized complicity of all men in the crimes of totalitarian regimes is extended to the victims and thus made really total."[26]

Survivors of genocide sometimes describe the moment when they realize that ethics no longer applies. For Innocent Rwililiza, the realization comes when his group of Tutsis, ragged after weeks hiding in the marsh, capture three of their Hutu attackers. He writes:

> We [Tutsis] seemed like animals because we no longer resembled the humans we had once been, and the Hutus, they had grown used to seeing us like animals. They had robbed the Tutsi of their humanity in order to kill them more comfortably, but they themselves had sunk lower than wild beasts because they no longer knew why they were killing, and because in doing so, they were becoming crazed.[27]

For the hunting Hutu neighbor, the hunted Tutsi were of no moral significance; for Rwililiza, the neighbor had lost the capacity for thought about what he himself was doing and so was crazed; for Rwililiza and his fellow Tutsi fugitives in their comportment to one another, even though they were undergoing the same disaster and ran together during the day, gathering each evening to discover who was left, they also knew that they would not stop to help the ones who became too weak to run. For all concerned, in their different ways, ethics was finished.[28]

Bruno Bettelheim locates the end of ethics at a particular moment in the process of humiliation as he experienced it in the camps. He writes:

> One had first and foremost to remain informed and be aware of . . . the point beyond which one would never, under any circumstances, give in to the oppressor, even if it meant risking and losing one's life. . . . This keeping informed and aware of one's actions—though it could not alter the required act, save in extremities—this minimal distance from one's own behaviour, and the freedom to feel differently about it

depending on its character, this too was what permitted the prisoner to remain a human being. It was the giving up of all feelings, all inner reservations about one's actions, the letting go of a point at which one could hold fast no matter what, that changed prisoner into moslem.[29]

Moslems, or *Muselmänner*, were prisoners driven to the edge of death in the camps but who continued to survive, neither dead nor quite alive, neither human nor nonhuman, capable neither of life nor of a human death. They were listless people who dragged themselves about. There were very many of them, and they are mentioned in testimonies from all the annihilation camps. The image is all the more powerful for being the image of a being the other prisoners did not even consider worthy of being looked at.[30] The *Muselmänner* vanished: first each one into the mass of those between life and death and eventually into bones and ash.[31]

What is vital for Bettelheim is not the single act one convinces oneself one cannot do but the ability to be conscious of one's acts at all. It is not so much a matter of picking the deed that is worse than all others as it is of realizing that in this place it is possible to lose the capacity for the minute transcendence that allows us to have a view of ourselves and to judge any of our own actions. Without it, we are no more than self-identical, collapsed upon ourselves so completely that judgment is no longer possible. The prisoner who has been forced beyond his point of no return is a *Muselmann*, the signal that ethics has been foreclosed.

For Bettelheim, however, the *Muselmann* is not an abstract or merely imagined (in the sense of concocted or chimerical) threat. What he describes is a phenomenon he witnessed, that is, people who had been forced too far, people no longer entirely recognizable as people, people who could not be helped. This last is crucial. He writes that the prisoners sometimes tried to be kind to the *Muselmänner*, but they no longer knew how to respond. Other witnesses report that prisoners judged them not worthy of being looked at, that capos were infuriated by them, and that the SS guards regarded them as trash. "Every group thought only about eliminating them, each in its own way."[32] It was impossible to do right by the *Muselmann*. Insofar as Bettelheim, or any prisoner, found himself unable to bear the sight of the *Muselmann*, the point of no return had already been passed. This was an other the prisoners could not permit themselves to see, since to acknowledge him would be to acknowledge the impossibility of an ethical response and a limit *of* ethics.

Giorgio Agamben forces the thought further, identifying the *Muselmann* as "a limit figure of a special kind, in which not only categories such as dignity and respect but even the very idea of an ethical limit lose their meaning."[33] This is right, if not in all the ways Agamben claims. Primo Levi, like Bettelheim, bears first-hand witness to the phenomenon of the *Muselmann*, describing him as "an emaciated man, with head dropped and shoulders curved, on whose face and in whose eyes not a trace of thought is to be seen."[34] For Jean Améry, the *Muselmann* is the staggering corpse.[35] Ryn and Klodzinski write that *Muselmänner* "became indifferent to everything happening around them. They excluded themselves from all relations to their environment."[36] Then, in the next moment, each witness describes the turn away: For Améry, the *Muselmann* is precisely what had to be excluded from his contemplations on Auschwitz and its realities.[37] Ryn and Klodzinski write: "No one felt compassion for the Muslim, and no one felt sympathy for him either."[38] Levi becomes one of the saved while the others drown. Indeed, for the prisoners intent on survival, the *Muselmann* is already drowned.

There comes a moment when Levi departs from description of the phenomenon and reaches for a figure to account for the *Muselmann*'s diminishment: He was "the man who had seen the Gorgon." Agamben pursues the thought, asking who or what in the camp is the Gorgon. But that question is a distraction. Instead, we should ask: How we can understand the effect of seeing the Gorgon? The *Muselmann* moves slowly about the camp, but he is petrified. To see the Gorgon is to succumb to the gaze that—it now turns out—the world had been directing at you since before you knew you had to resist and which it kept trained on you as you fought or hid. You were forced to relinquish law and mores, then one small dignity after another until you were clinging to a habit, a memory, an ethical commitment, indeed, any small capacity for self-awareness, and now the gaze exhausts that resistance and collapses you into what it had marked you as all along: cockroach, infestation, trash. If anything has been set in stone, it is the world's specification of what you are.[39]

Agamben's ethical thinking in response to testimony about the *Muselmann* is troublesome, though the ethics of the extreme case is a familiar tradition. In 1916 Wittgenstein writes:

> If suicide is allowed, everything is allowed. If anything is not allowed, then suicide is not allowed. This throws a light on the nature of ethics, for suicide is, so to speak, the elementary sin. And when one investigates it, it is like investigating mercury vapour in order to comprehend the nature of vapors.[40]

Dostoevsky had prepared the way for the formulation a generation earlier: Without God and immortal life, everything is permitted. For Wittgenstein, the reflection is not a matter of making an ethical inference but of documenting the stages of an incipient realization. Rather than a principle, the starting point is a phenomenon, an experience undergone in the form of the death by suicide of more than one friend, along with his brother's death, also suspected to have been by suicide. If suicide is permitted, then everything is permitted, and God is surely dead. And yet the death of God does nothing to eliminate our need to forbid some things or the impulse to identify a sin, a wrong, or an injustice *so to speak* that could be elementary *so to speak*, that is, that could be the immanent ground for permission and prohibition.[41] If only we can prohibit something, we can still have ethics. If we can indeed prohibit *some* one thing, it will be suicide, and the content of the ethics that ensues will trace itself to this elementary sin, which becomes the object of our investigation when we want to shed light on ethics in general. There is a danger in spending too long too close to these toxic mercury vapors. Besides, what will we learn about the nature of vapor by studying an element that behaves so idiosyncratically? For Wittgenstein, suicide is a sin, only more so, and located not at the end of ethics but at its very beginning.

Agamben retains this structure of permission and prohibition in the hope of hanging a new metaethics on an old frame. He writes:

> The atrocious news that the survivors carry from the camp to the land of human beings is precisely that it is possible to lose dignity and decency beyond imagination, that there still is life in the most extreme degradation. And this new knowledge now becomes the touchstone by which to judge and measure all morality and dignity.[42]

The *Muselmann* is Agamben's mercury vapor, the phenomenon from which witnesses kept their distance for fear of the danger it held for them, the phenomenon of a human being dismantled but in whom persists a flicker of life that demands something of us. The *Muselmann* is, so to speak, elementary. It does not let us ask "What's wrong with genocide?" but rather gives Agamben a figure to turn to in the hope of an immanent ground for ethics. However, the difference between this figure and Wittgenstein's example is that suicide can be called a sin because it can happen in an otherwise ethically coherent world, a shared world where the distinction between permitted and not permitted is meaningful. This does not rule out controversy; indeed, it is the condition for the possibility of ethical dispute. In contrast, we find ourselves struggling to find a vocabulary for the wrongness of genocide because this phenomenon does not challenge our judgments of what is permissible—we agree that if anything is forbidden, *this* is forbidden—but rather our estimation of what

is *possible*. We cannot hope to retrieve a ground for permission and prohibition from that scarcely imaginable world where every evil is possible.

For Arendt, the Nazi extermination camps were the places where all
evil became possible.[43] It initially seemed that *making everything possible*
meant creating a situation in which everything could be destroyed. What
in fact came to be in that place was a situation to which "neither political
nor historical nor simply moral standards" could apply. Not only could
a life be destroyed, but its destruction would not even rate as a human
death.[44] The beings finally exterminated were no longer natal beings, that
is, were no longer distinguishable from others, no longer capable of initi-
ating something new in the world, and so were no longer capable of mortality. It was a thoroughgoing annihilation—no commemoration was permitted, relatives are not informed, mourning was impossible.[45] The end of
these lives is accompanied by none of the social rituals that fit a death into
a scheme of meaning. Instead, measures were taken "to treat people as if
they had never existed and to make them disappear in the literal sense
of the word."[46] It turned out that everything could be arranged as though
they had never been. Arendt writes: "The killing of man's individuality, of
the uniqueness shaped in equal parts by nature, will, and destiny . . . creates a horror that vastly overshadows the outrage of the juridical-political
person and the despair of the moral person."[47]

## Genocide beyond the End of Ethics

When genocide threatens to exhaust our ethical categories, we respond
by stretching them, as if genocide were right at the end of ethics, just beyond its purview. We hope that with just a little more effort we will be able
to come up with a good response. But perhaps genocide is not right at the
end of ethics but projected far beyond it. Adorno writes that Hitler imposes on us a new categorical imperative: "to arrange [our] thoughts and
actions so that Auschwitz will not repeat itself, so that nothing similar
will happen."[48] The statement looks like a renovation of moral thinking,
a use of the familiar rationalist ethical formulation to affirm a new ethics
in the aftermath of an unimagined horror. Yet this is not a rationally con-
ditioned imperative. It is not generated by our reasoning selves and could
not have been generated by us; it is not an instance of autonomy, because
we take our cue from a world shaped by Hitler and the Nazis. But what
choice do we have? The Nazi genocide rearranged the world. Confronted
with the suffering of the camps, experiencing natural abhorrence at the
unbearable physical suffering of the victims, reason wavers, condemning

Auschwitz both as the site of the triumph of death over life and also as the place where death was made impossible.[49]

What is this Auschwitz? On the one hand, it is what occupies the theoretical position from which a new categorical imperative emerges, the place that, since Kant, had been occupied by pure practical reason. On the other hand, it is the phenomenon of a specific extreme suffering. More to the point, what is "the similar thing" that must not ever happen? It too has a double structure. It is a form, a negative idea that does not lie right at the end of ethics as the worst thing but is rather a vanishing point; we cannot see it, and we certainly cannot see beyond it. But Auschwitz cannot be an empty form any more than the camp in Poland that bore the name was just an abstracted theoretical construct. The imperative has content insofar as we know the suffering of the victims; we are commanded to experience and bear witness, to allow ourselves to be revolted by that suffering and to allow the affect to produce its moral result in the rearrangement of our thoughts and actions. Historically, *Auschwitz* is the name for the last, most extreme enactment of the Nazi genocide; ethically, it is the name signaling that ethics as we know it has been foreclosed.

The deaths suffered in Auschwitz were not deaths as we know them. To die in Auschwitz was to be denied the possibility of a human death, that is, to be denied a passing away that could be mourned, acknowledged, undergone as in some way an element of a human life. The camp was a genocidal mechanism for the destruction of humanity, of political, legal, and moral personhood so that what was finally exterminated was pure identity, mere identity, identity without a self.[50] For Adorno, the wrong of Auschwitz is experienced as affect, but as Kant knew, affect falls short of the demonstration of a norm. Yet, as J. M. Bernstein writes:

> There are no demonstrable proofs here; the force of the imperative, via practical abhorrence, depends on its being not logically demonstrable: structures of material inference leave gaps from the perspective of rational demonstrability; from the inside, conversely, there is no sense of a gap to be filled: right reasoning, again, occurs only from within ethical understanding and is not a route to it.[51]

What makes Adorno's categorical imperative new for ethics in the Kantian tradition is the fact that in the place of a pure abstraction of ultimate good there is not an abstraction but a figure and not a figure of good but of evil. Instead of a form that draws us on toward perfection, we have a historical figure that must be avoided at all costs but that itself cannot show *why* we must avoid it.

This is what makes Adolf Eichmann's invocation of Kant's categorical imperative so disturbing and so eerily plausible. Rational demonstrability is a matter of form. Its logic is sustainable even in the service of ends that revolt us. In the dock in Jerusalem, Adolf Eichmann was at pains to show that he was not an antisemite and that he was quite a respectable person, though one who also had been very effective in sending thousands of Jews to the extermination camps. Arendt writes: "He had not simply dismissed the Kantian formula as no longer applicable, he had distorted it to read 'Act as if the principle of your actions were the same as that of the legislator or the law of the land,' or . . . 'Act in such a way that the Führer, if he knew your action, would approve it.'"[52] Accounting for his own actions meant warping the Kantian scheme to fit them. If we take the perfectly good will as the vanishing point of Kant's moral philosophy, what Eichmann did when he claimed to follow the categorical imperative was to take on the form of Kantian moral reasoning but drastically foreshorten the perspective, placing the actual genocidal will of the Führer where the vanishing point of the regulative idea would be. This is what allowed Eichmann to present his moral landscape as coherent, despite the fact that it was a landscape dotted with death camps.

Here is the form and language of moral life used in the avowed service of a despicable end. The regulative idea, which relies in its abstraction on the concepts of universality and humanity as an end in itself, is replaced with the idea of *genos* and the figure of the perfected, purified German people. Pure *genos* turns out to be the *ir*-regulative idea, the idea that, once placed in the position of highest end, generates a vast, errant logic of eugenics, antimiscegenation, cleansing of territory, deportations, separation of races, disruption of inheritances, delineation of ghettos, establishing of camps, and mass annihilation. The regulative idea of the perfectly good will has no content; it is an *abstraction* determined by a *rule*. The example of Eichmann shows how abstraction cedes to figure and how good will guided by reason is replaced by the figure of a pure *genos*. It is a figure always ready to be loaded with features gathered from among the historical contingencies of the moment and to be deployed in the rhetorics of racism and supremacy: In 1915, the vision of a unified national Turkish territory; in 1936, the blond hair and sleek limbs of Leni Riefenstahl's Teutonic subjects; in 1994, the image of a line of pure Hutu blood. The process of generating and projecting such ideas, as well as the process of adjudicating competing ends, is not a formal and specifically not an individual exercise; it is part of the plural process of making, remaking, and unmaking the world.

## Genocidal Life: The Case of Sexual Violence

Genocidal violence is not a single phenomenon. It happens as lethal violence and as annihilation but also as territorial, carceral, and police violence; surveillance; torture; the threat of violence; eugenics; social disruption; cultural destruction—and as sexual violence. These are forms of violence that coincide, overlap, compound, and contradict each other, but while lethal violence produces death and annihilation grinds human bodies to a powder of ash and reduces human lives to nothingness, other forms of violence produce their genocidal effects by enforcing destructive modes of life. Territorial violence is the exclusion or expulsion of a group from a land or country, turning people into exiles, refugees, stateless, dispossessed, and displaced persons. Croats and Serbs were cleansed from Serbia and Croatia in the 1990s in order to produce ethnically clean territories; Eichmann's signal, career-making achievement was developing a bureaucratic system that would leave the city of Vienna *Judenrein*, purified of Jews; the Trail of Tears cleared Native Americans from their lands. Carceral violence clears space by confining portions of a population *within* the territory, though *outside* public life, that is, in camps, prisons, borstals, reservations, and detention centers. It imprisons life, creating detainees, criminals, and delinquents against which society must be defended. Aggressive, targeted policing subjects a group to state violence and denies them the legitimate protection of law enforcement. Surveillance contorts social relations, confounding the roles of police and neighbor, friend and relative; destroying privacy, trust, and loyalty; and fostering paranoia. Threatened violence produces lives constrained by fear and self-censorship. Eugenics manipulates and constrains us in what should be the free decision of whom to choose as the parents of our children. Social disruption deals social death. Cultural destruction eliminates identities. Sexual violence uses its victims' bodies against themselves and their communities by making them instruments of domination and destruction, and it generates life by force. In each case, what is destroyed by the destructive mode of life is a *world*.

Genocidal violence attacks worldliness, and the case of genocidal sexual violence shows quite precisely how this happens. The phenomenon also requires special attention here because it poses a hard case for democratic thinking by pitting the values of the *genos* against the *demos*, leading us into a confrontation with the genocide paradox.

Sarah Miller describes the harm suffered by rape victims in the Darfur conflict in terms that quickly reach beyond the familiar ethical categories of self and other to the category of world.[53] The women of Darfur were beaten, wounded, and raped by members of the Janjaweed. On one level, each assault is deeply personal, an attack that inflicts physical and psychological harm and also constitutes a moral injury, an assault on the victim's human dignity. The women return to their already distraught communities, some with scars on their bodies branding them publicly as having been raped, others pregnant, as their attackers threatened, "with an Arab baby, who can have this land." They appear to their relatives and neighbors as morally diminished; they appear to themselves as implicated in their own self-betrayal, in the way that torture victims can experience themselves as completely dominated, powerless, yet forced to participate in their own violation. On another level, the harm suffered is *relational*. We can think of the suffering of the singular victim as a *part* of the suffering inflicted on the community, a drop in its ocean of pain, but Miller shows a more complicated and more pernicious phenomenon. Sex is not merely a transaction between two people. It is a mode of relation, and the relations between sexual partners form a key network of community. Mass rapes hijack the reproductive capabilities of a group, both biologically by forcing pregnancy and culturally by displacing women from the crucial nodes of cultural transmission within families and kinship groups. When they return home, survivors may no longer occupy their roles as wives, mothers, sisters, and daughters in their patrilineal society. The status of rape victim is uncontainable; their wounded bodies are weaponized, sustaining the attack on the community even after the attackers have gone. Their suffering constitutes harm to themselves, reverberates through the community, and returns to them changed and amplified, damaging the relations that sustain their existence *and* that hold the generational community together. Both the strange and familiar child she might bear and her own body's displaced presence among them injure her *genos*.

While Miller treats both the harm to the individual and the relational harm to her and her community as instances of moral harm, Robin May Schott argues that genocidal rape and rape used as a weapon of war must be recognized as *politically* evil. Schott takes quite seriously Arendt's thought that human natality—that is, the newness of each one of us when we come into the world—is the existential signal that we each are capable of doing something new. This newness takes on its full significance in our second birth, that is, our birth into the political sphere, where we show that we can act in ways not wholly accounted for by a causal chain of events and in doing so show who we are. Indeed, these spontaneous actions serve to constantly reconstitute the political sphere, holding it open for action and for all comers. When Bosnian Serb leaders mandated enforced impregnation as a war strategy, they attacked natality. Schott writes: "When the human condition of natality is so transformed that it threatens the viability of the public world, then it also undermines the ability of a political community to guarantee rights."[54] A world in which conception can be conceived as a weapon of genocidal destruction and where leaders can issue such a mandate is also the war world where the Berberovics' neighbor can be shot in broad daylight, a young man can kick an elderly woman in the head as she lies on the ground, and a high-school teacher will rape his former students.[55]

Wars end, but when they leave behind a legacy of forced impregnation, they leave communities in the grip of the genocide paradox. The belligerents in the war in Bosnia imposed the ideology of pure *genos* determined by biology. It does not matter that any given victim identified himself in multiple, playful, biological, cultural, or ironic ways; attacked as a Muslim, he could only respond as a Muslim. The conflict produced identity-defining differences. As one witness put it, having been doctors working together at the hospital in Sarajevo, he and his colleagues became Serb doctors and Muslim doctors; there was no possible identification that did not include ethnicity. Under attack, as the world is violently reordered into genera, one commits to a *genos* one may have hardly thought of in times of peace.[56] Ethnic cleansing is the process of the expulsion of other genera and those marked as impure, closing the political space and constructing instead a national space for the homogenous *us* alone. When the ideology of purity dominates, the others' purity is the most valuable target; when genetic inheritance is the standard of purity, genetic pollution is the most deeply destructive weapon. Individual victims sustain atrocious injury; their communities, which they now have no choice but to understand as genera, are injured too. Schott's point is that the very possibility of building a political community is damaged by the ideology that has overdetermined the human condition of natality, reducing it to biological generation. If it is assumed that the question "Who are you?" is exhausted by pedigree, there is no space for spontaneous action and no conception of the political rights that would protect it as a human capacity.

## Ontology and Politics

What *is* wrong with genocide? Pronouncing genocide exotically, incomprehensively evil gets us nowhere, so the question persists. How does political thinking on genocide fare any better than a traditional ethical approach? I began by sketching an Arendtian distinction between ethics and politics, and now a more elaborate picture is needed. For Arendt, the wrong of genocide is its attack on worldliness. Existence is something none of us can ever choose for ourselves, and none of us may choose those with whom we will share the world or with whom we will have shared it. The great genocidal crime of the Nazis, their crime against humanity, was taking upon themselves the right to make that choice. Postponing for a moment the question of grounds, we can recognize this as at least a coherent claim. It is true that we share the world with a great many others whom we did not and could not choose, but it is also the case that, within the human world, we live in worlds—spaces, realms, spheres, cultures—where choice is permitted and situations in which it is required. We come to be privately, from and with people we could not have chosen; we emerge socially and can decide there who our friends are or whom to love. Eventually, in Arendt's schema, we show who we are by our words and deeds in the political realm, but she refuses to examine how those words and deeds are informed by the layers of familial and social experience that are the condition for their possibility. Home is where we live with our intimates; the social realm is where we spend time with people we like, those we choose as friends, lovers, partners, associates; the political sphere is where we are and act with and in the face of everybody, whoever they happen to be. We will not love or like all of them, but we must let them *be*. As political beings we must look at them, coexist with them, and presume to talk with them.

This is grounded in her most characteristic existential assertion, that is, that when each of us was born, the world had seen no one quite like us before. The fact of birth is the signal of our human condition of natality and plurality. We are all alike in our natal newness, and we are irreducibly distinct, not just as tokens of a type but as genuinely natal individuals: beings who were born on the earth. Worldliness consists in inhabiting a human world with other, irreducibly distinct humans. These are people we did not choose to be with because we did not choose existence. In fact, it makes no sense to say that we *did not* choose them, as though we might have chosen them or have chosen someone else; we *could not possibly have* chosen them because we *could not possibly have* chosen existence. The particulars or identities of those with whom we share the world are essentially contingent in the same way that our coming to be is essentially contingent.

How does this—or any—existential condition come to have political significance? As I noted in the Introduction, for Arendt, natality is signaled by birth and is in turn the signal of our ability to bring about something new, that is, our capacity for action; sharing this condition and this capacity signals the requirement that our shared world be open for all our actions. That is a lot of signaling, and a signal is not yet a norm. Seyla Benhabib writes: "It is the step leading from the constituents of a philosophical anthropology (natality, worldliness, plurality, and forms of human activity) to [an] attitude of respect for the other that is missing from Arendt's thought."[57] This *is* a problem for Arendt, so long as we look to her work for a derivation of norms. Hans Jonas finds himself in a similar position, and, unlike Arendt, he struggles openly with the problem. Over the course of several works he offers arguments for the essential value of human diversity, finally frankly confronting the general problem of grounding such arguments in the essay "Toward an Ontological Grounding of an Ethics for the Future." He acknowledges that biologism, subjectivism of values, and historical (and other) relativism are not susceptible to refutation and that his own version of humanism is similarly unassailable. Yet that is not to say that it is irrational or unphilosophical. Jonas could take a Nietzschean approach—"What have I to do with refutations!"[58]—and indeed he eventually says as much, albeit in more modest terms:

> My premises are, I believe, somewhat better thought out and do more justice to the total phenomenon of man and Being in general. But in the last analysis my argument can do no more than give rational grounding to an *option* it presents as a choice for a thoughtful person—an option that of course has its own inner power of persuasion. Unfortunately, I have nothing better to offer.[59]

Jonas's difficulty is embedded in the title of his essay: ". . . an Ontological Grounding of an *Ethics* for the Future." He does have something to offer here, but he offers it the wrong way, as the wrong thing. If he wants to *derive* an ethics, it's not surprising that he ends by turning up his palms. His description will never produce the sort of transcendent, transcendental claims that ethics reaches for as an ultimate grounding in order to avoid the accusation of trying to derive an "ought" from an "is." As an ethical claim, Jonas's defense does indeed involve a fallacy. But as a phenomenology of humankind that generates general, ontological claims, it produces, by his own description, an option, something for us to discuss. That is to say, it is a *political* option, the object of political judgment. To turn it into an ethical matter is to turn away from the work of politics.[60]

If we think of Arendt as offering a derivation of ethical rules, we encounter the same problem. The human conditions of natality, worldliness, plurality, and sharing are not a priori principles. They are generalized conditions that have been generated by phenomenological description, and they produce demands that will not be norms, since none will be self-evident rules for action or susceptible to proof. This is Arendt's antifoundationalism. The validity of political principles such as equality or diversity does not rely on the faultlessness of their derivation but rather "upon free agreement and consent; they are arrived at by discursive, representative thinking; and they are communicated by means of persuasion and dissuasion."[61] That is to say, we remain subject to the political hermeneutic that requires us to pay attention to the phenomena as we think about how to be together well, generationally. Generational being in the world is not a norm, but, as the temporal structure of how we come to be, how we are instituted, it makes us both vulnerable and liable to certain sorts of nonreciprocal demands.[62] This is the work of politics, and it is political thinking—that is, democratic thinking—that will have us confront the genocide paradox not as an exotic aberration but as embedded in our being together.

Yet, from the very beginning, real existing democracies mobilized against this realization. Etienne Balibar poses the question quite seriously: "Why is every democratic declaration of a new nation accompanied by a genocide?"[63] The world took up Lemkin's term after 1943 and began to use it for the horror that was before its eyes; in 1946, the states of the world, in near unanimity, condemned genocide as "shocking to the conscience of mankind."[64] But then began the diplomatic debate about what the object of the shock would turn out to be. What would the word mean? Unanimity became a task, and for two years diplomats and scholars negotiated which acts were so particularly shocking and what about them was unconscionable.[65] The universal desire to condemn was constantly jostled by particular desires to avoid self-incrimination on particular grounds, which became obvious in the campaign by the Soviet Union and its allies to remove reference to political groups but also in a lesser-known campaign by Western democracies to remove the category of cultural genocide.[66] The initial resolution stated that crimes of genocide had occurred "when racial, religious, political and other groups have been destroyed, entirely or in part." In the first full draft (the Secretariat Draft) a year later, the list had changed, and the purpose of the Convention was described as preventing "the destruction of racial, *national*, *linguistic*, religious or political groups of human beings."[67] Following the Soviet Union's arguments and eventual acquiescence on the part of the United States, the final version dropped mention of political groups, listing only "national, ethnical, racial or religious [groups]."

The strand of negotiation against the inclusion of cultural genocide was led by the United States, France, and Canada. The initial resolution included reference to the cultural contributions that different groups make to the flourishing of humankind, and the Secretariat Draft went on to elaborate three forms of genocide: physical genocide, including massacres and also the deprivation of all means of livelihood to produce slow death; biological genocide, perpetrated by restricting births; and cultural genocide, which destroyed the specific characteristics of a group by forced transfer of children, exile, repression of language, or the destruction of books and religious artifacts.[68]

Those who objected acknowledged the genocidal horrors of the camps and wanted to preserve the term for those specific acts, rejecting a continuum that could lead from there to the horrors of cultural destruction. The Danish delegate argued that "it would show a lack of logic and of a sense of proportion to include in the same convention both mass murders in gas chambers and the closing of libraries."[69] But what logic was being appealed to? The United States declared:

> The prohibition of the use of [a] language, systematic destruction of books, and destruction and dispersion of documents and objects of historical or artistic value commonly known in this Convention to those who wish to include it as "cultural genocide" is a matter which certainly should not be included in this Convention. The act of creating the new international crime of genocide is one of extreme gravity and the United States feels that it should be confined to those barbarous acts directed against individuals which form the basic concept of public opinion on this subject.[70]

It is not clear which public this declaration refers to, for others relied on other concepts. Pakistan took the position that "cultural genocide represented the end, whereas physical genocide was merely the means. . . . For millions of men in most Eastern countries, the protection of sacred books and shrines was more important than life itself; the destruction of those sacred books or shrines might mean the extinction of spiritual life."[71] China held that "cultural genocide might be even more harmful than physical or biological genocide, since it worked below the surface and attacked a whole population, attempting to deprive it of its ancestral culture and to destroy its very language."[72]

It appears to have been broadly accepted that cultures could be ranged on a scale from primitive to advanced and that "backward" cultures were subject to the logic of a civilization process. The Union of South Africa "wished to point to the danger latent in the provisions [on cultural genocide] where primitive or backwards groups were concerned."[73] Specifically, certain cultures would necessarily succumb to the civilizing action of the state. Iran was concerned that it would "have to be decided whether all cultures, even the most barbarous, deserved protection, and whether the assimilation resulting from the civilizing action of a State also constituted genocide."[74] Most telling is the fact that established democracies used the same premises. Australia's delegate, apparently speaking without irony, said that "genocide was such a vile act that even savages and wild beasts were incapable of committing it. War toughened soldiers had been struck with horror at the sight of the victims of genocide who were still alive."[75] Sweden pointedly expressed the anxiety of these democracies: "The question could arise whether, for example, the fact that Sweden had converted the Lapps to Christianity might not lay her open to the accusation that she had committed an act of cultural genocide." The modern state understood itself as having a need—even a duty—to establish a degree of homogeneity in its population in order to make of it a people. It was imperative to block the genocide continuum that would lead from the horrors of the camps to the horrors of what Western democracies regarded as the normal practices of state building.

Democracy asserts the priority of *demos* over *genos* in political life: In these negotiations on the concept of genocide, that assertion is indistinguishable from the assertion of one hegemonic *genos* over others in the name of democratic assimilation. The Canadian delegate's statement plainly enacts the collapse of *demos* into *genos*:

> The Government and people of Canada were horrified at the idea of cultural genocide and hoped that effective action would be taken to suppress it. The people of his country were deeply attached to their cultural heritage, which was made up *mainly of a combination of Anglo-Saxon and French elements, and they would strongly oppose the attempt to undermine the influence of those two cultures*, as they would oppose any similar attempt in any other part of the world.[76]

No mention is made of Canada's history of violence against native peoples; instead, the delegate noted "that he knew of no country where the government, and the people generally, were more concerned to ensure the preservation of the culture, language or religion of minority groups."[77]

With the exception of the transfer of children, all elements of cultural genocide disappeared from the final draft.[78]

Talk of *finality* is misleading here. In 1948, the Convention was put in place as an international legal document and greeted as a substantial achievement, but it is an end only in the sense that it is a notable point on an arc of the political hermeneutic of genocide. Efforts to discern, understand, and respond to the phenomenon would now necessarily pass through the Convention description while also, at the same time, through testimony of observers, survivors, and accused perpetrators, along with descriptions and redescriptions by nongovernmental organizations and state actors; meanwhile, political, diplomatic, and scholarly debate would revisit its language as a matter of hermeneutic ritual. Asking questions— What is genocide? What are the criteria? Does this case count?—may have the stated aim of elucidating a clear and powerful instrument against violence while simultaneously serving the purposes of exculpation and self-preservation. Asking after the *wrongness* of genocide runs this same risk of serving the interests of the powerful, but it has three important advantages. First, it forces us to a deeper level of analysis regarding how we value the *genos*. Second, it moves the conversation into the realm of politics and, thereby, third, leads democratic politics to confront the paradoxical relation of *demos* and *genos*.

# 4 / Democracy of Generational Beings

*Every human problem cries out to be considered on the basis of time, the ideal that the present always serves to build the future. And this future is not that of the* cosmos, *but very much the future of my century, my country, and my existence.*

—FRANTZ FANON, *Black Skin, White Masks*

*And yet we need the concept of democracy with its strange temporality for the critical function it performs, interrupting and casting suspicion on the rhetoric of democracy that engulfs us.*

—ROBERT BERNASCONI, "Rousseau and the Supplement to the Social Contract"

## The Democratic Paradox and the Genocide Paradox

Democracy is the struggle between and among commitments to *demos, genos,* and *cosmos.* It is a struggle—and this is the same thing—between the generational time of *genos* on the one hand and the cosmic time of the universe on the other. *Demos* came to be in an interruption, and interruption would seem to be the only contender for the title of a properly democratic temporality. Yet there is nothing proper about interruption. It is not its own way of being but cuts across temporalities, breaking into generational time on the one hand or distracting from the long, unknown *durée* of the universe on the other. It is also not distinctively or particularly democratic. In the absence of evidently democratic time, the challenge here, now, is to discern the shape of the problem of time for democracies.

The democratic struggle is a struggle in *imagination,* for what can the people look like when they are neither the self-same people of the *genos* nor all the people of the *cosmos*? It is an *existential* struggle, given the demand, which comes from the point of view of *genos,* that the people be *a* people with a principle that secures its identity over time and a competing demand from the point of view of the universe that the people be all people. And yet there are actually existing democracies, and in them the struggle is *experienced* as the struggle for autonomy in the face of the desire to belong in a way that is not the same as how we belong to our parents and children and also not how we belong to the universe. They are democracies not because they have triumphed in these struggles—to imagine people as free and equal, to be together over time, to share the experience of belonging—but because they persist in the effort.

The struggle happens on the *theoretical* level too. The tradition that looks backward, as Plato does, to a philosophical aristocracy projected into the past will show democracy as a degenerate form, succumbing to the excesses of individual freedom governed by appetite. A forward-looking tradition that identifies democracy as an ideal not yet reached, and perhaps unreachable, will show democracies constantly falling short of true equality and true freedom. A list of necessary and sufficient features culled from actually existing democracies—participation, representation, elections, rule of law, or peaceful succession, for example—will not do it justice, since any given list would be no more than an accumulation of empirical contingencies that do not amount to a principle of organization.

The struggle of *genos*, *demos*, and *cosmos* informs all democratic thought, but it comes closest to the surface in the tradition of radical democracy. Democracy struggles with and against the projection of its own perfection and the progress we may or may not make toward it; it interrupts *genos* life and insists on our freedom, here and now. Yet such anarchic individualist liberty soon confronts the plurality of *demotoi* who make up the *demos*, the many, all equal without being equivalent, all embedded in an array of nonreciprocal, asymmetrical relations, all existing according to the temporalities of generational life. The roots of radical democracy in the anarchist tradition are well documented by Todd May, and Rancière argues that "Democracy means this above all: anarchic 'government,' founded on nothing other than the absence of all title to govern."[1] What remains to be done is to take on the thought that democracy is the modification anarchism undergoes when it confronts the temporality of generational life. Failure to do so means that democracies remain theoretically entangled in *genos*-thinking and historically embroiled in genocidal violence.

In Chapter 3 we saw the nations of the world struggling in 1947 and 1948 to make a distinction between genocide, on the one hand, and the assimilation of difference that they regarded as an essential part of nation building, on the other. The anxieties that run through those debates are an index to genocidal violence in the histories of contemporary democracies.[2] Canada insisted on its respect for indigenous cultures while, between 1883 and 1996, the Canadian government removed 150,000 indigenous children from their homes and families and forced them to be educated in government- and church-run residential schools. Australia emphasized the horror of what had happened in the war in Europe while, between 1788 and 1930, there had been an estimated 250 massacres of aboriginal Australians by European settlers.[3] Britain was concerned about its colonies and made a point of rejecting a suggestion by the USSR that it had "some sinister motive for wishing to maintain the colonial clause" governing, among other things, extradition for crimes of genocide. The British delegate added that "the record of the United Kingdom with regard to its colonial peoples was sufficiently well known."[4] At this point, the British nation-state relied on an empire that ruled almost a quarter of the world's population. The expansion of democracy at home in the course of the nineteenth century (with the parliamentary reforms of 1832, for example) was matched by the progress of violent exploitation overseas. Between 1870 and 1914, millions of imperial subjects died of drought and famine even as they were being forcibly incorporated into a London-centered world economy;[5] Boer and African people were starved in concentration camps between 1899 and 1902; in 1947, as the discussion of the genocide convention was under way in the United States, the British partition of India was displacing 10 million people and would lead to the killing of an estimated 1 million people.

Meanwhile, contributions to the diplomatic debate by the United States show a remarkable *lack* of anxiety about the conflict between its history of both democratic innovation and violent oppression. The treatment of Native Americans or Black Americans was not addressed in the debates, and neither the United States nor any other country responded to the statement by the Women's International Democratic Federation that "Negro women in the United States were by far the least protected and most discriminated against minority group."[6] In 1951, the charge of genocide was brought against the United States by Black Americans, but the international community took no position; the institutions of American democracy did not understand themselves as having been called into question; and lynching, discrimination, and segregation continued. In fact, the United States embarked on a policy of international intervention conceived of as exporting democracy, a policy often experienced by its targets as a genocidal attack on their lives, their people, their way of being, and their mode of belonging.[7]

Can democracy survive such a history? Can it persist as a value? We will see in what follows how the thought of the "family" survives everything we know about the cruelties of real existing families, and the thought of "the family of humankind" may have work to do beyond or against the universalizing forces of hegemonic cosmopolitanism. In its own conflicted way, the idea of democracy can survive the confrontation with democracies' real violence and failures. It can do so as a figure of freedom and equality precisely in the avowed context of the history of democratic disappointments and disasters. Families are not always havens of care and protection, but they should be; democracies have not abolished genocidal violence, but they should have.

Earlier, I broached the paradox of democracy alongside William Connolly, who warns of the fury of self-assertion that threatens to swamp the public space if it admits *genos* as an identifier. The very institutions of democracy—majority rule, for example—compound the problem with their tendency to create perpetual minorities who will be marginalized, excluded, and eliminated until the *demos* itself is homogenized and translated into *genos*.[8] Connolly points to this as a social paradox that political theories either acknowledge and negotiate pluralistically or suppress behind the schema of an exclusive cosmopolitan universality.[9] Chantal Mouffe makes the same claim, arguing (after Schmitt) that the paradoxical character of liberal-democratic politics comes from the mistaken idea that we can preserve liberty understood *both* as belonging to the individual *and* in terms of our being in relation, as if they were the same thing. The paradox is something positive, for Mouffe, since it has the great advantage of frustrating liberal tendencies to total dissemination, on the one hand, and democratic tendencies to total closure, on the other.[10] Derrida will name it an aporia and will find sources for political theory in the thought of the friend when there is no friend, the guest who may also be the enemy, messianism without a messiah, and, most tellingly, the democracy that is always to come.

If we organized ourselves according to the *genos* alone, the fury of self-assertion could be just that—furious and assertive—and contestation between the genera could be all violent struggle for domination. If we organized ourselves according to the *cosmos* alone, the universal law would make both *genos* and *demos* irrelevant. The political theories that acknowledge some version of Connolly's paradox are theories that see the limitations of both *genos* and *cosmos*; one way to negotiate it pluralistically is to begin from the nonfoundation of the *demos*.

This is where the democratic paradox meets the genocide paradox. The problem comes into focus as the problem of democratic time. Democracy is the political manifestation of human plurality; the *demos* is not a *genos*, and *democracy* is not a synonym for *nation*-state. Moreover, belonging to the *demos* does not mean sharing a worldview. On the contrary, it means sharing a common world that cannot be fully seen from a single perspective. What it requires of its citizens is not obedience or loyalty but judgment; democratic citizenship relies on a developed capacity to judge reflectively, that is, to judge in the absence of a concept of rule.[11] In addition, our fellow democrats are people with whom we share no essence, origin, or destiny beyond being here now. Since the *demos* is constantly changing, losing the old ones and adding new ones by birth, migration, and expansion, a democracy must constantly decide how to sustain the impulse and practices that make its world. The newcomers keep coming, the generations keep overlapping, and the structure of *genos* is always at hand, offering a model for what it is to be in time but also, surreptitiously, offering itself as *what is* in time, proposing itself as the thing that needs to be kept going. We value generational being in ways that lead us to care about and care for the ones who came before and the ones who come after us, to bear the past and the future. But if we take on the genetic principle as determinative and apply the criterion of identity when we decide whom we belong with, whom we are responsible to and responsible for, then we submit the rhythms of generational care to the service of sheer self-assertion.

We value democratic liberty and equality and also the freedom to struggle over what they amount to, what their limits are, and for whom. After all, in political life, disputes and disagreements are our lot.[12] Models of democracy all make room for contestation and consider how to hold open the space for that contestation. Yet they fail to grasp the generational time of democratic life and the generational content of democratic contestation. Arendt, for one, understands that political life involves struggle (*agon*) and requires judgment without the direction of pregiven principles, and she thinks of it as structured by our being between past and future. Yet she excludes the generational *content* of our lives, that is, the particular mess of asymmetrical, nonreciprocal relations that create and sustain us even as they tug at us with demands both material and existential and threaten to smother us with expectations.

The danger of that exclusion is immense. As I have argued, we come to be in networks of enduring generational relations linking us to those (of us) who have gone and to others (of us) who have yet to come. If we fail to pay sustained attention to how we live in this structure and how we negotiate the demands it makes on us, we find ourselves unprepared for the theoretical work of understanding the relation of *genos* and violence, for seeing the work that it takes to keep things going and also the slow violence that destroys worlds, and for confronting the democratic deficits that make it so that belonging to the *demos* is experienced as an inadequate replacement for—or an irritating distraction *from*—*genos* life. It leaves us disastrously unprepared for the genocidal attackers' knock on the door—if not ours, then our neighbor's or the door of the family across town or across the border. It leaves us unprepared for the reassuring, pernicious appeal of the language of *them* and *us* by which democracies identify those who belong and those who don't. It abets our ignorance of the genocidal violence perpetrated in democracy's name.

## Genos and Cosmos

There is a solution to the genocide paradox that seems to be merely obvious. We should set aside our concern with the *genos* in human affairs, loosen our commitments to genetic identities, blur the very category of *genos*, and finally acknowledge one another simply, or at least principally, as fellow human beings. If we could only do this, the idea of attacking your *genos* on behalf of mine would lose sense, since we would belong not so much to this or that group but to humanity, the universe, or the earth. Yet, given what I have been arguing about *genos* and kinship, this may be too much to ask right away. In that case, we might take it on as an ideal that would serve as a guide to our living together, leading us to act in ways that gradually reduce the importance of *genos* and increase the value we place on the individual, on the one hand, and the cosmos, on the other. If this also seems too high a demand, we might allow ourselves to remain attached to the *genos* in certain ways and in certain aspects of our lives, so long as those attachments do not interfere with the overarching commitment to our human being and our belonging to the universe.

Objections to such cosmos-thinking revolve around three questions: (1) Can we be adequately motivated by an abstract concept of humanity? (2) What is lost when we reduce human being to the figure of the human as such? (3) What can the rights of human beings mean in the absence of an authority to defend them? Each one is at the same time a question about *genos*: (1) Is there a way of belonging to the *cosmos* that excites feelings that are a match to what we feel about belonging to a *genos*? (2) Human being as such includes a capacity for rationality and autonomy but is essentially generational, relational, and diverse; how does this structure political life? (3) Can the *cosmos* protect our rights, or must that task fall to the institutions of existing nation-states? In other words, when it comes to the political question, can *cosmos*-thinking carry us beyond *genos*-thinking?

Structures are already in place that aim to bring about an international cosmopolitan arrangement, not only the theoretical scaffolding of Enlightenment concepts of humanity, rationality, dignity, and universality but also worldly institutions built upon those concepts. December 10, 1948, the day after the ratification of the Genocide Convention, the General Assembly of the United Nations proclaimed the Universal Declaration of Human Rights with the aim of ensuring that every individual and every organ of society, keeping this Declaration constantly in mind, shall strive by teaching and education to promote respect for these rights and freedoms and by progressive measures, national and international, to secure their universal and effective recognition and observance.[13]

The Declaration declares us all free and equal in dignity and all entitled to the same rights and freedoms. The individual is the locus of value, and the just government or organ of society joins individuals in preserving the liberty of each citizen of the universe. The ideal toward which the document urges us is a universal respect for individual rights. We can understand as much, and we are surely inspired by the beautiful thought of the universe, but we may also find it, and the language of *all*, *everyone*, and *man*, too abstract to imagine and too empty to motivate us. We understand that the earth is populated by billions of people, and we can grasp the number in terms of orders of magnitude, but any image we have will be the image of something other than seven billion human beings.[14] "All humans" is not a category we can adequately populate in imagination, and we cannot love all humans as we love any given human.

In the face of the problem of motivation, the Declaration's Preamble quietly reverts to the language of *genos*, at first in the form of the appeal to *family*: "Whereas recognition of the inherent dignity and of the equal and inalienable rights of all members of *the human family* is the foundation of freedom, justice and peace in the world." The cosmopolitan principle of rights, which often presents itself as presuming the merest, barest individual, now presumes the shared experience and idea of family and feelings of care, protectiveness, and love. We all know what families are—we were each raised by *some*one—but we also know about the wretchedness of family life. We remember our own childhood hurts, and we know the stories from the fate of Iphigenia at the hand of her father, to Abel's at the hand of his brother, to Freud's "family romance" and Vinterberg's *Celebration*. Yet it will always be the case that those closest to us and those to whom we are most attached are the ones who can hurt us most—this is the nature of vulnerability—and somehow, *family* survives as a positive focus for our imagination. The cruelties of Agamemnon and Cain strike us as devastatingly cruel because of the gulf they open up between how those families are and the sense we have of how families ought to be. Thierry de Duve describes it in terms of respect: We are moved by the Declaration's thought of *the human family* as a basis for freedom, justice, and peace because our shared transcendental idea of family invokes feelings of benevolence, mutual support, and respect, feelings that we cannot count on being activated by the formal concept of universal rights or the regulative idea of a world populated by perfectly respectful and respectable humans alone.[15]

The fact that the cosmopolitan thinking of the Declaration on Human Rights finds moving expression in the language of family life is not fatal to its aim. On the contrary, the fact that a document addressed to all the people of the world should reach beyond the language of the individualistic strand of European Enlightenment is to its credit. Yet the appeal to family, whatever it will turn out to mean, leads the Declaration into troublesome entanglements. First, the primary feeling invoked by *family* is famously not respect but love. Even in its idealized form, family is far from being the scene of respect. We don't have sex with our partners out of respect or hold and feed our children out of respect. Young people are instructed to respect their elders, but that is not always where we find the motivation to care for our aging parents. Instead, we love our partners jealously, and our children ferociously, and care for our parents with affection, frustration, anger, and sadness, all at a level of intensity rarely matched in other scenes. The Declaration uses *the family of man* to invoke this loving intensity only to be then forced to temper it—if not replace it entirely—with the universalizable concept of respect. Second, inequality is inescapable in family life given the generational inequality of adults and children and the asymmetry of their relations. Can conjuring a network of inherently *un*equal relations lead us to affirm equal rights for all? Meanwhile, the advantage of invoking the family of man may have to do not only with parents and children but with a wider array of relations that bind together an extended family across time, drawing on feelings that include the sense of genealogical belonging I considered in Chapter 2 or security in the inheritance of a tradition and concern for its future. This means—third—that in addition to "benevolence, mutual support, and respect," which would no doubt incline us toward freedom, justice, and peace, we must also reckon with the struggles of being between past and future and feelings of love, security, anxiety, and belonging, which might not.

In Chapter 2, I distinguished between *my* people (plural) and *a* people (singular), that is, the group of related individuals tied together over some few remembered generations, on the one hand, and a larger set of unnamed or unindividuated ancestors, on the other. I noted in that chapter the tendency of *genos*-thinking to blur this distinction and to use the affective appeal of the first to motivate commitments to the second. When we are called to war, the summons comes not in terms of respect but in the words and images of patriotic love and the desire to protect our families and our way of life. When the Declaration on Human Rights refers to the human family, it is in order to motivate our commitment as individuals to our shared human existence; soon after, however, it once again appeals to *genos*-thinking, addressing us as *peoples* and *nations*. We must each and all be treated equally, and peoples and nations are charged as the agents of progress toward the goal of "universal and effective recognition and observance" of universal human rights. That is to say, the Declaration appeals to the thought of the *genos* (in its familial form) in order to motivate the *genos* (in its national form) to progress toward *cosmos*-thinking. In its effort to make up the motivation deficit of cosmopolitanism, it reinforces the thinking that opposes it.

If *genos*-thinking, *genos* identity, and the experience of *genos* life refuse to disappear in the face of cosmic law, perhaps they can be confined within the private or social realm identified by cosmopolitan political thought as their proper place. In the effort to avoid dividing the *cosmos* into *genera*, modern cosmopolitanism asks us to pause on the threshold of its public sphere, or behind a veil of ignorance, or at the edge of the ideal speech situation. There, we cloak our inherited identities and home in on what is most transparently communicable in the specificities of individual experience, paring ourselves down to the bare bones of human being. This human figure will have a certain role in understanding the theoretical construct of cosmopolitanism, but in terms of imagination, it will inevitably fall short. We do not inhabit identities as we wear our clothing, and we can imagine no bones bare enough. They will always be the bones of some sort of human being, and from Vitruvian Man to Le Corbusier's Modulator, it is no accident that the figure standing for Man has taken its particular manly shape, embodying power and privilege. Each time we imagine a bare human, we imagine too little of human existence.

*Cosmos*-thinking may not be a way to spring the trap of *genos*-thinking once and for all, but it does make up a broad set of interventions in relation to *genos*. Certainly, we cannot dismiss cosmopolitanism any more than we can do without the thought of a cosmic order, but the thought that it is the rational, evident, and operable solution to politics must be set aside, and its historical place in the European imperial project must not be neglected. It is not a transcendent concept ex machina (though it claims a transcendental role) but emerges in experience and imagination even as it takes form in theory.

After all, neither *genos* nor *cosmos* is a natural order. For instance, we can pinpoint a key moment when the naturalized order of *genos* was brought to light as such in the tradition of anthropological kinship studies. David Schneider could gather data in Yap in 1947 and 1948 and find in it evidence for a systematic account of Yap kinship structures.[16] Yet he would revisit the same data decades later and conclude that it showed an altogether different, recalcitrant set of relations that resisted systematization.[17] The initial model emerged in a context shaped by the Western kinship schema developed in the nineteenth century by Henry Lewis Morgan and others and by the presumption that its structures were—indeed, that they *must be*—universal. This is what Schneider rejected when he revisited his data, famously declaring in 1972: "*In the way in which Morgan and his followers have used it,* [kinship] *does not exist in any culture known to man.*"[18] Yet how did anthropologists come to find those Western kinship models to begin with? What regional ontology governed that research? What postulate guided their thinking? What *experience* of *genos* warrants the *concept* of *genos* that would in turn warrant the *experience* of *genos*?

*Cosmos* does not escape the same circularity. Cosmopolitan politics is not a matter of responding to the superstition or ideology of the *genos* with the evident truth of the *cosmos*. We can have an experience of *this*—of where we are, here and now—as an experience of *cosmos* only once we are equipped with the postulate of the universe as an ordered whole. No experience gives us the concept. We cannot read the order of the universe in the starry sky, the nest of a bird, or the sensations of holding a baby, but certain experiences—these ones, perhaps—can lead us to think that we are part of ordered nature. We cannot catalogue all of them or predict or—least of all—prescribe what they might be, but there are ways in which we encounter the world that guide us toward the postulates that in turn make possible the experience of cosmopolitan belonging: that nature is an ordered whole, that humans have a place in it, that all humans have a place in it equally. This is not a matter of proof. Nothing in our lived experience will *demonstrate* their truth or falsity, but as we set about trying to answer the question of how to live together, we cannot do without the postulate of the *cosmos*. The UN Declaration's deployment of *the family of man* is a reminder that we also cannot do without some form of the postulate of the *genos*.[19]

The sharper reminder took shape in the Genocide Convention itself, an address *by* the assembly of nation-states *to* itself as an assembly and to each of its members. It affirms the value of nations and "ethnical, racial, and religious groups" and points to the nation-state as the forum where prevention and punishment of genocidal attacks will happen. International cooperation is necessary, and international penal tribunals are anticipated, but the impetus for cooperation and the activation of international organs originate in the agency of the nation-state.

After all, though the idea of the *cosmos* propels the Declaration on Human Rights, the *cosmos* does not grant or protect our rights. Our status as human inhabitants of the universe cannot serve as the basis of our rights. As Arendt argues in *The Origins of Totalitarianism*, the Rights of Man have their ground in civil society and not the other way around.[20] We have rights insofar as we are specified, identified humans, and the mechanism for this identification has been the state. We have rights as citizens, and, since we still live in the age of the nation-state, we have rights as Turkish or Indonesian or US citizens.[21] There is no such thing as the citizen *as such* or a citizen of the world. Only by being marked for inclusion do we become the sort of beings—sorted, grouped, identified beings—who have rights. Belonging is a political and existential necessity.[22]

## *Genos* and *Demos*

If cosmopolitanism cannot cut the Gordian knot of the genocide paradox, should democracy not be able to undertake the work of unraveling it? Rancière argues that politics begins where biology ends, and he identifies the decisive moment where the one gives way to the other in Plato's *Laws*. Having enumerated the traditional qualifications for ruling—superiority by birth and superiority by knowledge—Plato adds "the choice of God," which is manifest in the drawing of lots. This is the democratic qualification. It is no discernable qualification at all. Thierry de Duve takes up the thought:

> However, how the emancipation of legitimate power from hereditary tribal authority should be conceived, and where one is to place the breaking point are open questions. I would place it inside the history of the concept of filiation—more precisely, of fatherhood, which is nowhere a simply biological concept—rather than conceive it as a break from filiation altogether, as Rancière does.[23]

De Duve holds out hope for a breaking point and anticipates it occurring at a place—imagined, existing, experiential, theoretical—to which biology and politics both lay full claim. This is exactly the sort of contested place where we might look for an escape from the genocide paradox, though it soon becomes clear that the break is never clean, and, instead, there is always a protracted unraveling and entangling. Biology never captured the full truth of fatherhood or of power in *genos*-based societies, and politics cannot leave biology behind; de Duve's argument suggests as much. *Bios* is not the sort of thing that ends as long as any of us live, and the history of democracy—starting with Kleisthenes—is the ongoing history of one break after another, all of them conceptually complicated and politically messy.

The law of the *cosmos* presents itself as natural law; the *genos* presents itself as the natural law as it governs the generation of sameness and difference over time. In contrast, the demes of Kleisthenes touched on in the Introduction required a set of unabashedly *un*natural decisions about democratic locales. In 510 BCE, Hippias the tyrant had been driven into exile, the Spartan soldiers who had helped the Athenian aristocrats overthrow him had left, and the aristocratic families were fighting among themselves for dominance. The *demos*—the Athenians who did not belong to the aristocracy and who had largely supported the tyrant—began to "get the worst of things."[24] Driven by claims that "there were many sharing in the politeia for whom it was not appropriate," a civic scrutiny (*diapsephismos*) was launched that would call out those of impure blood.[25] It was a paroxysm of *genos*-thinking. Phillip Manville writes in his history of Athenian citizenship:

> The "scrutiny" was not an orderly or parliamentary review of citizen lists (which did not exist at this time). It was a reign of terror, caught up in the bitter civil war among aristocrats, ruthless leaders striving for political power now that Hippias was gone. . . . Large number of Athenians were driven out or rendered legally vulnerable by this event. . . . It is against this background of the *diapsephismos*—a reign of terror in which "true" citizenship was a man's only defense—that the enormous popularity of Kleisthenes's reforms can be appreciated.

Kleisthenes "wished to mix them up so that more would share in the citizenship."[26] He declared an amnesty and, ignoring the four ancient Ionic tribes, which had been recognized by Solon, divided Attica into 139 demes, or districts, where every Athenian would register, every man selecting one as his home deme. Moreover, Kleisthenes allocated the demes among ten entirely new tribes. From that moment, an Athenian would belong to his distinctive *demos* in addition to his family or tribe and, most significantly of all, would be a participant in political life as a member of a *demos* and not as a member of a family. Athenian democracy could now distinguish itself from the violent familial struggles of earlier times and in other cities.[27] With this beginning, the polis sets itself at odds with *genos* and opens itself to new contingencies. Why ten tribes? Where were the boundaries of the demes? How would a person decide between registering where he lived and where he was born? In at least one node of the system, contingency appears to have been explicitly acknowledged and embraced as the rule of chance; according to Aristotle, demes were distributed among tribes by lot.[28]

This was a break, though hardly a clean one. The demes were artificial but often followed existing geographical or social boundaries. Every Athenian now took on a new mode of belonging, but as a supplement rather than a replacement to family belonging; he would now take on the name of his deme as part of his proper name, an *addition* to family name. (It appears that adoption of the new names was not immediate and never became widespread.) In many cases, the deme where a citizen chose to register was an area he already regarded as an ancestral homeland. More important than each of these, however, is the fact that at the moment of the reform, every man chose the deme to which he *and his descendants* would belong. The new mode of belonging, which aimed to dismantle the hereditary rule of the aristocratic families, immediately became a matter of inheritance. *Genos* reasserted itself in the *demos*.

But something new had happened, and heredity could no longer be asserted as the single criterion for political rule; shared genetic origin was no longer the basis for political life, and, however a *polis* would claim to be instituted, it could not be regarded as a matter of nature or necessity. Kleisthenes's reform gave Athenian citizenship and the city of Athens a new origin that was irreducibly contingent, incorporating into democratic life the anarchic moment that it would never leave behind and a tension that democratic thinking would work hard and hopelessly to undo.[29]

In this way, the *demos* inaugurates political existence precisely by not being a *genos*. More specifically—and this gets us right to the point—the *deme* inaugurated politics as a matter of place without touching on the question of time.[30] Kleisthenes's reforms punctuated the life of the city, suspending the rule that tied inclusion to descent, giving pause to those who had taken to obsessively examining the rolls, putting a stop to claims that the city was being infiltrated by impure blood, declaring an amnesty, and recalibrating the mechanism for the allocation of citizenship. The time of the city stopped. Every man selected his deme. Time began again, and it had the same generational structure through which authority had flowed before. Power continued to circulate and accumulate across generations, but now it came from a new origin, and, moreover, interruption was now available as a source of authority.

Put another way, political life is inaugurated in the break in the expected temporal flow of bequest and inheritance. The temporality of continuity and interruption applies to this inaugural moment, but this duality is not enough to serve as a model for democratic time. More accurately, it turns out to be *too much* as a model for democratic time. For Prince Hamlet, his father's death has left the state itself "disjoint and out of frame."[31] His tragedy originates in the fact that he, heir to a throne, remains subject to a hereditary, princely time that promises rectitude. In the face of disruption of that time, he becomes convinced that he was born to set it right; that is, (1) that it *can* be rectified, (2) that it was *he* who was born to set it right, and (3) that he was *born* to set it right. He assumes—on what grounds?— that time can and should be *in* joint and that he knows what it is for time to be right, to be rejoined, son following father, widowed queen remaining a widow, uncle staying in his place, prince becoming king. In contrast, democratic time promises no such rectitude; it offers no rectitude at all. There is no right democratic time; there is no democratic time, only, I argue, the question of time for democracies.

The deme, the first place of democracy, was "the country, divided into parts," though it would be a mistake to think of it as territory. There is no evidence of a survey having been conducted and no trace of boundary stones. In fact, their absence is specifically noted. There is also no evidence of a public archive recording deme boundaries. David Whitehead writes in *The Demes of Attica*: "Kleisthenes dealt with the demes as a series of isolated villages, not blocks of territory."[32] Without a boundary, without chorological studies, there was no implication that a rule for inclusion and exclusion would or could be read off the landscape. This was not a matter of dividing up a space by drawing lines through it but of designating the places of the *demos*. We can think of home as contained by four walls, on the one hand, or by a hearth, on the other; those who belong are identified as those who live within these walls or, alternatively, as those who gather around this home fire. In the same way, a political district might be defined by its borders, in the way counties and states are defined in modern polities, or it might be understood as centered on a place where people live together and gather to trade, work, perform religious rites, get into and out of disputes, and make decisions about their shared life. Many of Kleisthenes's demes hewed to more or less natural divisions and topographies, but this too can follow either the model of the four walls or the model of the hearth; a valley defined by the mountain ridges on either side or, otherwise, by the river running through it. The isolated village is not a space carved out by borders; it is the *place* where people come together as the *demos*.[33]

The compass of each administrative unit may have been both revolutionary and evolutionary, but if the demes were constituted in the last analysis by (revolutionary) fiat, the people of each district became a people, that is, instituted itself, in the aggregated decisions of those who became its members. All Athenians of any defensible status, even the many accused of impure birth, were permitted to choose and, in choosing, become members of a *demos* and part of the *polis*.[34] Yet soon—indeed, perhaps right away, and perhaps as an integral part of Kleisthenes's reform—the *demotoi*, or demesmen, were also expected to take note of immigrants settled in the district and to begin working out the rights allowed them and obligations required of them.[35] Even if there were no boundary stones, there was a requirement to keep track of who came and went from the place; being there and living there was not enough to permit one to belong to the *demos*.[36] This is what Schmitt will not let us forget: A democracy includes some and excludes others, but it has no evident internal criterion for doing so.[37]

As a historical interruption, the reforms took time, time for citizens to register, time—years and even decades—for the new order and the new nomenclature to be adopted. As an interruption of the social logic of belonging, it was over almost as soon it had begun. And yet, it was the break that set democracy in place: a-chronic, topographical democracy, with freedom at its core, the village as its hearth-shaped model, and no principle for its being in time. This was the anarchic element understood in relation to time: Membership was elective, its members were united by no *genos* but shared equality and difference, and they engaged *on that basis* in the political task of living together freely. Yet living has its own temporalities, and the figure of the *demos* does not hang in this state of interrupted animation for long. While the new *demotoi* take up questions of place and limits, and while they discuss the status of those who come from elsewhere, there is no pause in the arrival of newcomers by birth or in the departure of the old ones. The difference is that now, insofar as the community exists as a *demos*, the logic of the *demos* requires questions not asked before: What are they to us, the ones who came before and the ones yet to come, the old and the young, the dead and the not born? What is our responsibility to them? The *genos* had understood its very self as the answer to all these unspoken questions; from its point of view, each one is a question too far. We can say with Aristotle that the *genos* is the same "though some of [its members] are perpetually dying, others coming into the world, as we say that a river or a fountain is the same, though the waters are continually changing."[38] Yet, as he also points out, this cannot be assumed as the mode of being of a community of citizens. With the inauguration of politics in the wake of the democratic interruption, the *demos* encounters *its* old and young, *its* dead and those who will come, *its* newcomers by birth, expansion, and migration, and it must respond to them all democratically.

## The Problem of Time for Democracies

At stake here is not a conflict between times—then and now and to come, the world as it is and the world as it used to be and as it will be—but the relationship between different modes of being in time and different temporal events and practices.[39] If we start from the continuities of *genos*-time as the temporality of inheritance, belonging, and anticipation, then *demos*-time is overdetermined as the instant of break and interruption. This model has the apparent advantage of offering a way to resolve the paradoxes by releasing the tension between continuity and interruption, but the cost is high, no matter which way we try to achieve the resolution: We either collapse *demos* into *genos* and politics into a dimension of tribal, national, or otherwise essentialized life or we privilege democratic interruption as if it were the punctuation of time by eternity, reducing politics to miraculous, messianic interventions—if they ever come—and reduce political thinking to Schmitt's political theology.[40] Both result in the foreclosure of politics. The real advantage of the model instead lies in sustaining the tension as the condition for the possibility of multiple temporal practices. It means examining how we get on with things and keep things going in a way that is anarchic (vulnerable to interruption and constant refounding), generational (acknowledges the overlap of generations, the demands of care for the young and the old, the dead and those to come, and the work of bequest and inheritance), democratic (plural, contingent, and open to the expression of differing temporalities), and worldly (lodged in the scene for the making of meaning).[41]

At the beginning of this chapter, I described democracy as anarchism plus generational life. *Arkhe* is both *rule* and *origin*, and an-archism, strictly speaking, must separate these meanings with the greatest care. Anarchism rejects rule, including the rule of history, tradition, inheritance, and everything that draws its authority from a venerable origin. To be an-archic in the sense of *origin* means rejecting *the* origin and committing oneself instead to the origin that each of us is, to constantly starting over, cherishing above all the freedom of individuals, who come to be all the time, each one original. Anarchist temporality has a miraculous quality, but in the most human and mundane sense. An anarchist will not fret that time is out of joint; for anarchism (again, strictly speaking), time is never *in* joint. Yet what can this mean in the context of the overlapping time of generations? Even anarchists were infants once, and they have children, but there is no such thing as anarchist parenting. The proposition is as contradictory as the scene of a parent instructing her child: "Obey no authority!" While the anarchist principle values every free individual as a new beginning, when it meets the principle of generation it must consider both the old world into which each one arrives and the work of bringing each one up. The anarchist mother raises her child in a world that values his freedom, instilling in him the values that she hopes will lead him to reject authority and seek freedom as she does. She will have in mind the authority of state and church and their histories and traditions, but her tragedy is the tragedy of every generation as it ages: from the point of view of the young, she is history too.

For some, the child is the problem—or, rather, the Child, the figure of obligatory reproduction and the tyranny of the future, is the problem. Lee Edelman writes in *No Future: Queer Theory and the Death Drive*: "For politics, however radical the means by which specific constituencies attempt to produce a more desirable social order, remains at its core, conservative insofar as it works to *affirm* a structure, to *authenticate* social order, which it then intends to transmit to the future in the form of its inner Child."[42] As I noted in the Introduction, he is right to identify the impulse toward persistence that marks every new constitution; he is right to emphasize the continuity between the privatized realms of social reproduction and politics; he is also right to see the figure of the Child as enforcing the hetero-norms that overdetermine generational life as lived for the sake of persistence itself, requiring no end of sacrifice for the future. His response, in line with the antisocial thesis in queer theory, is a commitment to negativity and the antifutural time of the death drive. As such, the only time for politics is another sort of interruption, the time of now-and-no-more. Yet Jack Halberstam, attuned to the same negativity, finds time for queer youth; Carolyn Dinshaw responds with an examination of the relation of past and present and the queer desire for history; Elizabeth Freeman introduces the thought of temporal drag.[43] Lauren Berlant, professing a wary optimism in response to Edelman's pessimism, writes:

> I am committed to the political project of imagining how to detach from lives that don't work and from worlds that negate the subjects that produce them; and I aim, along with many antinormative activists, to expand the field of affective potentialities, latent and explicit fantasies, and infrastructures for how to live beyond survival, toward flourishing not later but in the ongoing now.[44]

Politically speaking, the Child is indeed the problem if understood as the unambiguous figure of a willed, prefigured future. Real existing children are more complicated; they present the possibility of preservation and conservation, to be sure, but also the natal promise of innovation and risk of wholesale destruction.[45] This anarchic moment is, as Judith Butler puts it, "a permanent principle of revolution within democratic orders."[46] If we understand democracy as only properly ordered by a democratic constitution and if we subscribe to a modern veneration of founding moments and founding documents, then constitutions risk becoming the place where natal, anarchic energy goes to die. I've noted that living individuals are not constituted but instituted, actively coming to be while also being passively shaped by structures of lived experience and consciousness that are not simply self-sufficient. Rather than natural essences or mere constructs of our social milieu, we are worldly people.[47] Better put, we are natural, social, and worldly. In the same way, *institution* leads us to the life of democracies. Political thinking that understands *revolution* as the moment of chaotic interruption and *constitution* as the (re)establishing of legal, political, and temporal order will, at its extreme, collapse the constitutional act into the constitutional document. In this case, the act of constituting a new mode of government is exhausted in the drafting and ratification of the document. The founding moment closes. Constitutional temporality tethers subsequent generations to that moment as the source of constitutional authority and political legitimacy.[48]

*Institution*, in contrast, refers to the event and practice of instituting; revolution is the opening gesture that *institutes* indeterminate possibilities. The drafting and ratification of a constitution—paradigmatically, the Constitution of the United States of America in 1789 and the French Constitution of 1791—is the process by which those possibilities are made determinate, instituted in the form of the practices, structures, that is, the institutions of government. A constitution that remains identified with the thinking of its framers is—within the time it takes for a generation to pass away—as dead as they are. But this is not its fate, and the constitutional document survives insofar as it is the work of institution and insofar as the process of amendment and interpretation becomes a generational practice of democratic inheritance.

Thomas Jefferson, writing in the aftermath of his own democratic intervention and keenly aware of the intensification of life he experienced in those years of public action, envisioned the revolutionary moment opening again in each generation. He writes indulgently of Shay's Rebellion of 1786: "God forbid we should ever go twenty years without such a rebellion. . . . The tree of liberty must be refreshed from time to time, with the blood of patriots and tyrants. It is its natural manure."[49] Yet what if subsequent revolutionary generations were to institute tyranny instead? What if the anarchic right not to be ruled were sacrificed by a new generation to the desire to be ruled by the demagogue? Could it be that the fundamental liberties guaranteed by a democratic constitution need to be protected from the *demos*?[50]

Yet every democratic instituting happens in the midst of generations. Remember that Plato dreamed of an *un*inherited city founded by banishing all adults, an imagined city whose Generation Zero would be told that they were born of the very soil of Athens. It is the most dramatic expression of his fear of democracy and politics, which always requires us to deal with newcomers by birth, migration, and expansion and to deal with adults as adults (as Arendt reminds us). Yet those adults live in a world also populated by the young and the old (as Joan Tronto reminds us), not to mention the dead (as Benjamin reminds us) and those to come (as Hans Jonas reminds us).[51] The people who enacted Kleisthenes's reform included grandfathers, fathers, and young men. The founders of the American Republic included Benjamin Franklin, who was seventy in 1776, Thomas Jefferson (thirty-three), and Thomas Lynch Jr. and Edward Rutledge (both twenty-six). John Adams (forty) describes the group as the "Fathers Brothers Disciples and Sons" with whom he shaped the new union. From the beginning, the *demos* is instituted among generations.[52] Also, what is done and said in the democratic intervention by that group of founders is witnessed by more than those present and heard by more than its immediate intended addressees.[53] "We the people" institutes a new form of citizenship, interpellating some as citizens, calling others to prepare themselves for the role when their generational time comes, while forcing still others to suffer the call as the pronouncement of their exclusion—intimate exclusion, in the case of women, or estranged, as in the case of foreigners, or both, carried to the extreme, in the case of enslaved people. These are *the misinterpellated*, the ones who hear the call that was not intended for them.[54] It is not wrong to worry, as Popper does, that generations who inherit constitutional democracy will use their inherited freedom to institute tyranny, but we should also worry that the founding generation instituted its own democratic tyranny. What becomes of the misinterpellated? What will happen when they show up, unbidden?

The rising generation, the sons and grandsons of the American Founders, heard their elders' address and prepared themselves for their inheritance.[55] Would the arrival of *their time* mean occupying institutions that were already complete in all their essentials? Would the city remain the same and be spared more democratic interruption? Jefferson hoped not, but he also knew that in the case of his new American state it would be impossible for it to remain unchanged because of the great incendiary built into it—and into his own family—by the refusal to confront the disaster of slavery. (Though, what can *own* and *family* mean when one family member owns the others as property?) Thirty years after Independence, and despite his admiration for rebellion in the abstract or in the form of a small rebellion by New England farmers, he was as eager as ever to avoid the coming rebellion that would risk presenting "our slaves with freedom and a dagger." "[What will happen] remains to be seen," he writes to Adams, "but I hope not by you and me. Surely, they will parlay awhile, and give us time to get out of the way."[56]

The founding sons received a state they did not make, a history they could not change, a world they were nonetheless inculcated into as their home, and a place where they belonged and that they experienced as belonging to them. Echoing through it was the address they heard as their title: "*We* therefore, the representatives of the United States of America in General Congress assembled, do in the name and by the authority of the good people of these colonies . . . that as free and independent states . . ." Derrida, in a lecture delivered in Virginia in 1976 under the title "Declarations of Independence" (that is, long before his analyses of the time of politics in *The Politics of Friendship*, *Spectres of Marx*, and *Rogues*), unravels the grammar of that inheritance. The *we* of the democratic interruption is surely a constative speech act; those who declare it are *describing* their existence as a free people. Yet it is also performative, drawing into existence this freedom and this people in the very act of declaring them free. Derrida writes: "One cannot decide . . . whether independence is stated or produced by this utterance. . . . The 'we' of the declaration speaks 'in the name of the people.' But this people does not exist. They do *not* exist as an entity, it does *not* exist, *before* this declaration, not *as such*." Indeed, he adds, the people gives birth to itself in this declaration, dissolving as they do so the links of colonial paternity or maternity.[57]

Yet, elsewhere in the same Declaration of Independence, the logic of brotherhood and the unbroken time of the *genos* reappear. Even as the grammar of the act announces the departure from *genos*-thinking, the vocabulary of blood bonds and white—indeed, English—supremacy reestablishes just such thinking.[58] The British are described in the document as consanguine brethren, possessed of native justice and magnanimity; the mercenaries sent against the colonists to do the work of death and desolation are noted to include "Scotch" and other foreigners; the "Indian savages" who inhabit the frontier are warlike and merciless; "our negroes," though conspicuously absent from the final draft of the Declaration, are implicated as those ready to be incited to domestic insurrection.[59] The *form* of the Declaration makes it an address to a people (*demos*) that both is and is not yet, but its *content* means that it would be heard by some as an address to them as the white or English people that they already embodied (*genos*). Some continue to hear it this way.

The Declaration of Independence articulates two dominant temporalities. According to one, the *genos* proceeds in lockstep with the naturalized order of generations according to which its past generated its present and its present generates its future. Our freedom is inherited from our forefathers. According to the other, the *demos* emerges not just as a matter of interruption but in the future anterior and, as it emerges, tries to extricate itself from *genos*-time; the people *will have had* the authority to authorize their own freedom only insofar as we, the future of those people, take them on as our past and authorize them *to have spoken* for us.[60] Every democratic generation must institute them, authorizing them to have spoken on our behalf, *whoever we have turned out to be. Genos* identity is received from the past, handed down to us and in us by our ancestors, and, insofar as we hear "We, the people" as "We, the *genos*" or "We, who know who we are," we make the claim for the fact of our freedom and our right to it ("we are, and ought to be free") *as if* we were descendants of Englishmen and not "negroes," "savages," and foreigners. On the *genos* model, ownership of the claim to freedom perpetuates self-identity with every generation, deepening its exclusions as it goes.[61]

When the misinterpellated arrive, they come as they are, and their coming does not just tweak or stretch the democracy but reopens its anarchic beginning. James Martel describes the phenomenon using Kafka's parable "Abraham." In the story, the famous Abraham hears the call and sets off to make the sacrifice that he believes has been asked of him by God. But the call has also been heard by several other Abrahams, all of whom, for one reason or another, don't get around to setting out with their sons. All, that is, except for one old Abraham with an unpromising child. He is also a man of faith but can't quite believe that God could possibly have meant him. What if he were to go the appointed place anyway, appearing with his child at the edge of the scene? Both Abrahams came because they believed that God had a plan. Now, if it turns out that God cruelly creates this sort of confusion or messes up this badly or doesn't have the whole picture, what have they been believing in all along? Thus, the free American, interpellated as citizen, is subjected to the rule (*arche*) of an archic institution, its overwhelming power and coherence. The arrival generations later of misinterpellated Americans throws the rule into question. The Founders used the language of *demos* to call up a *genos*. What happens when the *demos* shows up in the person of whomever?

The excluded take on democracy—take it on as an assumption and take it on in confrontation—as generational beings for whom the moment of founding is deferred: not we women, but our daughters' daughters; not we the enslaved, but our children's children; not we workers, who own nothing but our labor, but our working descendants. The arrival of democracy is deferred not by an action of theirs but by virtue of the place they occupy in a generational structure that produces and reproduces women and women's inequality, enslaved people and racism, and workers and workers' disenfranchisement but that is also—crucially—in principle open to other futures. Their admission, if and when it comes, is not merely an extension of the definition of *demos* but the creation of a new political realm into which the newcomers arrive not as additional interchangeable instances of the citizen as such but bearing the accumulated experience of historical exclusion.

The demes Kleisthenes created were expected to take up the question of migrants and others. Yet, despite the jolt of interruption, the rhythm of generation persisted, and when we pause in any given moment to tell an origin story and a history of what our real existing democracy has become—"Look who we have turned out to be!"—the *demos* model invokes the passive movement of generation to make possible a story of the progressive extension of ever more rights to ever more people. Instead of the future anterior, it recounts itself in the simple past tense. The revolution brought something new on the face of the earth, and some were invited into their time at the start, while others had to wait and insist. Their insistence sometimes had to take the form of sabotage, rebellion, and war, as well as speech and nonviolent action, and the suffering of those left out for so long may be irredeemable. But, the story goes, we've got to admit that our democracy is getting better and more democratic, all the time. Don't we?

In "Constitutional Democracy: A Paradoxical Union of Contradictory Principles?" Habermas prepares a structure for this democratic progress. The modern democratic origin is the dual event of the constitutional assemblies of Philadelphia and Paris, which set in train a "self-correcting historical process." He writes:

The allegedly paradoxical relation between democracy and the rule of law resolves itself in the dimension of historical time, provided one conceives the constitution as a project that makes the founding act into an ongoing process of constitution-making that continues across generations.[62]

The laws that govern the life of the *demos* emerge in the historical founding moment but are legitimated only in the process of building a tradition that holds open that founding so that each generation can actualize the principles of the constitution. That is to say, the founding is open, but only just wide enough. Beneath Habermas's argument lie two related assumptions that produce an essentially optimistic and conservative justification of constitutional inheritance: first, that subsequent generations will "start with the same standards as did the founders"; second, that the constitutional origin is exhaustive and remains the source of a singular, unfolding democratic tradition.[63]

The insidious danger of the justification is that it takes on the temporality of generation without reckoning with the phenomenon of *genos*. It treats expansion as a matter of numbers, as though including the members of a group long excluded would enlarge the *demos* but otherwise leave it largely unchanged. Among other things, it allows expansion to happen stepwise, embracing some individuals and some ways of being now but not others, making some wait and others wait longer, and allows us to point to each advance, even the admission of each token, as a step in the right direction. At its logical extreme it assumes that one becomes equal as a citizen by becoming indistinguishable from existing citizens, as if democratic diversity were indistinguishable from the general equivalence of liberal capitalism.[64] But it ignores the fact that, if *genos*-thinking provided the criterion for my violent exclusion, the injustice is compounded if I am forbidden to join the *demos* with my historical people *as a people*; the *demos* must not only be expanded but transformed.[65] Martin Luther King Jr. wrote in 1967: "Most whites in America proceed from a premise that equality is a loose expression for improvement. White America is not even psychologically organized to close the gap—essentially it seeks only to make it less painful and less obvious but in most respects to retain it."[66]

Understanding democratic temporality as progressive temporality means that every demand made now can be answered and contained in terms of *already, soon, not yet,* and *in due course,* masking deeper, more disruptive conflicts between temporalities. What some experience as gradual inclusion others undergo as the stalled time of trauma; what some regard as respect for traditional communities and old ways is experienced by others as condemnation to pastness and political irrelevance; what for some is reassurance of how far we have come is, for others, confusion about whether any distance has been traveled at all; what allows some of us to imagine that a little more effort will bring our democracy to completion, fulfilling its promise in the most expansive way, is what demonstrates to others that what was projected as a promise was only ever a lie.[67] Meanwhile, generations rise and pass. The hidden work of generation and maintenance keeps being done hour by hour according to universally recognizable rhythms of living and dying, to be sure, but also always in distinctive ways shaped by historical conditions of freedom and unfreedom, equality and inequality, domination and exploitation, hope and disappointment. One way and another, and another, and another, repetitions of the practices of generation and care make worlds, and make us.

# Conclusion: The Antigenocidal Democracy

How would we react to the prospect of the end of the world as we know it? Specifically, how we would respond to news that human fertility would end soon after we and everyone we knew were dead? In *Death and the Afterlife*, Samuel Scheffler asks us to consider what we would think about our lives now if the youngest people now on earth were to be the last generation of humans. Despite the fact that no one at all would be harmed in this scenario, the news would matter to us. In fact, Scheffler argues, the thought of the end of humanity would matter to us more than the fact of our own mortality, and this is because of how we make meaning. He writes:

> The expectation that others will survive me, that humanity will go on, is necessary for my valuing much of what I do, but the recognition that I will not survive, that my life will not go on, is likewise necessary for my valuing much of what I do. What I need is that I should die and that others should live.

From the moment we are born, we owe the world a death, and mortal life becomes meaningful against the background of human existence that preceded us and that will continue after we have gone. This is the "afterlife" of Scheffler's title. His thought experiments address us as individuals, as people with families and personal friends, and as members of *humanity*. Even though we know we are mortal, and even though we largely want to spare suffering to others in general and in particular, we also want our deaths to matter. We want to be able to imagine the people around us noticing that we have gone; the loss of us should give them pause, and we should be able to imagine them spending some respectable period of time in grief and mourning.

Yet Scheffler also acknowledges (eventually) that we find meaning in the existence and persistence of the *groups* to which we belong. Certainly, I should die and others should live, and universalist ethics will add: "whoever those others are." Yet, as I have argued, between humanity in the person of whomever, on the one hand, and the particular people I know and love, on the other, there are people, *my* people, most of whom I do not know but with whom I stand in a relationship of often passionate belonging. We give generational content to the placeholder "others who should live" in the form of the younger generations of people with whom we share the earth, certainly. We also imagine continuity in the shape of our offspring and younger relatives and friends, the ones most likely to preserve the knowledge *that* I lived, that is, to remember *me* and *my* having lived. But future generations also take on a distinct significance in the form of the others, who may or may not be relatives and may or may not have known me but with whom I will have had enough in common to suggest that *how I* lived might persist in *how they* live. We hope that things will keep going in some familiar ways so that, if I were somehow not to die, the world would remain recognizable as our world, and I could still feel at home in it. Scheffler puts it mildly: "This is a surprisingly powerful and comforting thought for many people."[1]

It is surprising only if we take the self-possessed individual as our starting point. Scheffler's realization of the power and comfort of the idea of the future world brings the thought experiment of individualism to its close. To singular, plural, generationally instituted beings, it is no surprise at all that the world matters, that we should care about the specificity of the worldly contexts in which we come to be, that those contexts are vulnerable, and that we are concerned for their future. Earlier, I used *culture*—culture anthropologically speaking—to describe the ways we live together generationally, and the term captures what would make the afterworld recognizable as still ours: familiar images, stories, rules, and rituals, all the way to the daily, barely noticed practices of social, private, household life. An attack on a culture—the destruction of religious buildings, suppression of language, outlawing of traditional practices—attacks the inheritance that passes between generations and harms the process of instituting the meaning of the group and also, thereby, the meaning of the lives of its members. This was central to the discussions of cultural genocide and the Genocide Convention.[2]

Culture is the process by which events and states of affairs acquire meaning. Yet even when it is broadly construed, the term does not always capture all that is involved in the sense of belonging in the world. Améry understood himself as deeply embedded in the culture of his homeplace, only to discover, when the Nazi flags appeared on their houses, that this was not his neighbors' understanding. Suddenly, details of his genealogy that he had regarded as mildly interesting now mattered to them more than anything else. The Austrian culture that he had regarded as his own was racialized and weaponized against him. For Scheffler, such change is a matter of values. For Shmuel Lederman, it identifies Améry and those like him as having a different perspective on the world, one informed by a different history and, I will add, a different temporality.[3] What had been important to him was the network of relationships that made up his community's being in that place together now; what was important to his neighbors—either what had become important in that moment of crisis or what had been so all along—was their relation to generations of Austrian ancestors. Once Nazis were in power, no other viewpoint and no other mode of being in time mattered.

Lederman's identification of the wrong of genocide draws on Arendt's understanding of the difference among human groups based on their different views of the shared human world.[4] The elimination of a group that shared a particular view is a loss to all humanity because it is the loss of a distinctive, irreplaceable perspective on the world. Yet can we be sure that we will know a distinctive perspective when we encounter one? The confidence that we will relies on the assumption that groups can express their worldview and that we can hear them. Focusing on the difference of temporalities helps here because of how difficult it is to give expression to another way of being in time.

Arendt stakes her claim for a worldly, antigenocidal politics in a gap between past and future. In a passage often cited, she describes the gap as the place for thinking but also as the gap that became relevant for political life when we no longer could rely on tradition to bridge it, that is, to ferry us from past to future almost without our knowing it. The gap and how to move in it became "a tangible reality and perplexity for all." She takes her cue from another parable of Kafka's:

He has two antagonists: the first presses him from behind, from the origin. The second blocks the road ahead. He gives battle to both. To be sure, the first supports him in his fight with the second, for he wants to push him forward, and in the same way the second supports him in his fight with the first, since he drives him back. But it is only theoretically so. For it is not only the two antagonists who are there, but he himself as well, and who really knows his intentions? His dream, though, is that some time in an unguarded moment—and this would require a night darker than any night has ever been yet—he will jump out of the fighting line and be promoted, on account of his experience in fighting, to the position of umpire over his antagonists in their fight with each other.[5]

However much we long for the peace of eternity, here is where we are and where our life and afterlife will be.[6] Here is where the meaning of things is to be worked out. Kafka's "he" is alone in the gap, which threatens to close around him at every moment, but we must imagine instead that he is there with others, that the past has the faces of his elders and forebears while the future looks like the young. We encounter the task of holding open the gap as singular plural beings who try to make a home in the world that was here before we came and that we hope will exist after we have gone. The new ones come charged with anarchic natal energy, which will be essential to the persistence of the world but which also carries the threat of revolutionary destruction.

Arendt lets us imagine three ways of inheriting the world. (1) If the old ones engage the young in the tradition by setting them the essentially conservative task of shoring up the old ways and living up to the example of heroic ancestors, the world may persist, and it may continue (at least for a time) to take a form the old would recognize. Alternatively, the older generation, having themselves inherited a world scarred by brutality and injustice, may throw up their hands in the face of that history and in the face of the puzzling, recalcitrant newcomers, leaving the rising generation on their own. This opens the possibility that (2) they will never hear the call to take responsibility and will neglect the task or that (3) the new ones may vent the force of their natal energy in sheer destruction. Tradition risks suffocating the world; unconcern risks neglecting it to death; revolution risks sending it up in flames.

What is a *demos* to do? Each democracy exists as a struggle to answer the question of how we are to live freely and equally, and what Arendt refers to as the awesome responsibility of democratic freedom is the call to respond democratically to the world as it is. This is not legal accountability or moral responsibility.[7] It cannot be contained within the familiar ethical system of intentions, actions, and their consequences. It is not a matter of feelings of guilt for our sins or the sins of our fathers or our people or humankind or of drawing blame on ourselves by declaring: "We are all guilty." After all, as Arendt observes sharply, such a declaration establishes a sentiment of solidarity with those who actually did wrong.[8] Instead, political responsibility has the structure of the constitutional responsibility that—in response to Aristotle's question of continuity— makes a new government responsible for the deeds and misdeeds of its predecessors. A revolutionary government may reject legal liability for the contracts entered into by the government it overthrows, but it remains *responsible* for the actions of previous governments. Thus, Napoleon assumed all that the historical state of France had done: *La France, c'est moi.* More precisely, a revolutionary government is responsible for the world that was created by its actions *and* by the actions of its predecessors. Since a democratic government acts as or on behalf of a *demos*, we citizens are responsible with a political, worldly responsibility that asks that we take up and take on what comes down to us.[9]

We are responsible for the gap and for how we occupy it. Arendt, with the help of Kafka, would have us bear up under the force of history, but, just as Kafka's "He" is a cipher, the words *we* and *us* are placeholders. Insofar as we hope that the world will remain in some way a home for us, we take responsibility for a human plurality extended over time and diverse across generations. Since it is a gap created by holding off the past and future that would otherwise crush us or overdetermine everything (which is the same thing for free beings), it is where we respond according to diverse temporalities. I have discussed what comes down to us as the world and as our democratic responsibility, but the *demos* also rules—the *kratos* in *democracy*—and so bequeaths and inherits rule. Rule cannot be divided up among the members of the *demos*, but it also cannot be exercised equally by all of the citizens all the time. Aristotle formulated the problem and gave a characteristically elegant response; we must take turns at ruling.[10] We take turns in the gap, and the generational patterns of circling in and out of positions of power, the overlapping arrival and departure of generations, the dynamic of symmetrical and asymmetrical relations, the networks of reciprocal and nonreciprocal obligations must all find expression in the democratic space.[11]

Arendt proposes three human temporalities (which cut across the three modes of inheriting), but not all are granted political status: the cyclical time of natural existence and the labor and consumption of our bodies (*bios*), the time of a human life (*zoe*) that forms an arc from birth to death, and the time of things and institutions that endure longer than a human life and give some measure of permanence to the human world. This is where we make meaning both in the constitutional decision that we are equal and free and in the telling of stories.[12] Indeed, the narrative of a heroic life, retold through generations, is a paradigm of meaning making for Arendt, but the capacity to do those deeds and tell those stories and the space in which action and storytelling can happen are fragile and always in need of protection.

Protection from what? Arendt fears that a life lived according to the temporal circle of the *bios*, which itself knows no gap, will trap us in the life of labor and consumption, expose us to existential loneliness, and make way for the designation of people and peoples as superfluous.[13] Lives are shed into oblivion. As a result, culture in the anthropological sense is of no interest, while culture understood as the production of artifacts and institutions that outlive us become her focus. Indeed, longevity is the value that leads her into a ranking of cultures where those who leave stone cathedrals are higher than those who build tents of cloth.[14] Yet Pericles, whose orations were paradigmatic for Arendt, was a man who was born and died and, in between, ate, slept, and had sex. Even he was somebody's child, raised in a customary way. He was a man who died in an epidemic. By designating these as simply material realities and consigning them to the private sphere, Arendt rejects the possibility that the temporality of natural life might also be expressed in democratic life. It is the price her political schema pays for preserving politics from the tendency of modern societies to transform all our activities into forms of repetitive labor and consumption. Yet she is not mistaken in pointing to a desire that our actions have an afterlife. This requires enduring objects and institutions—and languages and practices—that will sustain and in turn be sustained by a persisting world.

The details of what Pericles ate and when, who prepared his meals, who his parents were, where he slept and with whom, and who tended him when he got sick are the content of a world.[15] We labor and consume in meaningfully different ways, some more, some less free, some more, some less equal, some crushingly exploitative, some hidden within the four walls of domestic life, some on display as public rituals, all of them subject to the turns of nature as well as the multiple temporal requirements of markets, regulation, bodies, capital, salvations, inheritances, climates, desires, and generation. Arendt acknowledges the generational structure of worldly, political life but rejects the material content of generation—that is, all the culturally inflected practices that make up a form of generational life—as a mortal threat to politics. For her, the definition of political action is that it shows *who* I am, while the *genos* is the mark of a natural *what*. Missing is a consideration of how we make the distinction and how we make meaning. A politics that ignores the stuff of generational existence—even as it grasps its structure—will not recognize violence to our generational being when it sees it.[16]

Rejecting Arendt's cultural hierarchies, we can attend instead to the creation of meaning in the daily work of inheritance and adaptation, knowing that it is often indistinguishable from the labor of our bodies; what is attacked by genocidal violence and what we are responsible for in an existential-democratic way is, above all, the possibility of meaning making by which a mass of intergenerational relations comes to be a living world. This is the indispensable contribution of *The Human Condition*'s political schema; it forces us to rethink the ontological status of human relations. Lederman distills the thought very clearly. It is not a matter of responsibility for groups, as though they had independent reality; it is not responsibility for individuals, as though *they* had independent reality. Rather, he writes:

> Groups are the sum of their individual members and of the various kinds of relations these individuals create among themselves—their "in-between" space, as Arendt put it. . . . In their speech, action, creativity and their life with relation to both others and to their natural surroundings, individuals create more than their own life. They create a web of meaning, more often than not incredibly rich and sophisticated. It is this richness, irreducible to any individual life, elusive of any attempt to describe it in definitive terms, and open to us primarily through our actual and meaningful encounter with members of the group and their way of life, that is lost, or deeply endangered, when a genocide occurs.[17]

This is why attempts to define the sort of groups susceptible to genocide are never satisfactory and why the wording of the Convention on Genocide failed as a definition but succeeded as the opening of a decades-long debate. Rightly so. Lederman's insight leads us to think less in terms of relation—which remains in danger of being reduced to a *thing*—and more in terms of modes of relating, of being together in time.[18] Moreover, it lets us draw the question of genocide from the arena of international relations into domestic democratic life. As Arendt writes: "Strictly speaking, politics is not so much about human beings as it is about the world that comes into being between them and endures beyond them. To the extent that politics becomes destructive and causes worlds to end, it destroys and annihilates itself."[19]

The democratic polity is a world of worlds. Beyond its world-preserving imperative, it has no criterion for the subordination of individuals or groups or activities, and the patterns of subordination and domination evident in all existing democracies are always open to challenge *on democratic grounds*. What sets democracy apart is its necessary uncertainty, a temporal openness to a future *demos* that we might have to struggle to recognize, an unimagined democracy that, as Derrida puts it, is always to come.[20]

We know what violent failures of temporal openness in and by democracies look like. Many concern a democracy's constricted vision of its own future. Elections in Myanmar in 2015 ushered in a brief era of democracy, but, during that time, the country continued to rely on a 1982 Citizenship Law that reserved full citizenship to those whose families settled in the country before 1832 or who belonged to one of its 130 recognized ethnic groups. This list did not include Rohingya. Associate and naturalized citizenship was available for people who were residents in or before 1948. Few Rohingya knew of this law, and even fewer could meet the standards of proof needed. Even so, the Central Body could deny a citizenship application even if the criteria are met; the result is that Rohingya were excluded and left stateless.[21] The commitment to an imagined state without Rohingya paved the way for discrimination, attacks by the state, and the violent expulsions of 2017 and 2018.[22]

In the United States, a 2008 Census Bureau report estimated that in 2042, less than 50 percent of the population of the country would be white. This future—where "white Americans will be a minority in their country"—has proved intolerable to some.[23] In August 2017, armed white supremacists marched in Charlottesville, Virginia, chanting "You will not replace us" and "Jews will not replace us," refusing any future United States of America other than one dominated by a dreamed-of, self-identical community of white Americans. Heather Heyer was killed that day as she protested the nationalist demonstration.

Democracies' refusal to be haunted by their victims is part of the work of foreclosing certain futures. Where the governments of settler-colonial states have begun acknowledging past injustices, they have also worked to break the temporal continuity between this world and the world in which indigenous people were massacred, hunted, worked to death, and dispossessed and had their children stolen and their culture destroyed. In its submission to the Australian Reconciliation Convention in 1996, the government argued that when it came to evaluating the laws and practices of earlier times, "it is appropriate to have regard to the standards and values prevailing at the time of their enactment and implementation, rather than to the standards and values prevailing today."[24] Addressing the same Convention in 1997, Australian prime minister John Howard took care to emphasize the absence of moral responsibility, as though this were the only definition of responsibility: "Australians of this generation should not be required to accept guilt and blame for past actions and policies over which they had no control." If Aboriginal communities suffered inequality now, the problem was to be traced to their contemporary deprivation in the areas of health, housing, education, and employment with no further connection to be made to past injustices or a history of physical and cultural dispossession.[25]

When the triumphant refuse to countenance the past or to answer to the defeated and the dead, they can manage and diminish any resistant attachment to the past by commodifying and curating it as traditional, dismissing it as melancholic, and pathologizing it as trauma. Above all, it must not be granted the status of a coherent strategy of resistance. Certain liberal strands of democratic thinking will insist on "moving on" as the healthy, emancipatory response, but, as Rajana Khanna argues: "Melancholia is not simply a crippling attachment to a past that acts like a drain of energy on the present, even though it is indeed an impoverishment of the [Freudian] ego." In fact, undoing the ego is part of the movement toward the understanding of institution and coming-to-be that I have been arguing for here. Khanna continues: "Unlike arguments concerning melancholic affectation described as disabling in terms of imagining a politically different future, the affect of melancholia . . . points the way toward a political future free of the failures of postcolonial states and misguided biopolitics."[26] Refusing to mourn and move on from historical injustice might tie an *ego* to a dismantling and disabling past; it could open a *demos* to the question and the questionability of its past and future.

If democracies can open themselves to such questions; if they are capable of taking a distance from the state apparatus that fixes them in constitutional time; if they can prevent the practices of governing and the dynamics of the *demos* congealing into a set of concrete self-interests, can they be sure, then, of recognizing the destruction of worlds? Can we hear and understand when victims articulate their loss? The Crow, whose lives and culture revolved around the buffalo herds of the North American plains, were confined to a reservation beginning in 1868. Asked by a settler researcher for stories of his later life, Chief Plenty Coups replied: "When the buffalo went away the hearts of my people fell to the ground, and they could not lift them up again. After this, nothing happened."[27] Happenings, and stories of happenings, require a world in which to have meaning; for Plenty Coups, dispossession was the end of the world. Jonathan Lear terms this a crisis of intelligibility; its intractability is intensified by its being a crisis of temporal meaning. The question is not whether there is a democratic resolution to the crisis but whether a democracy can entertain such intelligibility and open itself to this temporality.

In the mountains of southern Peru, people of the Quechua-speaking community of Sonqo, interviewed in the 1970s, spoke of living in a *pacha*, or world, that was continuous with that of the Inca who fled the Spanish on paths through their land four hundred years before.[28] Conquest by the Spanish was specifically not the end of their world. In fact, they looked forward to the *pachakuti*, or cataclysmic world-reversal yet to come, a reversal that would strike down the Spanish and bring the Inca back. But they also worried about their children, who spoke Spanish, worked in Cusco, and no longer wore local alpaca clothing; the Inca would reject them when they returned.[29] Could they make sense of a future that would be a restoration for them but a catastrophe for the next generation, which inhabits two worlds? Can a democracy entertain this worldview and the temporality that shapes this anxiety?[30]

There are very many examples, but the simplest formulation might point to the deepest challenge. When Dolleen Tisawii'ashii Manning describes her mode of being-in-the-world, a mode of being she experiences as exclusive to the Anishinaabe, she describes it as informed by knowledges "passed between mnidoo ancestors, past and future, through the infinite and the simultaneous." Mnidoo—"All my relations / All my relatives, My all / My everything," animate, inanimate, immaterial—inaugurates a complex ontology, but the temporal challenge is in the thought of ancestors, *past and future*. Can a democracy entertain mnidoo temporality, a matter of neither pastness nor futurity nor temporal betweenness? Can democracy rise to being *with* rather than *between* past and future?[31]

There is no guarantee that it can. Indeed, it may be as difficult, albeit thanks to a different sort of ignorance, to grasp the always present everyday ways of being in time that underpin a life. The open democratic space, host to the expression of various temporalities, also covers over the work of maintenance that goes on just beyond the field of vision of political life, leaving the labor of keeping things going barely perceptible. We have seen democracy come into being by interrupting *genos* and by instituting the people who will turn out to have been the democratic people. We have seen how democracies claim the temporality of progress while blocking change; how Arendt envisioned political life in a temporal gap; how the temporalities of the gap included overlap and deferral, asymmetry and nonreciprocity; and how Derrida offers a thought of democracy anticipated.

What few democratic theorists but Arendt notice, and what she notes only in order to explicitly set it aside, is what Lisa Baraitser calls the time of on-go. We are responsible for the labor and work it takes to hold open the gap. Baraitser writes: "Maintenance is a bulwark against the time of entropy, and the propensity of all living systems to decay and eventually die. Maintenance requires an attachment to now-time that is not so much the time of the Benjaminian flash, but of the slow burn of one moment looking much like the next."[32] It is the temporality of what Joan Tronto famously defines as care: "the species activity that includes everything that we do to maintain, continue, and repair our 'world' so that we can live in it as well as possible."[33] Maintenance is the temporality of the care that props us up and keeps us going by tending relations among us.[34] From the point of view of politics, the daily, uneventful repetitions of this labor, its place in the most intimate spaces of our lives, its unproductive character, and its relentlessness all serve to press it below our line of vision and into the domestic realm of generational labor. But this is how Lederman's rich webs of meaning are built, and these activities do not fall out of history. This is the ongoing now that might beat us down with the rhythm of deadening, alienating labor or may permit our flourishing as engaged, creative workers. As Gail Lewis writes, the care that institutes us is refracted through the historical experience of our forebears, which may have imbued it with an ambivalence that has everything to do with race, gender, and the experience of colonialism and that seeps into the ways our lives were and are maintained by others and then into how we carry out that work of maintenance in turn. She adds: "Care is an arduous temporal practice that entails the maintenance of relations with ourselves and others through histories of oppression that return in the present again and again."[35]

Again, what is a *demos* to do? Arendt imagines it undertaking the work of maintaining—or conserving, destroying, or renewing—our worldly institutions as though they were edifices, setting the work of political maintenance apart from what Baraitser and others point to as the work of keeping things going. Bonnie Honig argues for an expansive understanding of what counts as an institution and thereby what counts as worldliness. After all, we furnish our world with objects (for Arendt, the work of our hands), including public things that by virtue of being shared things institute citizens as free and equal. This is true of anthems and public buildings but also the electrical power grid and railway stations. Honig writes: "[A democracy's public things] do not take care of our needs only. [As *our* things] they also constitute us, complement us, limit us, thwart us, and interpellate us into democratic citizenship."

Insofar as the *demos* takes care, it must decide on the form of public institutions and the extent of civil infrastructure, to be sure, but also, crucially, how we will share the work of keeping them going. If decisions about how to share democratic sovereignty are rightly made democratically, then decisions about our public works should not be handed over to the market or approached as matters of human capital or human resources. Indeed, Martel encourages us to understand "ordinariness as an unlikely but powerful bias from which to resist the blandishments of liberalism."[36] If democratic power is the sort of thing that is shared by taking turns, and if public infrastructure is the sort of thing we share by all using them when we need them, then what sort of shared thing is the work of democratic maintenance? Mierle Laderman Ukeles reminds us of the sourball of every revolution: "After the revolution, who is going to pick up the garbage on Monday morning?"[37] And every morning after that? If citizens are to appear in public space, ready for spontaneous action, who will keep things going at home? Who will make sure the children are fed and the old ones kept warm? Whose children? Which old folk?

We are familiar with the spectacle of the revolutionary beginnings of modern democracies, including the glorious violence of 1776 and 1789. We recognize catastrophic violence and violent events, but, as Rob Nixon warns, the ease of that recognition blinds us to the operation of slow violence, the attritional violence and destruction gradually disseminated over generations. We have trouble seeing it as violence at all. This is how the disastrous buildup of toxins in the land and sea and in the bodies of poor people across the Global South unfolds, producing suffering that goes largely unobserved, undiagnosed, and untreated. In the same way, if we think of genocides as outbursts of atrocious violence or hold Auschwitz as the paradigm, we will find it hard to acknowledge what happened in the slow poisoning of generations of Ogoni in Nigeria by Shell and Chevron or the quiet, slow deaths and the rotting worlds of Australian Aboriginal peoples as either genocidal or violent.[38]

If it is the case that democracy relies on a slow, dimly lit oppression that unfolds not only over there but also right here, just out of public view, how would we know? The antigenocidal democracy is centered on a public space of contestation, including contestation about violence. Its openness is a matter of receptivity to difference, a capacity to live with the uncertainty of the future and be host to many temporalities and the site of many worlds, but also an ability to hear the demands of those who see and bear *its* violence. Under the heading of peacetime violence, Nancy Scheper-Hughes writes of the hospitalized psychiatric patients in Italy so humiliated and deprived of dignity that each wished to be the next to die; unnamed and unregistered infants in Brazil allowed to starve in a situation of normalized and institutionalized indifference; the young men in postapartheid South Africa condemned, incarcerated, and killed as "dangerous young lions"; last-born sons of Irish farming families virtually forbidden to reproduce as a matter of sacrifice for the family's land and wealth. She invites us to consider the family resemblance between, on the one hand, public consent in the United States today for attacks by government agents on "illegal aliens" and the separation of families at the US-Mexico border and, on the other, the government sponsored genocide of the Trail of Tears. She describes the steady evolution of US prisons into alternative Black concentration camps. She warns of the dangers embedded in the overproduction of social science research on urban violence, an academic narrative that, refracted through mass media, feeds a popular sense of danger and fuels support for police brutality as a defense against urban anarchy.[39] After an unflinching description of the old-age home where her mother howled and thrashed in her bed and where her father would urinate in the wastepaper basket because the port-a-potty was placed too far away from his bed, and after acknowledging her own inability to have those still beloved old ones come to live with her, she asks us to consider "what kind of civilization and people have we become when we . . . can fall prey to a lethal passivity toward institutional practices which compromise and erode the humanity and personhood of our own parents."[40]

We might challenge a line of analogies that leads us so far from Auschwitz; we might fear for the loss of the power of the term *genocide*; we might ask whether each example comes from a democratic context and bears on the context of democratic violence at all. Scheper-Hughes responds: "The benefit [of asking ourselves these questions] lies in the ability to draw connections, make predictions, to sensitize people to *genocide-like* practices and sentiments hidden within the perfectly acceptable and normative behavior of ordinary, good-enough citizens."[41]

The antigenocidal democracy will take utterly seriously the fact that we come to belong in various worlds and also *how* we do so. What we must not underestimate is the ability of good-enough citizens to forget or fail to know the violences our belonging implies and the superfluousness it makes possible. The antigenocidal democracy will acknowledge that nonreciprocal, asymmetrical relations are the deep structure of generational being and also recognize the dynamic sophistication of the generational networks that worldly groups develop in response. It will confront its need to perpetuate its world of worlds, knowing that *genos* cannot be the model for its mode of generation. The *demos* will be a persistent question for it, taking shape in specific controversies about borders, citizenship, temporalities, and rule; the answers will be matters of judgment.[42]

It will forge equality in the midst of asymmetry and nonreciprocity, a form of equality that frustrates efforts to enforce the general equivalence that makes all of us interchangeable and each of us disposable—though some more so than others. It will take up its own work of inheritance, including the inheritance of injustices perpetrated and worlds destroyed, and recognize that its openness to the expression of other temporalities means that it will be haunted by its pasts, by the present suffering that hovers below the threshold of our ability to perceive, and by unknown futures. It means that democratic responsibility may not be a matter of politics between past and future but *with* past and future. It also means that it risks destroying itself in revolution or cosseting its institutions into irrelevance. That is the risk it must take as it holds open the space for contestation where it will resist the flare of political violence as well as the slow burn of disregard.[43] The antigenocidal democracy will know that it has no origin, no destiny, and no principle of rule, only shifting and layered responsibilities to the ones who have gone, the ones who are to come, the world we have in common, the world in which something of us might continue, and the world where we can hear the question of how we are to live together as a question of generation, that is, of what we owe the past, what we owe the future, and how we will hold open the world we received.

## Acknowledgments

I am very grateful to the communities, institutions, and the very many people who lent their help and support as I wrote this book. The Philosophy Department at Stony Brook and the Stony Brook Humanities Institute provided time to write. The New York Public Library; the Biblioteca Pública de Valencia, Spain; and the Wexford County Library, Ireland, provided space. The United States Holocaust Memorial Museum hosted a workshop on philosophical approaches to the genocidal in 2016, which I organized with Martin Shuster. Those two weeks working with Martin and an amazing group of thinkers turned out to be pivotal for this project. Several other communities have also been crucial: the Hannah Arendt Circle; the Society for the Philosophical Study of Genocide and the Holocaust; the Collegium Phaenomenologicum, particularly the three-week session devoted to Critical Phenomenology in 2019; the North American Society for Hermeneutics; the Society for Phenomenology and Existential Philosophy; the Institute for Genocide and Mass Atrocity Prevention, Binghamton University; the Radical Philosophy Association; the International Institute for Hermeneutics; the Anthropology and Phenomenology working group at Aarhus University, Denmark; and philosophy colloquia and workshops at Bard College, Boston College, Concordia University, DePaul University, Emory University, Fordham University, the Indian Institute of Technology Delhi, Loyola Marymount University Los Angeles, the New School, Northern Arizona University Flagstaff, Penn State University, Stony Brook University, SUNY New Paltz, SUNY Purchase, Texas A&M, the University of Oregon, and Université

Paris Sorbonne IV. In the time of COVID-19, online conversations kept people in touch and kept us all going, in particular Jason Throop's Team Phenomenology at the Anthropology Department at UCLA and Stony Brook's Critical Phenomenology group. Anonymous readers of the manuscript gave very helpful feedback. My thanks to all the Stony Brook MA and PhD students with whom I have had the privilege of thinking philosophically and generationally and who have been relentless in pushing my thinking in new directions, especially Hannah Bacon, Eva Boodman, Adam Blair, Erik Bormanis, maggie castor, Mike Chiddo, Tim Cuffman, Jeffrey Epstein, Juan Guerrero, Jake Hook, Adam Israel, Leah Kaplan, Willow Mindich, Phillip Nelson, Helen Ngo, Phillip Opsasnick, Emilia Russo, and Kyle Tanaka. Thanks to James Wheeler for editorial help. Particular thanks also to Jay Bernstein, Alissa Betz, Emma Bianchi, Peg Birmingham, Patrick Burns, Ed Casey, Harvey Cormier, Megan Craig, Bob Crease, Cecilie Eriksen, Matthias Fritsch, Lisa Guenther, Robert Harvey, Gregg Horowitz, Richard Kearney, Eva Kittay, Tom Lay, Sarah Lilly, Shmuel Lederman, Gary Marmorstein, Eduardo Mendieta, Martin Shuster, Lorenzo Simpson, Tony Steinbock, Dimitris Vardoulakis, and Thomas Wentzer.

When each of us is born, the world has never seen anyone quite like us before, as Hannah Arendt puts it. The words are a curious and lovely echo of a phrase often used by Peig Sayers of the Blasket Islands when she speaks of the dead: "We will not see the like of them again." James O'Byrne, Marie Hayes O'Byrne, and Vincent O'Byrne are gone now. We miss them and won't see anyone quite like them again, to be sure, but they have left their mark in us and on the world. Love to John O'Byrne, the kin keeper, Michael O'Byrne, who helps us all keep it real, and Miriam O'Byrne, who, in person, letters, phone calls, texts, and video chats, is always there. Finally, love and appreciation to Michael Beck and Sophia Beck—every day.

# Notes

## Introduction: Democracy and *Genos*

1. Claude Lefort, *Democracy and Political Theory*, trans. David Macey (Oxford: Oxford University Press, 1988), 19.

2. Chantal Mouffe, *The Democratic Paradox* (London: Verso, 2000), 2.

3. In response, Wendy Brown argues for a reinvestment in the principles and practices of democracy while acknowledging that individual freedom might not be its reward.

4. On the question of inclusion in and exclusion from the demos, see Carl Schmitt, *The Crisis of Parliamentary Democracy*, trans. Ellen Kennedy (Cambridge, MA: MIT Press, 1988), 9. See also Chantal Mouffe, "Schmitt and the Paradox of Liberal Democracy," in *The Democratic Paradox*, 36–59.

5. See Hannah Arendt, *The Human Condition* (Chicago: University of Chicago Press, 1958); Jürgen Habermas, "Constitutional Democracy: A Paradoxical Union of Contradictory Principles?," *Political Theory* 29, no. 6 (December 2001): 766–81; John Rawls, *A Theory of Justice*, original ed. (Cambridge, MA: Harvard University Press, 2009).

6. There is a great deal of interesting work being done in this field. See the essays collected in José M. Medina, John J. Stuhr, and Jessica Wahman, eds., *Cosmopolitanism and Place* (Bloomington: Indiana University Press, 2017); Walter Mignolo, "Cosmopolitanism and the De-Colonial Option," *Studies in Philosophy and Education* 29, no. 2 (March 2010): 111–27, https://doi.org/10.1007/s11217-009-9163-1; Eduardo Mendieta, "From Imperial to Dialogical Cosmopolitanism," *Ethics & Global Politics* 2, no. 3 (January 1, 2009): 241–58, https://doi.org/10.3402/egp.v2i3.2044.

7. William Connolly, *Identity/Difference: Democratic Negotiations of Political Paradox* (Minneapolis: University of Minnesota Press, 2002), xv.

8. Lewis R. Gordon, *Freedom, Justice, and Decolonization* (New York: Routledge, 2020), 114.

9. Lee Edelman puts it very simply: "For politics, however radical the means by which specific constituencies attempt to produce a more desirable social order, remains, at its core, conservative insofar as it works to *affirm* a structure, to *authenticate* social order, which it then intends to transmit to the future in the form of its inner Child." Lee Edelman, *No Future: Queer Theory and the Death Drive* (Durham, NC: Duke University Press, 2004), 2–3.

10. See James Clifford, "Taking Identity Politics Seriously: 'The Contradictory, Stony Ground . . . ,'" in *Without Guarantees: In Honor of Stuart Hall*, ed. Paul Gilroy, Lawrence Grossberg, and Angela McRobbie (London: Verso, 2000), 94–112.

11. Payam Akhavan, *Reducing Genocide to Law: Definition, Meaning, and the Ultimate Crime* (Cambridge: Cambridge University Press, 2012), 11.

12. In the *New York Times* in June 2021, Nicholas Kristof writes: "In 2021 the United States and other countries have declared that China is committing genocide against ethnic Uyghurs—yet nothing much changes. That passivity discounts the horror of genocide, the ultimate crime." Nicholas Kristof, "A Journey through Atrocities," *New York Times*, June 13, 2021.

13. On the use of *genos*, see the note at the end of this chapter.

14. See Michael Mann, *The Dark Side of Democracy: Explaining Ethnic Cleansing* (Cambridge: Cambridge University Press, 2005).

15. An excellent model here is Amy Allen, *The End of Progress: Decolonizing the Normative Foundations of Critical Theory* (New York: Columbia University Press, n.d.), https://www.degruyter.com/document/doi/10.7312/alle17324/html.

16. See Guenther, "Critical Phenomenology," in *Fifty Concepts for a Critical Phenomenology*, ed. Weiss et al. (Evanston, IL: Northwestern University Press, 2020), 11–16; Alia Al-Saji, "A Phenomenology of Hesitation: Interrupting Racializing Habits of Seeing," in *Living Alterities: Phenomenology, Embodiment, and Race* (Albany: State University of New York Press, 2014), 133–72; Michel Foucault, *Society Must Be Defended: Lectures at the College de France 1975–1976* (New York: Picador, 2003), 242–54.

17. Matthias Fritsch writes: "Given its central emphasis on temporality in the constitution of a human world—from Husserl's time-consciousness to Heidegger's historicity, from Arendt's natality to de Beauvoir's reflections on aging, from Levinas' fecundity to Derrida's living-on—the phenomenological tradition, broadly construed, may be expected to offer central insights into intergenerational relations." Personal communication, December 2015.

18. See *Symposium* 207, 208. Note also Harvey Lomax's account of Nietzsche's horror at death as making him *will* hopelessly the eternal return. J. Harvey Lomax, "Nietzsche & the Eternal Recurrence," *Philosophy Now* 29 (November 2000): 20–22.

19. See Anne O'Byrne, "Symbol, Exchange, and Birth," *Philosophy and Social Criticism* 30, no. 3 (May 2004): 355–73.

20. See Samuel Scheffler, *Death and the Afterlife*, ed. Niko Kolodny, 1st ed. (New York: Oxford University Press, 2013).

21. My thanks to Maggie Castor for showing me this.

22. Regarding the thought of social ontology and ontology socialized, see Carol Gould, *Marx's Social Ontology: Individuality and Community in Marx's Theory of Social Reality* (Cambridge, MA: MIT Press, 1978).

23. See Hannah Arendt, "The Crisis in Education," in *Between Past and Future* (New York: Penguin, 1968), 173–96.

24. On the relation between figure and background, see Jean-Luc Nancy and Philippe Lacoue-Labarthe, *Scène* (Paris: Détroits, 2013).

25. Martin Heidegger, *Being and Time*, trans. John Macquarrie and Edward Robinson (New York: Harper & Row, 1962), 384.

26. The fact that Heidegger insists in *Being and Time* that being-toward-death is not experienced in the deaths of others is what blocks the way to an understanding of generation and makes it possible for him to propose that our relation to the generations of the dead is a relation to the gallery of heroes of our people. What remains unexamined is the process of mourning, commemoration, narration, redemption, and nation building by which such galleries are assembled. For groups denied mourning and who lack the institutions of a *people*, the dead are still waiting for redemption.

27. Hannah Arendt, *The Origins of Totalitarianism* (New York: Houghton Mifflin Harcourt, 1973), 452. See also Judith Butler, *Frames of War: When Is Life Grievable?* (New York: Verso, 2016).

28. Heidegger, *Being and Time*, sect. 47. See also Hans Ruin, *Being with the Dead: Burial, Ancestral Politics, and the Roots of Historical Consciousness* (Stanford, CA: Stanford University Press, 2019).

29. See Zoe Waxman, "Testimony and Representation," in *The Historiography of the Holocaust*, ed. Dan Stone (London: Palgrave Macmillan, 2004).

30. Orlando Patterson, *Slavery and Social Death* (Cambridge, MA: Harvard University Press, 1982).

31. See Jean-Luc Nancy, *Being Singular Plural* (Stanford, CA: Stanford University Press, 2000).

32. He writes in *Philosophical Rudiments Concerning Government and Society* that the condition on which a mother, or another, chooses to do so is that "being grown to full age he become not her enemy." Thomas Hobbes, *The English Works of Thomas Hobbes of Malmesbury* (Bohn, 1841), 2:116.

33. Hobbes knew this but tried to capture its implications in the structure of contract and the great implausibility of tacit consent.

34. François Jacob, *The Logic of Life: A History of Heredity* (New York: Vintage, 1976), 28.

35. See Arendt, "The Crisis in Education."

36. Walter Benjamin, "Theses on the Philosophy of History," in *Illuminations*, ed. Hannah Arendt, trans. Harry Zohn (New York: Schocken, 1969), 253–64.

37. See Elaine Scarry, *The Body in Pain: The Making and Unmaking of the World* (Oxford: Oxford University Press, 1985).

38. Matthias Fritsch, "Natal Alienation and Intergenerational Relations," presented at the Annual Meeting of the Society for Phenomenology and Existential Philosophy, Atlanta, GA, October 2015.

39. See, for instance, the contributions to John K. Roth, *Genocide and Human Rights: A Philosophical Guide* (London: Palgrave Macmillan, 2005). See also Mohammed Abed, "Clarifying the Concept of Genocide," *Metaphilosophy* 37, no. 3–4 (July 1, 2006): 308–30, https://doi.org/10.1111/j.1467-9973.2006.00443.x, where the author works to discern which groups can be thought of as susceptible to genocide and which cannot.

40. Debra Bergoffen, *Contesting the Politics of Genocidal Rape: Affirming the Dignity of the Vulnerable Body* (New York: Routledge, 2012).

41. See Rebecca Hamilton, "Inside Colin Powell's Decision to Declare Genocide in Darfur," *Atlantic*, August 17, 2011, http://www.theatlantic.com/international/archive/2011/08/inside-colin-powells-decision-to-declare-genocide-in-darfur/243560/.

42. See Abed, "Clarifying the Concept of Genocide."

43. Raphael Lemkin, *Axis Rule in Occupied Europe* (1944). Cited in Samantha Power, *A Problem from Hell* (New York: Basic Books, 2013), 42.

44. Troy Davis was executed by the US state of Georgia in 2011.

45. Richard Bernstein, *Violence: Thinking without Banisters* (London: John Wiley & Sons, 2013). Bernstein reminds us that, on the one hand, all designations of groups harbor the possibility of violence and, on the other, that the reign of violence renders moot all subtleties of identification and all authority over one's own identity.

46. Inge Deutschkron, *Ich Trug Den Gelben Stern* (Köln: Verlag Wissenschaft und Politik, 1983).

47. Annie L. Burton et al., *Women's Slave Narratives* (Mineola, NY: Dover, 2006), 61.

48. Sarah Clark Miller, "Moral Injury and Relational Harm: Analyzing Rape in Darfur," *Journal of Social Philosophy* 40, no. 4 (2009): 63-64, https://doi.org/10.1111/j.1467-9833.2009.01468.x.

49. This theme is pursued by "intentionalist" thinkers in genocide studies. See R. J. Rummel and Irving Louis Horowitz, *Death by Government: Genocide and Mass Murder since 1900* (New York: Routledge, 2017), https://doi.org/10.4324/9780203793756.

50. Christopher R. Browning, *Ordinary Men: Reserve Police Battalion 101 and the Final Solution in Poland* (New York: HarperCollins, 2017).

51. See Martin Shuster's arguments for rethinking our understanding of agency in the face of genocides in Anne O'Byrne and Martin Shuster, eds., *Logics of Genocide: The Structures of Violence and the Contemporary World* (New York: Routledge, 2020).

52. Federico Finchelstein notes this coherence: "Only fascists can explain to themselves the meaning of victimization. For non-fascists in general, and their victims in particular, the Holocaust makes no sense." Federico Finchelstein, "The Holocaust as Ideology: Borges and the Meaning of Transnational Fascism," *Dapim: Studies on the Shoah* 25 (2011): 278-79.

53. Brian Keenan, *An Evil Cradling* (New York: Random House, 2015).

54. James Hatley, *Suffering Witness: The Quandary of Responsibility after the Irreparable* (Albany: State University of New York Press, 2012), 63.

55. O'Byrne and Shuster, eds., *Logics of Genocide*, 8.

56. Elizabeth A. Povinelli, *Economies of Abandonment: Social Belonging and Endurance in Late Liberalism* (Durham, NC: Duke University Press, 2011), ix.

57. R. J. Rummel and Irving Louis Horowitz, *Death by Government: Genocide and Mass Murder since 1900* (New York: Routledge, 2017); R. J. Rummel, *Power Kills: Democracy as a Method of Nonviolence* (Oxford: Transaction, 2003).

58. Larry May, *Genocide: A Normative Account* (Cambridge: Cambridge University Press, 2010), 11.

59. See Peter Novick, *The Holocaust in American Life* (New York: Houghton Mifflin Harcourt, 2000).

60. This is part of May's complaint. Writers tend to be beholden to the sentiments of survivors, which prevents them adopting a rational rather than emotional approach. This assumes that emotion and rationality can be separated.

NOTES TO PAGES 24–26 / 171

61. The Philosopher's Index lists nine books or articles on genocide published before 1980, nineteen in the 1980s, sixty-five in the 1990s, 246 in the 2000s, and 204 in the 2010s.

62. "What [William Taft IV, legal adviser to Powell] does conclude however, is that a finding of genocide in Darfur could 'act as a spur to the international community to take immediate and forceful actions to respond to ongoing atrocities.' Powell took this advice to heart, hoping that by using the word genocide he would move other nations on the UN Security Council to act. There are more and less charitable ways of understanding Powell's decision: As a laudable and historic pushing of the boundaries in a genuine effort to stop genocide; as a misguided, or even self-serving, attempt to avoid the risk of a Rwanda-like shaming when the story of Darfur was eventually written; or as an endeavor to claim the moral high-ground in the midst of the war on terror that ultimately undermined the power of the genocide label. What is not in question is Powell's strategy of using the determination to spur other countries to act in Darfur failed. . . . Though reaching different conclusions on whether or not to apply the genocide label, the decision of both Democratic and Republican administrations alike were influenced more by what they believed a genocide determination would mean in terms of action rather than by a strict interpretation of the evidence they had before them. The results to date suggest that neither Rwandans nor Sudanese have been well-served by such instrumentally-motivated avoidance, or use, of the g-word." Hamilton, "Inside Colin Powell's Decision to Declare Genocide in Darfur."

63. Bruce Wilshire, *Get 'Em All! Kill 'Em!* (Lanham, MD: Lexington, 2005), 134.

64. As another example, see Tony Barta's study of the settler determination to take aboriginal land in Australia and its genocidal consequences. Tony Barta, "Relations of Genocide: Land and Lives in the Colonization of Australia," in *Genocide and the Modern Age: Etiology and Case Studies of Mass Death* (Syracuse, NY: Syracuse University Press, 2000), 237–51.

65. The critical phenomenology of generation I have in view inevitably intersects with Foucault's thinking of biopolitics and biopower. Foucault explicitly rejects the phenomenological approach (see Michel Foucault, *The Order of Things: An Archaeology of Human Sciences* [New York: Knopf Doubleday, 2012], xv) but also makes clear that the element of phenomenology that he objects to is the absolute priority of the observing subject. This is not the place to work it out in full, but I would argue that the signal achievement of phenomenology is the displacement of the subject in favor of the intentional object, and the achievement of critical phenomenology is to put the method to work in making the connection between describing and changing the world. For a reading of Foucault's treatment of phenomenology in *The Order of Things*, see Johanna Oksala, *Foucault on Freedom* (Cambridge: Cambridge University Press, 2005), 40–70. See also Rudi Visker, *Truth and Singularity: Taking Foucault into Phenomenology* (Berlin: Springer Science & Business Media, 2000).

66. See Lisa Guenther, "Six Senses of Critique for Critical Phenomenology," *Puncta* 4, no. 2 (n.d.): 5–23, https://doi.org/10.5399/PJCP.V4I2.2. See also Al-Saji, "A Phenomenology of Hesitation."

67. For a more thoughtful response, see Alan Gewirth, "Is-Ought Problem Solved," *Proceedings of the American Philosophical Association* (1974).

68. See Dermot Moran, "'Let's Look at It Objectively': Why Phenomenology Cannot Be Naturalized," *Royal Institute of Philosophy Supplement* 72 (2013): 104, https://doi.org/10.1017/S1358246113000064.

172 / NOTES TO PAGES 26–33

69. Matthias Fritsch addresses this concern unflinchingly. See Matthias Fritsch, "Ontological Problems Call for Ontological Approaches," in *Taking Turns with the Earth: Phenomenology, Deconstruction, and Intergenerational Justice* (Stanford, CA: Stanford University Press, 2018), 40–43.

70. Moran, "'Let's Look at It Objectively,'" 104.

71. Note that the project of structuralism is understood by Jean-Claude le Milner in strikingly similar terms: "L'idée centrale [du structuralisme]: intégrer au domaine de la science galiléenne, originellement liée à la seule nature, des objets censés relever de la culture, sans pourtant qu'ils soient du même coup « naturalisés ». . . . Ainsi était remise en cause non seulement l'antique opposition phusis/thesis, mais aussi toutes ses variantes modernes (nature-convention, nature-histoire, nature-culture, etc.). Pour qu'une telle décision fût légitime, il fallait oser innover. La nouveauté, de proche en proche, affecta la notion de science galiléenne elle-même, puis la théorie de la connaissance empirique, pour toucher enfin, quoique avec retenue, à l'ontologie." Abstract of Jean-Claude le Milner, *Le peripile structural: figures et paradigm* (Paris: Seuil, 2002).

72. See Jean-Luc Nancy, *The Sense of the World* (Minneapolis: University of Minnesota Press, 1997).

73. Hannah Arendt, "Truth and Politics," in *Between Past and Future: Eight Exercises in Political Thought* (New York: Penguin, 1968), 238.

74. For a sophisticated investigation of the relation of ontology and normativity, see Fritsch, *Taking Turns with the Earth.*

75. Fritsch, *Taking Turns with the Earth.*

76. See Don Beith, *The Birth of Sense: Generative Passivity in Merleau-Ponty's Philosophy* (Athens: Ohio University Press, 2018).

77. I follow Rancière in using *politics* and *democratic politics* interchangeably. Jacques Rancière, *Aesthetics and Its Discontents*, trans. Steven Corcoran (Cambridge: Polity, 2009).

78. There are others who make similar arguments in terms of our living according to many rationalities. We might approach a mode of being in time as a mode of understanding the world. For example, see T. M. S. Evens, *Two Kinds of Rationality: Kibbutz Democracy and Generational Conflict* (Minneapolis: University of Minnesota Press, 1995), 85–117.

79. See Z. Bauman, *Postmodernity and Its Discontents* (New York: New York University Press, 1997).

80. Lauren Berlant and Lee Edelman, *Sex, or the Unbearable* (Durham, NC: Duke University Press, 2014), 20, 58.

81. R. Lemkin, *Totally Unofficial: The Autobiography of Raphael Lemkin*, ed. D. L. Frieze (New Haven, CT: Yale University Press, 2013), 180–85.

## 1. *Genos*

1. R. Lemkin, *Axis Rule in Occupied Europe: Laws of Occupation, Analysis of Government, Proposals for Redress* (Washington, DC: Carnegie Endowment for International Peace, Division of International Law, 1944), 79.

2. "Moreover . . . the broad 'O' in the middle of the word 'genocide' is always used in words to convey the meaning of a large object, and this is very appropriate to this case. Genocide conveys the concept of destroying great masses of peoples of a nation." R. Lemkin, *Totally Unofficial: The Autobiography of Raphael Lemkin*, ed. D. L. Frieze

(New Haven, CT: Yale University Press, 2013), 181. For Lemkin's own account of his generation of the term, see Lemkin, *Totally Unofficial*, 180–86; and Lemkin, *Axis Rule in Occupied Europe*, 79ff.

3. Emile Benveniste, *Indo-European Language and Society*, trans. Elizabeth Palmer (London: Faber and Faber, 1973), 207–8, 257–59.

4. Lemkin, *Axis Rule in Occupied Europe*, 79.

5. Cortés is reported to have told Charles V that he could not describe certain things he saw in America: "I do not know the words by which they are known." See Andrea Giunta, "Strategies of Modernity in Latin America," in *Beyond the Fantastic: Contemporary Art Criticism from Latin America*, ed. Gerardo Mosquera (Cambridge, MA: MIT Press, 1996), 53. Cited by Juan Carlos Guerrero Hernández, "Mutilated Bodies and Memories of Violence: Displacements and Contestations of Representations of Violence, in Contemporary Video Art and Photography in Colombia, 1993–1998," PhD diss., Stony Brook University, Department of Art and Art History, 2015, 83. See http://legacy.fordham.edu/halsall/mod/1520cortes.asp.

6. Gunnar Broberg, "Homo Sapiens: Linnaeus's Classification of Man," in *Linnaeus: The Man and His Work*, ed. Tore Frangsmyr (Canton, MA: Science History Publications, 1994), 157.

7. See Barbara Cassin et al., *Dictionary of Untranslatables: A Philosophical Lexicon* (Princeton, NJ: Princeton University Press, 2014), 757.

8. Georges Canguilhem, *Knowledge of Life* (New York: Fordham University Press, 2008); Michel Foucault, *Society Must Be Defended: Lectures at the College de France, 1975–1976* (New York: Picador, 2003); François Jacob, *The Logic of Life: A History of Heredity* (New York: Vintage, 1976); Samuel Talcott, "Errant Life, Molecular Biology, and Biopower: Canguilhem, Jacob, and Foucault," *History and Philosophy of the Life Sciences* 36, no. 2 (October 1, 2014): 254–79.

9. Michel Foucault, *The Order of Things: An Archaeology of Human Sciences* (New York: Knopf, 2012), xviii.

10. For Foucault, it is a matter of language, which it certainly is. Foucault explicitly rejects the phenomenological approach because of its concentration on the subject and its postulation of a transcendental subjectivity, but those criticisms are less pertinent once phenomenology develops the thought of intersubjectivity and being-with and the more it is understood in terms of hermeneutics.

11. See Foucault, *The Order of Things*, xxiv.

12. Note the parallel between the structure described here and the one Arendt identifies when she writes: "There is something here [in the camps] that should never be involved in politics as we used to understand it, namely all or nothing—all, and that is an undetermined infinity of forms of human living-together, or nothing, for the victory of the concentration-camp system would mean the same inexorable doom for human beings as the use of the hydrogen bomb would mean the doom of the human race." Hannah Arendt, *The Origins of Totalitarianism* (New York: Houghton Mifflin Harcourt, 1973), 443.

13. Primo Levi, *The Drowned and the Saved* (New York: Summit, 1988), 85.

14. See the note at the end of Chapter 1 on the use of *genos*.

15. Aristotle, *Categories*, trans. W. D. Ross (London: Metheun, 1971), 1b25–28.

16. Porphyry, *Introduction*, trans. Jonathan Barnes (Oxford: Clarendon, 2006), 0, 15.

17. Hacking cites Simplicius (fl. 530), "who wrote an exemplary account of different ways of reading the Categories, [and] reports that Porphyry studied their intermediate

role between words and things." Ian Hacking, "Trees of Logic, Trees of Porphyry," in *Advancements of Learning: Essays in Honour of Paolo Rossi*, ed. J. Heilbron (Florence: Olshki, 2007), 230. See also Porphyry, *Introduction*, 1, 15.

18. Porphyry, *Introduction*, 1, 18.

19. Porphyry, *Introduction*, 3, 15–20.

20. Porphyry, *Introduction*, 4, 21–32.

21. See Hacking, "Trees of Logic, Trees of Porphyry."

22. Eco briefly explores the possibility of using probrium rather than differentia to produce a definition of a genus, concluding: "The nature of probrium remains mysterious, both in Aristotle and in Porphyry, since it looks like something midway between an essential and an analytic property and an encyclopedic and a synthetic one." Umberto Eco, *Semiotics and the Philosophy of Language* (Bloomington: Indiana University Press, 1986), 60.

23. Eco, *Semiotics and the Philosophy of Language*, argues that this procedure of differentiation cannot produce a definition. "As a matter of fact, all the instances of a Porphyrian tree, following a common standard, aim at showing how man can be defined and are therefore incomplete" (61). For Eco, this is a difficulty, but the proliferation of difference and the frustration of the work of definition are to be welcomed for existential purposes.

24. Annamieke Verboon, "The Medieval Tree of Porphyry: An Organic Structure of Logic," in *The Tree: Symbol, Allegory, and Structural Device in Medieval Art and Thought*, ed. A. Worm and P. Salonis (Brepols: Turnhout, 2014).

25. Note that this is the same era when *arbores juris*, or Trees of Consanguinity, began to appear. See Annamieke Verboon, "The Medieval Tree of Porphyry: An Organic Structure of Logic," in *The Tree: Symbol, Allegory, and Structural Device in Medieval Art and Thought*, ed. A. Worm and P. Salonis (Brepols: Turnhout, 2014), 95–116.

26. Aristotle, *Categories*, trans. Ross, 23.

27. Porphyry observes that the same differentia are often observed in many species, "as four-footed in many animals which differ in species" (18.20). Aristotle also notes this in *Categories* 1b 15ff. See Eco, *Semiotics and the Philosophy of Language*, 62.

28. Kant understands his table of categories to be aiming at the same thing as Aristotle's categories, "though very distant . . . in execution." Immanuel Kant, *Critique of Pure Reason*, ed. and trans. Paul Guyer and Allen Wood (Cambridge: Cambridge University Press, 1998), A80, B106. See A81, B107 for his critical assessment of the flaws of Aristotle's system of categories, all traceable to the fact that he had no principle.

29. Eco, *Semiotics and the Philosophy of Language*, 66.

30. Eco, in *Semiotics and the Philosophy of Language*, having argued vigorously for the untenability of the Porphyrian mode of differentiation, acknowledges the possibility of the type of argument I make here. Porphyry's model failed, according to Eco, because it tried to understand semantic representation in the format of a dictionary rather than an encyclopedia. However, for all that, dictionary-like representations can be used a suitable tools for certain tasks (84). "Thus, if the encyclopedia is an unordered set of markers (and of frames, scripts, text-oriented instructions), the dictionary-like arrangements we continuously provide are transitory and pragmatically useful hierarchical reassessments of it" (85).

31. Aristotle, *Categories*, trans. Ross, 2.

32. Hacking reflects on the "incomplete sense" discernable in Ramon Llull's "*Arbor naturalis, arbor logicalis*." Hacking writes: "The strange mixture of vivid concrete

example and evocative abstract structure makes Llull dangerously tantalizing and conceptually difficult. Frances Yates confessed that when she first encountered Llull she thought the whole symbolic system was mad. Slowly it came to make an incomplete sense. The best explanation, at least of Llull's 'Natural and Logical Tree,' is in Johnston's aptly titled *The Spiritual Logic of Ramón Llull*." Hacking, "Trees of Logic, Trees of Porphyry," 247. See Mark David Johnston, *The Spiritual Logic of Ramon Llull* (London: Clarendon, 1987).

33. Hacking, "Trees of Logic, Trees of Porphyry," 252, traces a line of inheritance of the Porphyrian practice of generating categories by division—if not the image of the Porphyrian tree—through Peter Ramus (1515–1572), "a radical reformer of scholastic logic . . . it leads not as far as Linnaeus but to the man who made possible Linnaeus's classification of plants by sexual parts, namely Andrea Cesalpino (1519–1603)."

34. Carl von Linné, *Linnaeus' Philosophia Botanica*, trans. Stephen Freer (Oxford: Oxford University Press, 2005), 259.

35. Linné, *Linnaeus' Philosophia Botanica*, 172.

36. See Londa Schebinger, *Plants and Empire: Colonial Biprospecting in the Atlantic World* (Cambridge, MA: Harvard University Press, 2004), esp. chap. 5, "Linguistic Imperialism," 194–225.

37. Hamburgische Berichte, 1735, No. 75, 20 September, 618–19. Quoted in M. S. J. Engel-Ledeboer, "Carl Linnaeus and the Systema Naturae," in *Systema Naturae*, 8. For an extensive treatment of the economic interest that propelled the work, see Lisbet Koerner, *Linnaeus: Nature and Nation* (Cambridge, MA: Harvard University Press, 2009).

38. Carl von Linné, *Systema Naturae, 1735: Facsimile of the First Edition with an Introduction and a First English Translation of the "Observationes,"* ed. H. Engel, trans. M. S. J. Engel-Ledeboer (De Graaf, 1964), 19.

39. Linné, *Systema Naturae*, 18.

40. Linné, *Systema Naturae*, 19.

41. Linné, *Linnaeus' Philosophia Botanica*, 113. Kant will later make the same complaint about Linnaeus: "We do not have as yet a system of nature. In the existing so-called system of this type, the objects are merely put beside each other and ordered in sequence one after another. . . . True philosophy, however, has to follow the diversity and the manifoldness of matter through all time." Immanuel Kant, *Physische Geographie*, p.160; quoted in Emmanuel Eze, *Achieving Our Humanity: The Idea of the Post-racial Future* (New York: Routledge, 2001), 103.

42. Linné, *Linnaeus' Philosophia Botanica*, 23

43. Linné, *Linnaeus' Philosophia Botanica*, 31.

44. Linné, *Linnaeus' Philosophia Botanica*, 29.

45. Linné, *Linnaeus' Philosophia Botanica*, 49.

46. Linné, *Linnaeus' Philosophia Botanica*, 175. Linnaeus was too late to help Cortés in his particular predicament, but his system was later vigorously applied to the botanical discoveries of the New World. Daniela Bleichmar writes of the "botanical conquistadors" of the eighteenth century, for example. Daniela Bleichmar, "Botanical Conquistadors," in *Worlds of Natural History*, ed. H. A. Curry et al. (Cambridge: Cambridge University Press, 2018), 236–54. In some instances there is a linguistic gulf: Most Australian aboriginal languages were destroyed in the course of colonization, and today most Australians commonly refer to plants by their Linnaean names. In other instances, native names survived within the nomenclature devised by Europeans. Juan Guerrero writes of the work of Jose Celestino Mutis, who led the Spanish Royal

Botanical Expedition to New Granada (1782–1816): "We must recall Jaime Peralta's finding concerning the naming of some species of animals, that Mutis had no other option than to follow the names given by natives. That is the case of the large species of bird known as *Chauna Chavaria*; 'chavaria' was the name the natives had for it." Guerrero Hernández, "Mutilated Bodies and Memories of Violence," 84. Jaime Peralta, "De 'delirios ignorantes' a 'cultas reflexiones': la Ilustración europea y la apropiación de los saberes de la periferia colonial," *Fronteras de la Historia* 19, no. 1 (2014), 82; see also Andrea Giunta, "Strategies of Modernity in Latin America," in *Beyond the Fantastic: Contemporary Art Criticism from Latin America*, ed. Gerardo Mosquera (Cambridge, MA: MIT Press, 1996), 53. Indeed, as José Alejandro Restrepo comments, from the point of view of native botanical knowledge, "Linnaeus was another Chinese encyclopedist." José Alejandro Restrepo, *Musa paradisíaca: una video-instalación* [exhibition catalog] (Bogotá: Colombia: Instituto colombiano de cultura, 1997), 9.

47. "Observationes," in *Systema Natura*, 19.

48. Linné, *Linnaeus' Philosophia Botanica*, 224, 219.

49. Linné, *Linnaeus' Philosophia Botanica*, 219.

50. Linné, *Linnaeus' Philosophia Botanica*, 245. Freer's translation announces but does not explain the decision to translate Linnaeus's Latin *differentiae* as *definitions* rather than *differences*. I have reversed the decision here, to preserve the ambiguity.

51. Linné, *Linnaeus' Philosophia Botanica*, 220.

52. The *Paradoxa* were dropped from the sixth edition, in 1748.

53. Frangsmyr, ed., *Linnaeus: The Man and His Work*, 177.

54. A. O. Lovejoy, *The Great Chain of Being: A Study of the History of an Idea* (Cambridge, MA: Harvard University Press, 2009), 57.

55. Broberg, "Homo Sapiens," 179, writes: "The temptation to anthropomorphize these animals that were different from other marine creatures may be briefly illustrated by a note in *Iter Lapponicum* referring to the intercourse of seals: the female lies 'wide open' and the male '*ut homo*' embraces her." *Iter Lapponicum* (1913), 211.

56. The footnote appears in the tenth edition, but the English translation, published by Turton in 1800, has the entry for the white dolphin as the last text in the Mammalia section.

57. Broberg, "Homo Sapiens," 185. The girl was almost certainly Amelia Lewsam or Newsham, who was a Black albino and had been brought from Jamaica in 1754. She would have been nine or ten years old when Linnaeus heard of her.

58. Jami Weinstein, "Vital Ethics: On Life and In/Difference," in *Against Life*, ed. Alastair Hunt and Stephanie Youngblood (Evanston, IL: Northwestern University Press, 2016), 89.

59. Immanuel Kant, *Critique of Judgment*, trans. Werner S. Pluhar (Indianapolis, IN: Hackett, 1987), 168.

60. Ernst Cassirer, *The Problem of Knowledge: Philosophy, Science, and History since Hegel*, trans. William H. Woglom and Charles W. Hendel (New Haven, CT: Yale University Press, 1950), 124.

61. See Kant, *Critique of Judgment*, 168. Although this remark is in the *Critique of Judgment*, it occurs in the Preface, at a moment when Kant is describing what was achieved by the *Critique of Pure Reason*, that is, the identification of cognition as the proper domain of the understanding.

62. Kant, *Critique of Pure Reason*, A646, B674. Kant makes the observation quoted from Lovejoy above in different terms when he describes reason preparing the field for

the understanding by supplying the principles of sameness of kinds (homogeneity), variety (specification), and the affinity of all concepts (continuity). A657–58.

63. Another reading of this passage in the first *Critique* would show Kant breaking down Nature into elements that are pure (at least in principle) in a way analogous to the chemical process of fractionation by which a compound is separated into its constituent elements. This might be done for the sake of purity but also for the sake of knowing the makeup of the compound and freeing its components for new combinations. See S. Müller-Wille and H.-J. Rheinberger, eds., *Heredity Produced: At the Crossroads of Biology, Politics, and Culture, 1500–1870* (Cambridge, MA: MIT Press, 2007), 126, where this analogy is cannily used to offer a new account of the eugenically inflected discussions of heredity in the late nineteenth and early twentieth centuries.

64. Kant, *Critique of Pure Reason*, A654/B682.

65. Kant, *Critique of Pure Reason*, A646/B674.

66. Kant, *Critique of Pure Reason*, A668-669/B695-696.

67. Cassirer, *The Problem of Knowledge*, 124–29.

68. Jennifer Mensch, *Kant's Organicism: Epigenesis and the Development of Critical Philosophy* (Chicago: University of Chicago Press, 2013), 99.

69. Mensch, *Kant's Organicism*, 100.

70. A line of fertile mules would allow Buffon to show apparently disparate species to be in fact varieties of older, degenerated lines. Mensch, *Kant's Organicism*, 101. See also Mensch's elegant account of this moment in the development of Kant's thought: "Kant's argument from experience to its grounds thus led past both chance and mechanism when accounting for divergence, tracing itself back to an idea of natural providence as alone capable of grounding the unity and difference of humankind" (107).

71. Mensch, *Kant's Organicism*, 106.

72. Mensch, *Kant's Organicism*, 102,107.

73. Kant, *Critique of Judgment*, 418. See Staffan Müller-Wille and Hans-Jörg Rheinberger, *A Cultural History of Heredity* (Chicago: University of Chicago Press, 2012), 35, for a cultural historical account of how development and reproduction feature in the development of Kant's thought of natural purpose.

74. Kant, *Critique of Judgment*, 420n.

75. Kant, *Critique of Judgment*, 419.

76. Cassirer, *The Problem of Knowledge*, 126.

77. Mensch, *Kant's Organicism*, 151.

78. Robert Bernasconi has written extensively on the subject of Kant and race. See in particular Robert Bernasconi, "Kant as an Unfamiliar Source of Racism," in *Philosophers on Race: Critical Essays* (Oxford: Wiley-Blackwell, 2002), 145–65. See also Raphael Lagier, *Les races humaines selon Kant* (Paris: PUF, 2004); Peter McLaughlin, "Kant on Heredity," in *Heredity Produced*, 277–92.

79. Linné, *Linnaeus' Philosophia Botanica*, 185,183. He adds: "The reasons are to be sought in [my] *Critica botanica*."

80. The life and death of Linnaeus's family name is poignant. In Sweden in the late seventeenth century, family names were relatively rare, and Carl Linnaeus's father Nils would have been known in early life by first name and patronym: Nils Ingmarsson. However, in order to attend university, he had to acquire a family name, and he chose to name himself, and thereby his line, after the linden tree that grew on his family's land at Jonsboda. Other family had appealed to the tree in the same way, creating the names Lindelius and Tiliander out of its name in Swedish (*lind*) or Latin (*tilia*). Wilfrid

Blunt, *Linnaeus: The Compleat Naturalist* (Princeton, NJ: Princeton University Press, 2001), 12. He passed on the name Linnaeus (later ennobled as von Linné) to Carl and his four siblings. All but one of Carl's sons died in infancy, and the surviving son did not marry, so the von Linné family name persisted for just two generations. Carl's brother Samuel had seven daughters and five sons. Only one son reached maturity, and he died without marrying. Thus, the Linnaeus family name existed for no more than three generations. See http://www.linnaeus.uu.se/online/life/4_1.html.

81. Note the title of Julian Huxley's biography: Krishna R. Dronamraju, *If I Am to Be Remembered: The Life and Work of Julian Huxley* (Singapore: World Scientific, 1993).

82. Jacob, *The Logic of Life*, 19-20.

83. G. G. Simpson, *Principles of Animal Taxonomy* (New York: Columbia University Press, 1961), 53.

84. As a young man, Linnaeus describes plant sex voluptuously: "The actual petals of the flower contribute nothing to generation, serving only as the bridal bed which the great Creator has so gloriously prepared, adorned with such precious bedcurtains, and perfumed with so many sweet scents that the bridegroom and bride may therein celebrate their nuptials with the greater solemnity. When the bed has thus been made ready, then is the time for the bridegroom to embrace his beloved bride and surrender himself to her." *Praeludia Sponsaliorum Plantarum*, 1729, quoted in Blunt, *Linnaeus*, 33; and Guerrero Hernández, "Mutilated Bodies and Memories of Violence, 78. Nonetheless, Caspar Friedrich Wolff comments tartly: "[Linnaeus] may well know how to copulate, but has no understanding of the theory of generation." *Theorie der Generation* (1764): In 2 Adh, erkl. U. bewiesen (Berlin: Bernstiel, 1764), 25. Cited in Müller-Wille and Rheinberger, *A Cultural History of Heredity*, n31.

85. See Hacking, "Trees of Logic, Trees of Porphyry."

86. For the origin of the (biological) concept of reproduction in Buffon's work, see McLaughlin, "Kant on Heredity," 173-79.

87. Charles Darwin, *The Origin of Species* (London: John Murray, 1859), 172.

88. Larry Douglas Smith, "Fitzroy and the Fuegians: A Clash of Cultures," *Anglican and Episcopal History* 59, no. 3 (1990): 386-403.

89. On traveler naturalists, see Jacob, *The Logic of Life*, 162.

90. See Dilthey's contemporary efforts to make history scientific in *Über das Studium der Geschichte der Wissenschaften vom Menschen, der Gesellschaft und dem Staat* (GS 5:31-73) (1875).

91. Foucault, *The Order of Things*, 367-73.

92. See Cassirer, *The Problem of Knowledge*, 159.

93. Jacob, *The Logic of Life*, 166.

94. Darwin, *The Origin of Species*, 334.

95. Darwin, *The Origin of Species*, 335.

96. Darwin, *The Origin of Species*, 340.

97. This is the claim later made for it by Julian Sachs in *Geschichte der Botanik vom 16. Jahrhundert bis 1860*, S. 204, cited by Cassirer, *The Problem of Knowledge*, 157. See also 168n25, citing Sachs sec 12, 115, and elsewhere.

98. Cassirer, *The Problem of Knowledge*, 169.

99. Jacques Monod, *Chance and Necessity: An Essay on the Natural Philosophy of Modern Biology* (London: Penguin, 1997), 165.

100. Müller-Wille and Rheinberger, *A Cultural History of Heredity*, 160,

101. On the Human Genome Project, see "The Dream of the Human Genome" in Monod, *Chance and Necessity*, 165, 61–83; Müller-Wille and Rheinberger, *A Cultural History of Heredity*, 211, and Evelyn Fox Keller, "Nature, Nurture, and the Human Genome Project," in *The Code of Codes*, ed. Daniel J. Kevles and Leroy Hood (Cambridge, MA: Harvard University Press, 1992), 281–99.

102. Cassirer, *The Problem of Knowledge*, 166.

103. Cassirer, *The Problem of Knowledge*, 171

104. Cassirer, *The Problem of Knowledge*, 173.

105. Linnaeus had already split apart causal relationships and classificatory relationships, that is, the causal relationship of producing another individual and the classificatory relationship of identity by virtue of having descended from a common ancestor. Specific differences were passed on from generation to generation under all circumstances and obeyed universal laws; differences between varieties emerge in particular circumstances. Müller-Wille and Rheinberger, *A Cultural History of Heredity*, 33.

106. Luigi Cavalli-Sforza, Paolo Menozzi, and Alberto Piazza, *The History and Geography of Human Genes* (Princeton, NJ: Princeton University Press, 1994), 13–16. For a more detailed account of the fate of mutations, see Luigi Cavalli-Sforza and Francesco Cavalli-Sforza, *The Great Human Diasporas: The History of Diversity And Evolution* (New York: Basic Books, 1995), 77–105.

107. Darwin, *The Origin of Species*, 349.

108. As Buffon worried, "nature can vary her works *ad infinitum*." Quoted in Jacob, from Buffon's *Introduction a l'histoire des minéraux: Oeuvres complètes* (a), VI, 24.

109. The evolutionary taxonomist G. G. Simpson acknowledges as much and is taken to task for his "semi-scientific" approach by Bunge and Mahner: "Instead of attempting to eliminate this prescientific arbitrariness—Simpson's euphemism—the element of *art* in systematics—it is something hailed as a virtue." See Mahner and Bunge, eds., *Foundations of Biophilosophy* (Berlin: Springer, 2013), 251–52.

110. *Classical genetics* refers to the discipline that came into existence in the wake of Gregor Mendel's experiments with pea hybrids. Mendel's research was published in 1865, but genetics only became a coherent discipline in the first decade of the twentieth century. It provided the context for all biological research into heredity from that time until its working paradigms were left behind with the advent of new gene technologies in the 1970s. According to Müller-Wille and Rheinberger, these meant that genetics became less a matter of the science of producing "test-tube conditions under which the molecules of the organism and their reaction sequences assumed the status of objects of scientific investigation . . . now molecular technologists assembled molecules that carried genetic information and used the milieu of the cell as an appropriate technical medium for reproduction of these molecules, for expressing them, and for investigating the effects of their products." Müller-Wille and Rheinberger, *A Cultural History of Heredity*, 189; see also 4. Concerning the different accounts of evolutionary phenomena in classical genetics and its successor discipline, see the example of the birds and marsupials of Australia in Stephen Jay Gould, "Evolution and the Triumph of Homology," *American Scientist* 74, no. 1 (1986): 68.

111. Jacob, *The Logic of Life*, 203.

112. Müller-Wille and Rheinberger, *A Cultural History of Heredity*, 128, 137.

113. Pigluicci indicates a more nuanced account of the use of models in biology. "On the use of models in biology and science generally, Gavrilets (1997) concluded that

a model's predictive ability—the gold standard in disciplines such as physics—is not necessarily its most important contribution to science, as models in biology are more often useful as metaphors and tools to sharpen one's thinking about a given problem." Massimo Pigliucci, "Phenotypic Plasticity," in *Evolution: The Extended Synthesis*, ed. Massimo Pigliucci and Gerd Müller (Cambridge, MA: MIT Press, 2010), 374.

114. Massimo Pigliucci, "Species as Family Resemblance: The (Dis)Solution of the Species Problem?," *BioEssays* 25, no. 6 (n.d.): 596.

115. Mary Jane West-Eberhard, *Developmental Plasticity and Evolution* (Oxford: Oxford University Press, 2003), 34–35.

116. Theodore Garland and Scott A. Kelly, "Phenotypic Plasticity and Experimental Evolution," *Journal of Experimental Biology* 209 (2006): 2344, https://doi.org/10.1242/jeb.02244.

117. Maynard V. Olson, "When Less Is More: Gene Loss as an Engine of Evolutionary Change," *American Journal of Human Genetics* 64, no. 1 (January 1, 1999): 21–22, https://doi.org/10.1086/302219.

118. See Melanie L. J. Stiassny, "Atavisms, Phylogenetic Character Reversals, and the Origin of Evolutionary Novelties," *Netherlands Journal of Zoology* 42, no. 2 (1991): 260–76, https://doi.org/10.1163/156854291X00324.

119. "Even though extinction is typically considered as absolute, following admixture, fragments of the gene pool of extinct species can survive for tens of thousands of years in the genomes of extant recipient species." Alex Barlow et al., "Partial Genomic Survival of Cave Bears in Living Brown Bears," *Nature: Ecology and Evolution*, August 27, 2018, https://doi.org/10.1038/s41559-018-0654-8. There is also evidence of the persistence of Neanderthal DNA in modern non-African humans. R. E. Green et al., "A Draft Sequence of the Neandertal Genome," *Science* 328 (2010): 710–22.

120. John Protevi, *Life, War, Earth* (Minneapolis: University of Minnesota Press, 2013), 204.

121. Hermann Muller, "Our Load of Mutations," *American Journal of Human Genetics* 2, no. 2 (1950): 111–76.

122. Jacob, *The Logic of Life*, 90–91.

123. Foucault, *The Order of Things*, 74.

124. OC I, 64, Quoted in Jacob, *The Logic of Life*, 47.

125. Linné, *Linnaeus' Philosophia Botanica*, 305. Quoted in Jacob, *The Logic of Life*, 50.

126. Jacob, *The Logic of Life*, 100.

127. Jacob, *The Logic of Life*, 120.

128. Michel Foucault, *The History of Sexuality*, vol. 1: *The Will to Knowledge* (New York: Penguin, 2008), 137.

129. Jacob, *The Logic of Life*, 205–6.

130. Foucault, *The Order of Things*, 347, 355; Michel Foucault, *The Archaeology of Knowledge* (New York: Knopf, 2012), 186.

131. Quoted in Stuart Elden, *Foucault: The Birth of Power* (Hoboken, NJ: John Wiley & Sons, 2017), 14. Elden adds: "As Foucault's reading notes attest . . . heredity is a theme that links madness, medicine, crime and sexuality as well as the specialized knowledge of biology. That would encompass aspects of all of his major works, from the early 1960s to the 1980s."

132. Jacob, *The Logic of Life*, 307.

133. Catherine Malabou, "Philosophers, Biologists: Some More Effort If You Wish to Become Revolutionaries!," *Critical Inquiry* 43 (Autumn 2016): 203.

134. Jacob, *The Logic of Life*, 309–10.

135. Jacob, *The Logic of Life*, 312–17.

136. Gould, "Evolution and the Triumph of Homology," 66.

137. As are Mahner and Bunge's claims for their version of cladistics taxonomy: "Our taxonomy has been developed independently since it flows naturally from our ontology. Moreover, it is based on logical and ontological reasons, whereas traditional pattern cladism appears to be inspired by empiricism and falsificationism. . . . Since the taxa of cladistics classification are defined by lawfully related properties, they are . . . examples of biological kinds *sensu lato*." Mahner and Bunge, *Biophilosophy*, 248–49.

138. Gould, "Evolution and the Triumph of Homology," 63.

139. See Anthony Appiah, "The Uncompleted Argument: Du Bois and the Illusion of Race," *Critical Inquiry* 12, no. 1 (1985): 26, https://doi.org/10.2307/1343460.

140. Carol Kaesuk Yoon, *Naming Nature: The Clash between Instinct and Science* (New York: Norton, 2010), 4.

141. See Lulu Miller, *Why Fish Don't Exist: A Story of Loss, Love, and the Hidden Order of Life* (New York: Simon and Schuster, 2021).

142. See Bernasconi, "Kant as an Unfamiliar Source of Racism."

143. R. C. Lewontin, "The Apportionment of Human Diversity," in *Evolutionary Biology*, ed. T. Dobzhansky, M. K. Hecht, and W. C. Steere (New York: Springer, 1972), https://doi.org/10.1007/978-1-4684-9063-3_14.

144. "1998 AAA Statement on 'Race,'" *Anthropology Newsletter* 39, no. 9 (1998): 3.

145. Siddhartha Mukherjee, *The Gene: An Intimate History* (New York: Simon and Schuster, 2016).

146. Nicholas Wade, *A Troublesome Inheritance: Genes, Race, and Human History* (New York: Penguin, 2015).

147. Georg Forster, "Guiding Thread to a Future History of Humankind (1789)," in *Georg Forsters Werke*, ed. Akademie der Wissenschaften der DDR, later Berlin-Brandenburgische Akademie der Wissenschaften (Berlin: Akademie Verlag, 1958), 8:193.

148. This is despite the fact that the results of basic scientific research may turn out to be powerful elements in technological developments. Quoted by Hannah Arendt, *The Human Condition* (Chicago: University of Chicago Press, 1998), 231.

149. Müller-Wille and Rheinberger, *A Cultural History of Heredity*, 195, point out that the distinction between basic science and applied research may be moot after the founding of Genentech in 1976 and the increasing market orientation of genetic research since then.

150. Indeed, the tree needs its own justifications. It has always had a branching habit, but much has changed since Darwin sketched a set of relations at the beginning of *Origins*. Although the successor NSF project abandons the tree figure in favor of the title "Genealogy of Life," or "GoLife," the Tree of Life name persists despite the fact that it has rarely looked like a tree. The Tree of Porphyry and biblical genealogical trees all had strong trunks from which branches sprang, but Darwin's diagram instead suggests a Bush of Life, throwing out many scions from the start. Some of the wide gaps left by extinctions have been filled in by paleontology. What used to be known as microbial dark matter—dark because unculturable and all but impossible to study—is now being brought to light and is turning out to account for most of the biological species

diversity on Earth. The enormous outgrowth that is the figure of that diversity now dwarfs the rest of the bush. Moreover, microbes turn out to transmit genetic material not only vertically but also horizontally; a branch can cross its origin and grow back into or through its sister branches.

151. The National Science Foundation of the United States describes the Assembling the Tree of Life (ATOL) project in this way: "A flood of new information, from whole-genome sequences to detailed structural information to inventories of earth's biota to greater appreciation of the importance of lateral gene transfer in shaping evolutionary history, is transforming 21st century biology. Along with comparative data on morphology, fossils, development, behavior, and interactions of all forms of life on earth, these new data streams make even more critical the need for an organizing evolutionary context. Phylogeny, the genealogical map for all lineages of life on earth, provides an overall framework to facilitate biological information retrieval, prediction and analysis. Currently, single investigators or small teams of researchers are studying the evolutionary pathways of heredity usually concentrating on taxonomic groups of modest size. Assembly of a framework phylogeny, or Tree of Life, for all major lineages of life requires a greatly magnified effort, often involving large teams working across institutions and disciplines. This is the overall goal of the Assembling the Tree of Life activity. The National Science Foundation announces its intention to continue support of creative and innovative research that will resolve evolutionary relationships for large groups of organisms throughout the history of life. Investigators also will be supported for projects in data acquisition, analysis, algorithm development and dissemination in computational phylogenetics and phyloinformatics." http://www.nsf.gov/pubs/2010/nsf10513/nsf10513.htm.

152. An Zelter, 29, Januar 1830, *Goethes Briefe* XLVI 223, quoted in Cassirer, *The Problem of Knowledge*, 166.

153. See Pigliucci, "Species as Family Resemblance," 596, on the difficulty of discerning species empirically and of defining species theoretically. The article contains a survey of nine common definitions of species and a critical assessment of each.

154. Note that charts developed by physicians and eugenicists in the late nineteenth century were less linear, suggesting an attempt to capture a whole network of kin relationships around the patient. Müller-Wille and Rheinberger, *A Cultural History of Heredity*, 121–22.

## 2. How Much Kin Does a Person Need?

1. See Jennifer Mensch, *Kant's Organicism: Epigenesis and the Development of Critical Philosophy* (Chicago: University of Chicago Press, 2013), 106. "The discovery worth announcing in 1775 . . . was thus an increasing sense on Kant's part of the positive explanatory role that could be played by teleology in the search for a rationally unified order, for something that was at work in the nature of the human being as much as it was in 'Nature herself.'"

2. In his 1775 essay on race, Kant wrote: "It is clear that the cognition of things as they are now always leaves us desirous of the cognition of that which they once were and of the series of changes they underwent to arrive at each place in their present state." Immanuel Kant, "Of the Different Races of Human Beings," in *Anthropology, History, and Education*, ed. Günter Zöller and Robert B. Louden (Cambridge: Cambridge University Press, 2007), 89.

3. Nicholas Thomas (1996), quoted in Stephan Palmié, "Mixed Blessings and Sorrowful Mysteries: Second Thoughts about 'Hybridity,'" *Current Anthropology* 54, no. 4 (2013): 463–82, https://doi.org/10.1086/671196.

4. See Palmié, "Mixed Blessings and Sorrowful Mysteries."

5. See Greg Bird, *Containing Community: From Political Economy to Ontology in Agamben, Esposito, and Nancy* (Albany: SUNY Press, 2016), 287.

6. *Oxford English Dictionary*, 20 vols. (Oxford: Oxford University Press, 1989).

7. Hans-Georg Gadamer, *Truth and Method* (London: A&C Black, 2013), 459.

8. Hans-Georg Gadamer, *Truth and Method*, 319.

9. Shannon Hoff, "Rights and Worlds: On the Political Significance of Belonging," *Philosophical Forum* 45, no. 4 (2014): 355–73.

10. Gadamer, *Truth and Method*, 295.

11. Jean Améry, "How Much Home Does a Person Need?," in *At the Mind's Limit*, trans. Sidney Rosenfeld and Stella P. Rosenfeld (Bloomington: Indiana University Press, 1980), 55.

12. See Martin Shuster, "A Phenomenology of Home: Jean Améry on Homesickness," *Journal of French and Francophone Philosophy* 24, no. 3 (February 24, 2017): 117–27.

13. See Staffan Müller-Wille and Hans-Jörg Rheinberger, *A Cultural History of Heredity* (Chicago: University of Chicago Press, 2012), 122. See also Tamara Hareven, "The Search for Generational Memory: Tribal Rites in Industrial Society," *Daedalus* 107 (1978): 137–49. See also Gil Anidjar, *Blood: A Critique of Christianity* (New York: Columbia University Press, 2014).

14. Catherine Nash explores the contexts that continue tend to complete the circle and those that tend to keep it open: "As the language of genealogy travels with Irish roots tourists and through electronic networks, the implications of genealogical practices and identifications can mutate so that what may be a politically regressive turn to ethnic purity and racial discourse in one context can, in another, productively unsettle older exclusive versions of belonging. For both individual and collective identities, genealogical projects can have unsettling results." Catherine Nash, "Genetic Kinship," *Cultural Studies* 18, no. 1 (January 1, 2004): 1–33, https://doi.org/10.1080/0950238042000181593.

15. Kant, *Anthropology, History, Education*, 158.

16. Ludwig Wittgenstein, "I: A Lecture on Ethics," *Philosophical Review* 74, no. 1 (1965): 8, https://doi.org/10.2307/2183526.

17. Sigmund Freud, *Civilization and Its Discontents* (New York: Norton, 1989), 11. Hortense Spillers reads this Freudian image as an analogy for undifferentiated identity. Hortense J. Spillers, "Mama's Baby, Papa's Maybe: An American Grammar Book," *Diacritics* 17, no. 2 (1987): 72, https://doi.org/10.2307/464747.

18. PBS, *Finding Your Roots | Deepak Chopra's Ancestral Pilgrimage*, PBS, 2014, https://www.youtube.com/watch?v=SHwlPTgmxOk.

19. Hoff, "Rights and Worlds," 360.

20. I depart here from Hoff's (and Gadamer's) hermeneutic presumption of meaningful *wholes*. If pressed, I would sacrifice the familiar language of meaning for the awkward—but more accurate—language of *sense*. We make sense of the world as embodied, sensing beings, and our sense making is not a matter of finding the relation of a part to a whole and does not rely on a wholeness or completion of meaning. We

arrive organized for sense; sense is always under way. Jean-Luc Nancy writes: "We are the sense of the world."

21. Adam Blair, "Review of Don Beith's *The Birth of Sense: Generative Passivity in Merleau-Ponty's Philosophy* (978-0-8214-2310-3)," *Continental Philosophy Review* 51, no. 3 (September 1, 2018): 469–74, https://doi.org/10.1007/s11007-018-9447-7.

22. Barbara Cassin et al., *Dictionary of Untranslatables: A Philosophical Lexicon* (Princeton, NJ: Princeton University Press, 2014), 758.

23. See the entry for *atavus* in C. T. Lewis and C. Short, *Latin Dictionary: Based on Andrews's Edition of Freund's Latin Dictionary* (Oxford: Oxford University Press, 1963).

24. The sociobiologist R. I. M. Dunbar writes of the selection of an ancestor as the unifying element of a kinship group: "What is particularly interesting in this context is that it makes very little difference whether the members of the kinship group are themselves directly related to that 'ancestor' or not, since beyond about four generations removed in time the coefficients of relationship between two individuals are so low that they are, to all intents and purposes, unrelated. Indeed, it makes little difference whether that ancestor actually existed or not: the sun, the moon and Mother Earth are as functional in this context as one's great-great-great-grandfather." R. I. M. Dunbar, "Sociality among Humans and Non-Human Animals," in *Companion Encyclopedia of Anthropology*, ed. Tim Ingold (London: Taylor & Francis, 1994), 775.

25. Mann works this out in terms of micro- and macro-scale analysis. Michael Mann, *The Dark Side of Democracy: Explaining Ethnic Cleansing* (Cambridge: Cambridge University Press, 2005), 10.

26. See Anthony Appiah, "The Uncompleted Argument: Du Bois and the Illusion of Race," *Critical Inquiry* 12, no. 1 (1985): 26, https://doi.org/10.2307/1343460.

27. My thanks to Emanuela Bianchi for her formulation of this problem. Emanuela Bianchi, "Genos and Kratos: Kinship between Nature and Power," New York University, November 21, 2016.

28. Other kin-like relationships were typically corralled under the heading of *fictive kin*, a term that has fallen out of use in anthropology.

29. Claude Lévi-Strauss, *The Elementary Structures of Kinship*, rev. ed. (Boston: Beacon, 1969), 480.

30. David M. Schneider, *A Critique of the Study of Kinship* (Ann Arbor: University of Michigan Press, 1984), 201.

31. Anidjar, *Blood*, 39.

32. Claude Meillassoux, *Mythes et limites de l'anthropologie: le sang et les mots* (Page deux, 2001), 14.

33. Anidjar, *Blood*, 39n14.

34. Howard Eilberg-Schwartz, *The Savage in Judaism: An Anthropology of Israelite Religion and Ancient Judaism* (Bloomington: Indiana University Press, 1990).

35. Meillassoux, *Mythes et limites de l'anthropologie*.

36. Eilberg-Schwartz, *The Savage in Judaism*, 174. See also Anidjar, *Blood*, n72.

37. See Carol Delaney, "Cutting the Ties That Bind: The Sacrifice of Abraham and Patriarchal Kinship," in *Relative Values: Reconfiguring Kinship Studies* (Durham, NC: Duke University Press, n.d.), 445–67.

38. See Sigmund Freud, *Totem and Taboo and Other Works*, in *The Standard Edition of the Complete Psychological Works of Sigmund Freud* (London: Hogarth, 1955), vol. 13. I have developed this reading in more detail elsewhere. Anne O'Byrne, "Communitas and the Problem of Women," *Angelaki* 18, no. 3 (September 2013): 125–38.

39. Peggy McCracken, *The Curse of Eve, the Wound of the Hero: Blood, Gender, and Medieval Literature* (Philadelphia: University of Pennsylvania Press, 2010), 61.

40. Evelyn Fox Keller, *The Century of the Gene* (Cambridge, MA: Harvard University Press, 2002), 2–10.

41. Keller, *The Century of the Gene*, 133–47.

42. "First DNA Exoneration, Center on Wrongful Convictions: Bluhm Legal Clinic, Northwestern Pritzker School of Law," http://www.law.northwestern.edu/legalclinic/wrongfulconvictions/exonerations/il/gary-dotson.html.

43. On the transition from blood to genetics as a signal of race and inheritance, see Camisha Russell, *The Assisted Reproduction of Race* (Bloomington: Indiana University Press, 2018).

44. Nelson, *The Social Life of DNA*, 163.

45. See Michelle Alexander, *The New Jim Crow: Mass Incarceration in the Age of Colorblindness* (New York: New Press, 2012). See also Ava DuVernay, dir., *Thirteenth* (Netflix, 2016), https://www.netflix.com/title/80091741.

46. Luigi Luca Cavalli Sforza and Francesco Cavalli-Sforza, *The Great Human Diasporas: The History of Diversity and Evolution* (New York: Basic Books, 1995), 106.

47. One of the largest—if not the largest—popular genetic analysis brands, 23andMe, gives a direct response to Sforza and Cavalli-Sforza's question, indeed offering to identify one's maternal and paternal haplogroups. "Maternal haplogroups are families of mitochondrial DNA types that all trace back to a single mutation at a specific place and time. By looking at the geographic distribution of mtDNA types, we learn how our ancient female ancestors migrated throughout the world." 23andMe, "Customer Stories," https://www.23andme.com/stories/.

48. See Jonathan Marks's observations regarding the use of color-coded biogeographical world maps. Jonathan Marks, "'We're Going to Tell These People Who They Really Are': Science and Relatedness," in *Relative Values: Reconfiguring Kinship Studies*, ed. Sarah Franklin and Susan McKinnon (Durham, NC: Duke University Press, 2001), 371.

49. Sforza and Cavalli-Sforza, *The Great Human Diasporas*, 237.

50. Sforza and Cavalli-Sforza, *The Great Human Diasporas*, 257. The human genome project conducted by Celera and completed in 2000 used samples from five people. "Whose Genome Is It Anyway?," *Genome News Network*, http://www.genomenewsnetwork.org/articles/02_01/Whose_genome.shtml.

51. Marks, "'We're Going to Tell These People Who They Really Are,'" 368.

52. Jenny Reardon, "Race without Salvation: Beyond the Science/Society Divide in Genomic Studies of Human Diversity," in *Revisiting Race in a Genomic Age*, ed. Barbara A. Koenig, Sandra Soo-Jin Lee, and Sarah S. Richardson (New Brunswick, NJ: Rutgers University Press, 2008), 308.

53. Debra Harry and Frank Dukepoo, *Indians, Genes, and Genetics: What Indians Should Know about the New Biotechnology* (Nixon, NV: Indigenous Peoples Coalition against Biopiracy, 1998).

54. Marks, "'We're Going to Tell These People Who They Really Are,'" 376–77.

55. For a discussion of why these two changes were decisive and for a critical assessment of the Genographic Project, see Kimberly TallBear, *Native American DNA: Tribal Belonging and the False Promise of Genetic Science* (Minneapolis: University of Minnesota Press, 2013), 143–76.

56. Quoted in TallBear, *Native American DNA*, 146.

186 / NOTES TO PAGES 81–86

57. TallBear, *Native American DNA*, 147. See also V. Y. Mudimbe, *The Invention of Africa: Gnosis, Philosophy, and the Order of Knowledge* (Bloomington: Indiana University Press, 1988).

58. TallBear, *Native American DNA*, 149. On the history of racial science, see also Jonathan M. Marks, *Human Biodiversity: Genes, Race, and History* (New Brunswick, NJ: Transaction, 2001); Jenny Reardon, *Race to the Finish: Identity and Governance in an Age of Genomics* (Princeton, NJ: Princeton University Press, 2009); Nancy Stepan, *Idea of Race in Science: Great Britain, 1800–1960* (New York, 1982); George W. Stocking, *Race, Culture, and Evolution: Essays in the History of Anthropology* (Chicago: University of Chicago Press, 1968).

59. Cece Moore, http://www.pbs.org/weta/finding-your-roots/blog/season-wrap -finally-dna-takes-center-stage/.

60. The first genealogical shows Gates undertook focused on African Americans in particular. Later, he established a genetic analysis research brand, African DNA.

61. "Season Wrap-Up: Finally! DNA Takes Center Stage | Finding Your Roots," PBS, http://www.pbs.org/weta/finding-your-roots/blog/season-wrap-finally-dna-takes -center-stage/.

62. "Video: Educator Geoffrey Canada on His Complicated Slave Ancestry," *Finding Your Roots* (blog), March 27, 2012, http://ec2-54-235-253-171.compute-1.amazonaws .com/weta/finding-your-roots/both-sides-of-slavery/1330/.

63. Salon Staff Writer, "Ben Affleck: 'I Didn't Want Any Television Show about My Family to Include a Guy Who Owned Slaves. I Was Embarrassed,'" *Salon*, April 22, 2015, http://www.salon.com/2015/04/22/ben_affleck_i_didnt_want_any _television_show_about_my_family_to_include_a_guy_who_owned_slaves_i_was _embarrassed/.

64. Dorothy Roberts, *Fatal Invention: How Science, Politics, and Big Business Re-Create Race in the Twenty-First Century* (New York: New Press, 2011), 297.

65. See, for example, Nicholas Wade, *A Troublesome Inheritance: Genes, Race, and Human History* (New York: Penguin, 2015). Many of the scientists whose work was used in the book have protested its conclusions. See Michael Balter, "Geneticists Decry Book on Race and Evolution," *Science | AAAS*, August 8, 2014, http://www.sciencemag .org/news/2014/08/geneticists-decry-book-race-and-evolution. Meanwhile, in an interview with *Der Spiegel*, Craig Venter said: "We have, in truth, learned nothing from the genome other than probabilities. How does a 1 or 3 percent increased risk for something translate into the clinic? It is useless information." Craig Venter, "SPIEGEL Interview with Craig Venter: 'We Have Learned Nothing from the Genome,'" *Spiegel Online*, July 29, 2010, http://www.spiegel.de/international/world/spiegel-interview-with -craig-venter-we-have-learned-nothing-from-the-genome-a-709174-2.html.

66. Roberts, *Fatal Invention*, 299.

67. Hoff, "Rights and Worlds," 363. Hoff uses "intermateriality" to describe Merleau-Ponty's project. See "The Body as an Object and Mechanistic Physiology" and "The Spatiality of One's Own Body and Motricity," in Maurice Merleau-Ponty, *Phenomenology of Perception*, trans. Donald A. Landes (London: Routledge, 2013).

68. In this case I follow Jacqueline Stevens in preferring the term *genetic parents* to natural, birth, or biological parents. See Jacqueline Stevens, "Methods of Adoption: Eliminating the Genetic Privilege," in *Adoption Matters: Philosophical and Feminist Essays*, ed. Sally Anne Haslanger and Charlotte Witt (Ithaca, NY: Cornell University Press, 2005), 70.

69. Whether this experience begins at birth or over the course of gestation is not a decisive question here. Bearing a child, whether genetically related or not, can be understood here in terms of holding, feeding, and sustaining.

70. Dunbar, "Sociality among Humans and Non-Human Animals," 774.

71. Alan Barnard, "Rules and Prohibitions: The Form and Content of Human Kinship," in *Companion Encyclopedia of Anthropology*, ed. Tim Ingold (London: Taylor & Francis, 1994), 786.

72. For a more recent version of the argument regarding the value of knowing one's biological forebears, see J. David Velleman, "Family History," *Philosophical Papers* 34, no. 3 (November 1, 2005): 357–78, https://doi.org/10.1080/05568640509485163.

73. E. Wellisch, "Children without Genealogy—A Problem of Adoption," *Mental Health* 12, no. 1 (1952): 41–42.

74. H. J. Sants, "Genealogical Bewilderment in Children with Substitute Parents," *British Journal of Medical Psychology* 37, no. 2 (June 1, 1964): 133–42, https://doi.org/10.1111/j.2044-8341.1964.tb01981.x.

75. Sants, "Genealogical Bewilderment in Children with Substitute Parents," 143.

76. Sants, "Genealogical Bewilderment in Children with Substitute Parents," 133.

77. Kimberly Leighton, "Addressing the Harms of Not Knowing One's Heredity: Lessons from Genealogical Bewilderment," *Adoption & Culture* 3, no. 1 (2012): 63–107, https://doi.org/10.1353/ado.2012.0010.

78. Sigmund Freud, "Family Romances," in *The Standard Edition of the Complete Psychological Works of Sigmund Freud* (London: Hogarth, 1959), 9:238.

79. Sants, "Genealogical Bewilderment in Children with Substitute Parents," 134, 138.

80. Narelle Grech, quoted in Blankenhorn, quoted in Leighton, "Addressing the Harms of Not Knowing One's Heredity."

81. Leighton, "Addressing the Harms of Not Knowing One's Heredity."

82. Alondra Nelson, *The Social Life of DNA: Race, Reparations, and Reconciliation After the Genome* (Boston, Mass.: Beacon Press, 2016), 93.

83. Nelson, *The Social Life of DNA*, 99.

84. Nelson, *The Social Life of DNA*, 77, 93. See Nash, "Genetic Kinship." See also Alys Eve Weinbaum, *Wayward Reproductions: Genealogies of Race and Nation in Transatlantic Modern Thought* (Durham, NC: Duke University Press, 2004).

85. Nelson, *The Social Life of DNA*, 17.

86. Jeanette Edwards and Marilyn Strathern, "Including Our Own," in *Cultures of Relatedness*, ed. Janet Carsten (Cambridge: Cambridge University Press, 2000), 149–66.

87. Jeanette Edwards and Marilyn Strathern, "Including Our Own," 159.

88. Frederick Douglass, *Autobiographies* (New York: Library of America, 1994), 15–16.

89. Douglass, *Autobiographies*, 16.

90. Orlando Patterson, *Slavery and Social Death* (Cambridge, MA: Harvard University Press, 1982).

91. See Spillers, "Mama's Baby, Papa's Maybe," 76.

92. Patterson, *Slavery and Social Death*, 7.

93. Ethics used to offer the example of being born blind while others are born with sight as a natural injustice, but ableism has changed that conversation so thoroughly that the example is obsolete. See Ramon M. Lemos, "The Concept of Natural Right," *Midwest Studies in Philosophy* 7, no. 1 (1982): 133–50.

94. Difference—the specific differences between us—are generated under specific conditions, however, and what is important for Patterson is how those conditions are structured and what ties come into being with a new being. The concept is difficult to make sense of in any case, since I can claim no injustice in being born with a certain eye color. It is the work of no agent, the result of no action, and fulfills no contract. It is not a matter of division or distribution of a good. The contingent differences of birth are the condition for the possibility of injustice and also therefore the condition for the need for justice. It is also, as we will see later, the condition for our experiencing affection toward one person and not toward another without ever giving an account of it. On the one hand, whom we love cannot be legislated, which will be crucial for Arendt's and others' arguments against antimiscegenation laws as well as for later arguments in favor of same-sex marriage. Love cannot be commanded, and, much as we might wish, we cannot claim injustice in not being loved. On the other hand, nature knows no justice and persists in distributing characteristics—height, talents, the elements of amiability—in an unequal way. The result is the human condition of plurality, specifically the plurality of differences.

95. Spillers, "Mama's Baby, Papa's Maybe," 76.

96. Patterson, *Slavery and Social Death*, 8.

97. "Kinship relations were thus constructed in law as a source of confinement without shelter, or constraint without protection, for any child born to a slave woman, while the father's right to choose or 'elect' his children was guaranteed absolutely." Lisa Guenther, "Fecundity and Natal Alienation: Rethinking Kinship with Levinas and Orlando Patterson," *Levinas Studies* 7, no. 1 (June 13, 2014): 22.

98. "The Moynihan Report: An Annotated Edition," *Atlantic*, September 2015, https://www.theatlantic.com/politics/archive/2015/09/the-moynihan-report-an -annotated-edition/404632/.

99. Spillers, "Mama's Baby, Papa's Maybe," 75.

100. Quoted in David W. Blight, *Frederick Douglass: Prophet of Freedom* (New York: Simon and Schuster, 2018).

101. Claudia Card, "Genocide and Social Death," *Hypatia* 18, no. 1 (February 1, 2003): 74, https://doi.org/10.1111/j.1527-2001.2003.tb00779.x.

102. Hoff, "Rights and Worlds," 390.

103. Janet Carsten, *After Kinship* (Cambridge: Cambridge University Press, 2004), 139–40.

104. Barbara Bodenhorn, "'He Used to Be My Relative': Exploring the Bases of Relatedness among Inupiat of Northern Alaska," in *Cultures of Relatedness*, ed. Janet Carsten (Cambridge: Cambridge University Press, 2000), 128–48. If the kinship among the Inupiat is signaled by blood, it is now the blood of the hunted whale. For additional examples, see Sarah Franklin and Susan McKinnon, *Relative Values: Reconfiguring Kinship Studies* (Durham, NC: Duke University Press, 2002).

105. Janet Carsten, "Introduction: Cultures of Relatedness," in *Cultural Relatedness: New Approaches to the Study of Kinship* (Cambridge: Cambridge University Press, 2000), 18.

106. Thanks to maggie castor for pointing this out.

107. Kath Weston, *Families We Choose: Lesbians, Gays, Kinship* (New York: Columbia University Press, 1991), 27.

108. See Bersani's assessment of "the rage for respectability . . . in gay life" in Leo Bersani, *Homos* (Cambridge, MA: Harvard University Press, 1996).

109. Weston, *Families We Choose*, 34.

110. Bersani, *Homos*, 164.

111. Quoted in Bersani, *Homos*, 75.

112. Lee Edelman, *No Future: Queer Theory and the Death Drive* (Durham, NC: Duke University Press, 2004).

113. Bersani, *Homos*, 41.

114. Savannah Shange, "Play Aunties and Dyke Bitches: Gender, Generation, and the Ethics of Black Queer Kinship," *Black Scholar* 49, no. 1 (2019): 40–54, https://doi .org/10.1080/00064246.2019.1548058.

115. Gloria Anzaldúa, *Borderlands: The New Mestiza* (Aunt Lute Books, 2012).

116. Sarah Brophy, *Witnessing AIDS: Writing, Testimony, and the Work of Mourning* (Toronto: University of Toronto Press, 2004), 13.

117. Derek Jarman, *Modern Nature* (Minneapolis: University of Minnesota Press, 1992), 69.

118. Weston, *Families We Choose*, 184.

119. Edelman, *No Future*, 31, quoting Guy Hocquenghem, *Homosexual Desire* (Durham, NC: Duke University Press, 1993), 138, 147.

120. Bersani, likewise, does not eschew relation but insists on "a massive re-defining of relationality." Bersani, *Homos*, 75.

121. Cited in Shmuel Lederman, "A Nation Destroyed: An Existential Approach to the Distinctive Harm of Genocide," *Journal of Genocide Research* 19, no. 1 (January 2, 2017): 113, https://doi.org/10.1080/14623528.2016.1250473.

122. See Uma Narayan's warning against assuming that cultures can be approached as homogenous wholes. Uma Narayan, *Dislocating Cultures: Identities, Traditions, and Third World Feminism* (New York: Routledge, 2013).

123. Card, "Genocide and Social Death," 74.

124. Vincent Brown, *The Reaper's Garden: Death and Power in the World of Atlantic Slavery* (Cambridge, MA: Harvard University Press, 2008), 56n78.

125. Brown, *The Reaper's Garden*, 261.

126. This is the central tenet of Card's argument in Card, "Genocide and Social Death."

127. Toni Morrison, *Beloved* (New York: Vintage, 2004).

128. This formulation seems to neglect the amount and variety of often hidden work that is required to keep things going. I will return to this in Chapter 4. See Lisa Baraitser, "Touching Time: Maintenance, Endurance, Care," in *Psychosocial Imaginaries*, ed. Stephen Frosch (London: Palgrave Macmillan, 2015), 21–47.

129. Hatley in this work reinterprets *genos* in a way that coincides with my shift here from *genos* to *kin*. I would happily adopt his beautiful description of *genos* as a description of what I understand here by *kin*: "A human *genos* can be seen as a wave of memory, insight, and expectation coursing through time, a wave that lifts up and sustains the individuals of each succeeding generation, even as those individuals make their own particular contributions to or modifications of that wave." James Hatley, *Suffering Witness: The Quandry of Responsibility after the Irreparable* (Albany, NY: SUNY Press, 2012), 61.

130. Hatley, *Suffering Witness*, 30. See also Donna Haraway's lyrical recognition of the dynamism of kin: "Kin is a wild category that all sorts of people do their best to domesticate. Making kin as oddkin rather than, or at least in addition to, godkin and genealogical and biogenetic family troubles important matters, like to whom one is

actually responsible." Donna J. Haraway, *Staying with the Trouble: Making Kin in the Chthulucene* (Durham, NC: Duke University Press, 2016).

## 3. What's Wrong with Genocide?

1. US Holocaust Memorial Museum, "The Aftermath of the Holocaust: Personal Histories," https://www.ushmm.org/exhibition/personal-history/media_oi.php ?MediaId=1116&th=camps. Testimony of Doriane Kurz, Bergen-Belsen survivor.

2. Jean Hampton makes this point about the wrongness of rape. Jean Hampton, "Defining Wrong and Defining Rape," in *A Most Detestable Crime: New Philosophical Essays on Rape* (Oxford: Oxford University Press, 1999), 134.

3. UN International Criminal Tribunal for the former Yugoslavia, http://www.icty .org/sid/10124.

4. See Jacqueline Stevens, "The Friends of War and Genocide," in *Logics of Genocide* (New York: Routledge, 2020).

5. Quoted by Lawrence Wechsler, *Vermeer in Bosnia* (New York: Knopf, 2007) 22. See also Alfred van Cleef, *De Verloren Wereld van de Familie Berberovic* (Taal: Meulen-hoff Boekerij, 1999).

6. I do not wish to suggest that the Bosnian War is explained by the spontaneous resurgence of racial and ethnic identities after the death of Tito and the end of the Cold War. See Mira Bogdanović, "The Rift in the Praxis Group: Between Nationalism and Liberalism," *Critique* 43, no. 3–4 (October 2, 2015): 461–83, https://doi.org/10.1080/ 03017605.2015.1099850.

7. Berel Lang opted not to use the title "What's So Bad about Genocide, Any-way?" for the first chapter of *Genocide: The Act as Idea*, choosing instead "The Evil of Genocide." He points out, though, that the aim of the chapter and the book is indeed to discover what is distinctive—so bad or wrong—in the act of genocide. Berel Lang, *Genocide: The Act as Idea* (Philadelphia: University of Pennsylvania Press, 2017), 19. See also Lederman's review of the work: Shmuel Lederman, "What's So Bad about Geno-cide, Anyway?," *Journal of Genocide Research* 20, no. 3 (July 3, 2018): 429–33, https://doi .org/10.1080/14623528.2018.1445421.

8. In her work on war rape, Robin May Schott makes a case for extending the use of the moral/theological term *evil* from ethics into social analyses (in the concept of social death) and into political thinking. Ethical approaches to the phenomenon of rape (also common in genocidal contexts) needed to be supplemented by social and, in particular, political approaches. In the context of her enquiry, thinking of politics as supplementary was not inappropriate, but I wish to make the stronger claim here precisely in order to let political existence show itself most clearly. Robin M. Schott, "War Rape, Social Death, and Political Evil," *Development Dialogue* 55 (March 2011): 47–62.

9. Hannah Arendt, "Collective Responsibility," in *Essays in Understanding, 1930–1945* (New York: Schocken, 1994), 153.

10. Hannah Arendt, *The Promise of Politics* (New York: Knopf, 2009), 175.

11. My thanks to Thomas Wentzer for this formulation. See Wentzer's work on human plurality and humans as responsive beings in Thomas Schwarz Wentzer, "Ap-proaching Philosophical Anthropology: Human, the Responsive Being," in *Finite but Unbounded: New Approaches in Philosophical Anthropology* (Berlin: De Gruyter, 2017), 25–46, https://doi.org/10.1515/9783110523812-003.

12. For Arendt's thinking on the despotism of the good, see Hannah Arendt, *Between Past and Future: Eight Exercises in Political Thought* (New York: Penguin, 1968), 241; Hannah Arendt, *On Revolution* (New York: Penguin, 1963), 84; Hannah Arendt, *The Human Condition*, 2nd ed. (Chicago: University of Chicago Press, 1998), 77; Hannah Arendt, *Responsibility and Judgment* (New York: Schocken, 2005), 123, 125.

13. For an indication of the distinctiveness of Arendt's existential understanding of politics, see Shmuel Lederman, "A Nation Destroyed: An Existential Approach to the Distinctive Harm of Genocide," *Journal of Genocide Research* 19, no. 1 (January 2, 2017): 112–32, https://doi.org/10.1080/14623528.2016.1250473.

14. For a detailed account of the actions of local leaders in the face of pressure from the planners of the Rwanda genocide, see Scott Straus, *The Order of Genocide: Race, Power, and War in Rwanda* (Ithaca, NY: Cornell University Press, 2013).

15. Ella Myers provides an excellent assessment of this phenomenon in Ella Myers, *Worldly Ethics: Democratic Politics and Care for the World* (Durham, NC: Duke University Press, 2013). See also Judith Butler, *Precarious Life: The Powers of Mourning and Violence* (New York: Verso, 2004); William E. Connolly, *A World of Becoming* (Durham, NC: Duke University Press, 2011); Simon Critchley, *Infinitely Demanding: Ethics of Commitment, Politics of Resistance* (London: Verso, 2014); Ewa Plonowska Ziarek, *An Ethics of Dissensus: Postmodernity, Feminism, and the Politics of Radical Democracy* (Stanford, CA: Stanford University Press, 2001). See also the collection of essays in Marjorie Garber, Beatrice Hanssen, and Rebecca L. Walkowitz, eds., *The Turn to Ethics* (London: Routledge, 2013). On questions of intergenerational justice as they emerge under the heading of ethics and/or politics and engage questions of democratic temporality, Matthias Fritsch's work is unsurpassed. Matthias Fritsch, *Taking Turns with the Earth: Phenomenology, Deconstruction, and Intergenerational Justice* (Stanford, CA: Stanford University Press, 2018).

16. I use frame here in Butler's sense. Judith Butler, *Frames of War: When Is Life Grievable?* (New York: Verso, 2016).

17. See "Reflections on Violence and Non-violence" in Richard J. Bernstein, *Violence: Thinking without Banisters* (London: John Wiley & Sons, 2013). See also Butler, *Precarious Life*.

18. In the same way, Descartes reminds us that we can understand what a chiliagon is yet be unable to imagine the difference between it and a figure with 999 sides.

19. Christopher R. Browning, *Ordinary Men: Reserve Police Battalion 101 and the Final Solution in Poland* (New York: HarperCollins, 2017).

20. Tony Barta, "Relations of Genocide: Land and Lives in the Colonization of Australia," in *Genocide and the Modern Age: Etiology and Case Studies of Mass Death* (Syracuse, NY: Syracuse University Press, 2000), 238. Cited in Guenter Lewy, "Can There Be Genocide without the Intent to Commit Genocide?," *Journal of Genocide Research* 9, no. 4 (December 1, 2007): 664, https://doi.org/10.1080/14623520701644457.

21. Nasrin Siraj and Ellen Bal, "'Hunger Has Brought Us into This Jungle': Understanding Mobility and Immobility of Bengali Immigrants in the Chittagong Hills of Bangladesh," *Social Identities* 23, no. 4 (July 4, 2017): 404–6, https://doi.org/10.1080/13504630.2017.1281443.

22. Donald Bloxham and A. Dirk Moses, eds., *The Oxford Handbook of Genocide Studies* (Oxford: Oxford University Press, 2010), 6. On the thought of institutional agency, see Rocío Zambrana, "Genocide and Agency in the Americas: Methodological Considerations," in *Logics of Genocide*, ed. Anne O'Byrne and Martin Shuster (New

York: Routledge, 2020). See also Martin Shuster, "Philosophy and Genocide," in *The Oxford Handbook of Genocide Studies*, ed. Donald Bloxham and A. Dirk Moses (New York: Oxford University Press, 2010).

23. See Rosalind Hursthouse, *On Virtue Ethics* (Oxford: Oxford University Press, 1999).

24. Arendt identifies this as the death of the moral person. "The alternative is no longer between good and evil, but between murder and murder." Hannah Arendt, *The Origins of Totalitarianism* (New York: Houghton Mifflin Harcourt, 1973), 452.

25. Hannah Arendt, "Personal Responsibility under Dictatorship," in *Responsibility and Judgment* (New York: Schocken, 2005), 17–49.

26. Arendt, *The Origins of Totalitarianism*, 452.

27. Jean Hatzfeld, *Life Laid Bare: The Survivors in Rwanda Speak* (London: Other, 2013), 103.

28. Perhaps it is not accidental that Rwililiza's testimony does not include any detail of the fate of his attackers. Also, the transformation is not instantaneous. Arendt analyzes the system that made people superfluous under Nazism. See Arendt, *The Origins of Totalitarianism*. The sociologist Scott Straus details the process by which Tutsi became targets in specific local contexts. Straus, *The Order of Genocide*, 17–40.

29. Bruno Bettelheim, *The Informed Heart: Autonomy in a Mass Age* (New York: Free Press, 1960), quoted in Giorgio Agamben, *Remnants of Auschwitz: The Witness and the Archive* (London: Zone, 1999), 56.

30. Agamben, *Remnants of Auschwitz*, 43.

31. Agamben in particular insists that *Muselmänner* were those who did not return and so could never testify for themselves. Yet, puzzlingly, an afterword to *Remnants of Auschwitz* consists of testimonies of former self-described *Muselmänner*. See Robert Harvey's incisive response to this turn in Agamben's argument in Robert Harvey, *Witnessness: Beckett, Dante, Levi, and the Foundations of Responsibility* (New York: Bloomsbury Publishing USA, 2010), 66.

32. Ryn and Klodzinski, 127, cited in Agamben, *Remnants of Auschwitz*, 43.

33. Agamben, *Remnants of Auschwitz*, 63.

34. Levi, *Survival in Auschwitz*, 90, quoted in Agamben, *Remnants of Auschwitz*, 44.

35. Amèry, *At the Mind's Limit*, 9, cited in Agamben, *Remnants of Auschwitz*, 41.

36. Ryn and Klodzinski, *An die Grenze zwischen Leben und Tod*, 94, quoted in Agamben, *Remnants of Auschwitz*, 43.

37. Amèry, *At the Mind's Limit*, 9, quoted in Agamben, *Remnants of Auschwitz*, 41.

38. Agamben, *Remnants of Auschwitz*, 43.

39. My thanks to Kyle Tanaka for the provocation for this thought.

40. Ludwig Wittgenstein, *Notebooks, 1914–1916* (Chicago: University of Chicago Press, 1984), 10.1.17.

41. The same impulse was at work in Orlando Patterson's appeal to "natural injustice" discussed in Chapter 2. Orlando Patterson, *Slavery and Social Death* (Cambridge, MA: Harvard University Press, 1982).

42. Agamben, *Remnants of Auschwitz*, 69.

43. But fifty years later, Alain Badiou, revolting against conservatism, sees "the possibility of the impossible" as what is exposed by "every loving encounter, every scientific re-foundation, every artistic invention and every sequence of emancipatory politics . . . the sole principle of an ethics of truths." Alain Badiou, *Ethics: An Essay on the Understanding of Evil*, trans. P. Hallward, (London: Verso, 2002), 59.

44. Levi, *Survival in Auschwitz*, 90.

45. Arendt, *The Origins of Totalitarianism*, 452.

46. Arendt, *The Origins of Totalitarianism*, 442.

47. Arendt, *The Origins of Totalitarianism*, 454–55.

48. Theodor Adorno, *Negative Dialectics* (London: Routledge, 2003), 365.

49. "Auschwitz stands accused on two apparently contradictory grounds: on the one hand, of having realized the unconditional triumph of death against life; on the other, of having degraded and debased death. Neither of these charges—perhaps like every charge, which is always a genuinely legal gesture—succeeds in exhausting Auschwitz's offense, in defining its case in point." Agamben, *Remnants of Auschwitz*, 81.

50. Arendt, *The Origins of Totalitarianism*, 453.

51. J. M. Bernstein, *Adorno: Disenchantment and Ethics* (Cambridge: Cambridge University Press, 2001), 390.

52. Hannah Arendt, *Eichmann in Jerusalem* (New York: Penguin, 1963), 136.

53. Sarah Clark Miller, "Moral Injury and Relational Harm: Analyzing Rape in Darfur," *Journal of Social Philosophy* 40, no. 4 (2009): 504–23, https://doi.org/10.1111/j.1467-9833.2009.01468.x.

54. Schott, "War Rape, Social Death, and Political Evil," 58.

55. Susan Sontag, *Regarding the Pain of Others* (New York: Macmillan, 2004), 90.

56. Schott, "War Rape, Social Death, and Political Evil," 58.

57. Seyla Benhabib, *The Reluctant Modernism of Hannah Arendt* (London: Rowman & Littlefield, 2003), 296. See also Linda Zerilli's response to Benhabib's argument in Linda M. G. Zerilli, *A Democratic Theory of Judgment* (Chicago: University of Chicago Press, 2016), 276–77.

58. Friedrich Nietzsche, *On the Genealogy of Morals*, trans. Walter Kaufmann (New York: Knopf, 2010), 18.

59. Hans Jonas, "Toward an Ontological Grounding of an Ethics for the Future," in *Mortality and Morality: A Search for Good after Auschwitz* (Chicago: Northwestern University Press, 1996), 108.

60. See Linda M. G. Zerilli, "What a Political Claim Is," in *Feminism and the Abyss of Freedom* (Chicago: University of Chicago Press, 2005), 165ff.

61. Hannah Arendt, "Truth and Politics," in *Between Past and Future: Eight Exercises in Political Thought* (New York: Penguin, 1968), 243. See also Lederman, "A Nation Destroyed."

62. Matthias Fritsch's work, drawing on Derrida's *Rogues* and *Spectres of Marx*, is informative here. See Fritsch, *Taking Turns with the Earth*, 154–85. Fritsch will usually describe them as *ethical* demands in the context of his argument for intergenerational justice, but, like Derrida, he resists any question of a bright line between ethical and political thinking. Indeed, at certain moments Derrida will use the terms *ethicopolitical*, *juridico-ethico-political*, and *historico-political*. For another argument for my preference for *political*, one that responds specifically to these moments, see Anne O'Byrne, "Possible: On Rodolphe Gasché's Deconstruction, Its Force, Its Violence," *Philosophy Today* 63, no. 1 (n.d.): 243–53, https://doi.org/10.5840/philtoday2019631257.

63. Etienne Balibar and Immanuel Wallerstein, *Race, Nation, Class: Ambiguous Identities* (New York: Verso, 1991), 53.

64. Hirad Abtahi and Philippa Webb, *The Genocide Convention: The Travaux Préparatoires*, 2 vols. (New York: Brill, 2008), 34.

65. For a sketch of these debates, see the series of readings assembled in Chapter 1, "Concepts," in Jens Meierhenrich, *Genocide: A Reader* (Oxford: Oxford University

Press, 2014), 57–105. The UN documents concerning the diplomatic negotiations are gathered in Abtahi and Webb, *The Genocide Convention.*

66. Hirad Abtahi and Philippa Webb, "Secrets and Surprises in the Travaux Préparatoires of the Genocide Convention," in *Arcs of Global Justice: Essays in Honour of William A. Schabas* (Oxford: Oxford University Press, 2018), 305.

67. UN Secretary-General, "Draft Convention on the Crime of Genocide" (UN, June 26, 1947), https://digitallibrary.un.org/record/611058.

68. UN Secretary-General, "Draft Convention on the Crime of Genocide," 26–29.

69. E. S. Skallerud, "'Acts Shocking to the Conscience of Mankind': Why Norway Voted to Delete Cultural Genocide from the 1948 Genocide Convention" (Oslo, University of Olso, 2019), 158, https://www.duo.uio.no/bitstream/handle/10852/75292/1/HUMR5200-Candidate-8008.pdf.

70. Abtahi and Webb, *The Genocide Convention*, 983.

71. Abtahi and Webb, *The Genocide Convention*, 1502.

72. Abtahi and Webb, *The Genocide Convention*, 833.

73. Skallerud, "'Acts Shocking to the Conscience of Mankind,'" 17.

74. Skallerud, "'Acts Shocking to the Conscience of Mankind,'" 178.

75. Abtahi and Webb, *The Genocide Convention*, 2054.

76. Skallerud, "'Acts Shocking to the Conscience of Mankind,'" 33.

77. Abtahi and Webb, *The Genocide Convention*, 1224.

78. Voting in favor of removing Article III on cultural genocide were: South Africa, the United Kingdom, the United States, Australia, Belgium, Bolivia, Brazil, Canada, Chile, Denmark, the Dominican Republic, France, Greece, India, Iran, Liberia, Luxembourg, the Netherlands, New Zealand, Norway, Panama, Peru, Siam, Sweden, and Turkey. Voting against: USSR, Yugoslavia, Byelorussian SSR, China, Czechoslovakia, Ecuador, Egypt, Ethiopia, Lebanon, Mexico, Pakistan, the Philippines, Poland, Saudi Arabia, Syria, Ukrainian SSR. Abstentions: Venezuela, Afghanistan, Argentina, Cuba. Thirteen delegates were absent.

## 4. Democracy of Generational Beings

1. Jacques Rancière, *Hatred of Democracy*, trans. Steven Corcoran (London: Verso, 2006), 48. Todd May, *The Political Thought of Jacques Rancière: Creating Equality* (Edinburgh: Edinburgh University Press, 2008).

2. See note 77 in Chapter 3.

3. Lyndall Ryan, "Digital Map of Colonial Frontier Massacres in Australia, 1788–1930," *Teaching History* 54, no. 3 (2020): 13–20, https://doi.org//doi/10.3316/informit.515797928995944.

4. Hirad Abtahi and Philippa Webb, *The Genocide Convention: The Travaux Préparatoires*, 2 vols. (New York: Brill, 2008), 2070.

5. See Mike Davis, *Late Victorian Holocausts* (London: Verso, 2001), 9.

6. Abtahi and Webb, *The Genocide Convention*, 474.

7. See Alexander George, *Western State Terrorism* (London: Polity, 1991). See also Adam Jones, *Genocide, War Crimes, and the West* (London: Zed, 2004).

8. As Michael Mann points out: "Democracy has always carried with it the possibility that the majority will tyrannize the minority, and that possibility carries more ominous consequences in certain types of multi-ethnic environments." If I find myself excluded from a persistent majority, the *demos* has been taken over, or taken apart, by *genos*. Mann's

"multi-ethnic" environment is a political context where points of view have consolidated into identities and come to be fixed in place in the guise of historically given ethnicities or naturally given races. Democracy's reliance on majority rule is an opportunity for corruption, this time by the rule of the *genos*. Michael Mann, *The Dark Side of Democracy: Explaining Ethnic Cleansing* (Cambridge: Cambridge University Press, 2005), 2.

9. William Connolly, *Identity/Difference: Democratic Negotiations of Political Paradox* (Minneapolis: University of Minnesota Press, 2002), xv.

10. Chantal Mouffe, *The Democratic Paradox* (London: Verso, 2000), 10–11.

11. Linda M. G. Zerilli, *A Democratic Theory of Judgment* (Chicago: University of Chicago Press, 2016), 265. See also Engin Isin's historical work on the many ways in which citizenship has been instituted and granted in the face of noncitizens: "Being political, among all other ways of being, means to constitute oneself simultaneously with and against others as an agent capable of judgment about what is just and unjust." Engin Isin, *Being Political: Genealogies of Citizenship* (Minneapolis: University of Minnesota Press, 2002), x.

12. "Both perfect liberty and perfect equality become impossible. But this is the very condition of possibility for a pluralist form of human existence in which rights can exist *and* be exercised, in which freedom and equality can somehow manage to coexist." Mouffe, *The Democratic Paradox*, 10–11.

13. "Universal Declaration of Human Rights," October 6, 2015, http://www.un.org/en/universal-declaration-human-rights/.

14. Note the analogy to Descartes's chiliagon. We can understand what a one-thousand-sided figure is, but we cannot imagine one that would be distinguishable from one with 999 sides.

15. Thierry de Duve, "Aesthetics as the Transcendental Ground of Democracy," *Critical Inquiry* 42, no. 1 (September 1, 2015): 151, https://doi.org/10.1086/682999.

16. David M. Schneider, "The Kinship System and Village Organization of Yap, West Caroline Islands, Micronesia: A Structural and Functional Account" (Harvard University, 1949). See also Schneider, "Yap Kinship Terminology and Kin Groups," *American Anthropologist* 55, no. 2.1 (June 1953).

17. David M. Schneider, *A Critique of the Study of Kinship* (Ann Arbor: University of Michigan Press, 1984).

18. David M. Schneider, "What Is Kinship All About?," in *Kinship Studies in the Morgan Centennial Year*, ed. Priscilla Reining (Washington, DC: Anthropological Society of Washington, 1972), 50. Italics in the original.

19. de Duve, "Aesthetics as the Transcendental Ground of Democracy," 155.

20. Hannah Arendt, *The Origins of Totalitarianism* (New York: Houghton Mifflin Harcourt, 1973), 290–302. This argument is also made in "Who Is the Subject of the Rights of Man?," in Jacques Rancière, *Dissensus*, trans. Steven Corcoran (London: Bloomsbury, 2010), 64.

21. Etienne Balibar drives the argument further in "(De)Constructing the Human as Human Institution: A Reflection on the Coherence of Hannah Arendt's Practical Philosophy," *Social Research* 74, no. 3 (2007): 733–34, arguing that Arendt's "idea of rights is indistinguishable from the construction of the human, which is the immanent result of the historical invention of (political) institutions. Humans simply *are* their rights." Thanks to Phillip Nelson for this reference.

22. This argument has been pursued in many different ways. See Ayten Gündoğdu, *Rightlessness in an Age of Rights: Hannah Arendt and the Contemporary Struggles of*

*Migrants* (Oxford: Oxford University Press, 2015); Jill Stauffer, *Ethical Loneliness: The Injustice of Not Being Heard* (New York: Columbia University Press, 2015); Jennifer Gaffney, "Another Origin of Totalitarianism: Arendt on the Loneliness of Liberal Citizens," *Journal of British Society for Phenomenology* 47, no. 1 (2016): 1–17; Shmuel Lederman, "A Nation Destroyed: An Existential Approach to the Distinctive Harm of Genocide," *Journal of Genocide Research* 19, no. 1 (January 2, 2017): 112–32, https://doi .org/10.1080/14623528.2016.1250473.

23. de Duve, "Aesthetics as the Transcendental Ground of Philosophy," 162.

24. Herodotus, quoted in Phillip Brooke Manville, *The Origins of Citizenship in Ancient Athens* (Princeton, NJ: Princeton University Press, 1990), 174.

25. *Constitution of Athens* 13.5.

26. *Constitution of Athens* 21.2.

27. Nicole Loraux, *Born of the Earth*, trans. Selina Stewart (Ithaca, NY: Cornell University Press, 2000), 53. For Isocrates, from whom Loraux draws this claim, the violence depicted in the tragedies was characteristic of earlier times and other cities.

28. Some scholars agree that this was the case, but others think it unlikely, given that the actual distribution produced ten tribes that were more or less equal in population and also a geographical arrangement that would appear to have favored the Alkmeonids, the family to which Kleisthenes himself belonged. See John Thorley, *Athenian Democracy* (London: Routledge, 1996), 25.

29. Rancière, *Hatred of Democracy*, 7.

30. Clive Barnett argues that theorists of radical democracy such as Laclau and Mouffe are committed to an overly spatial understanding of democracy. Attending to the place rather than space of democracy substantially deflects his critique. See Clive Barnett, "Deconstructing Radical Democracy: Articulation, Representation, and Being-with-Others," *Political Geography* 23, no. 5 (2004): 517, https://doi.org/10.1016/j .polgeo.2004.01.004.

31. *Hamlet*, 1.2.

32. David Whitehead, *The Demes of Attica, 508/7–ca. 250 B.C.: A Political and Social Study* (Princeton, NJ: Princeton University Press, 2014), 28.

33. For more on the distinction between space and place, see E. Casey, *The Fate of Place: A Philosophical History* (Berkeley: University of California Press, 2013).

34. Manville, *The Origins of Citizenship in Ancient Athens*, 191.

35. Whitehead, *The Demes of Attica*, 81.

36. It is not clear how disputes were settled—or avoided—at the time of the reform. There is evidence that later, at least in the scrutiny of 346–345, when deme membership was already long established, everyone's status was voted upon by the members of the deme. Manville, *The Origins of Citizenship in Ancient Athens*, 174.

37. Citizens of democracies have proved adept at discovering grounds for inclusion and exclusion, as though those grounds were ready at hand. For a history of this phenomenon see Isin, *Being Political*.

38. *Politics*, 1276a–b.

39. See Clive Barnett, "Temporality and the Paradoxes of Democracy," *Political Geography* 24, no. 5 (2006): 645.

40. Horst Bredecamp, "From Walter Benjamin to Carl Schmitt, via Thomas Hobbes," trans. Melissa Thorson Hause and Jackson Bond, *Critical Inquiry* 25, no. 2 (Winter 1999): 251–54.

NOTES TO PAGES 141–44 / 197

41. Barnett, "Temporality and the Paradoxes of Democracy," 641–47. See also John Dunn, "How Democracies Succeed," *Economy and Society* 25, no. 4 (1996): 511–28, cited in Barnett.

42. Lee Edelman, *No Future: Queer Theory and the Death Drive* (Durham, NC: Duke University Press, 2004), 3.

43. Carolyn Dinshaw et al., "Theorizing Queer Temporalities: A Roundtable Discussion," *GLQ* 13, no. 2–3: 177–95. See also Jack Halberstam, *In a Queer Time and Place: Transgender Bodies, Subcultural Lives* (New York: New York University Press, 2005), 152–87.

44. Lauren Berlant and Lee Edelman, *Sex, or the Unbearable* (Durham, NC: Duke University Press, 2014), 5.

45. See Hannah Arendt, "The Crisis in Education," in *Between Past and Future* (New York: Penguin, 1968), 173–96. Anne O'Byrne, *Natality and Finitude* (Bloomington: Indiana University Press, 2011), 65–68.

46. Alain Badiou et al., *What Is a People?* (New York: Columbia University Press, 2016), 51.

47. See Don Beith, *The Birth of Sense: Generative Passivity in Merleau-Ponty's Philosophy* (Athens: Ohio University Press, 2018), particularly chap. 4, "The Intercorporeal Institution of Agency." See also Adam Blair, "Review of Don Beith's *The Birth of Sense: Generative Passivity in Merleau-Ponty's Philosophy* (978-0-8214-2310-3)," *Continental Philosophy Review* 51, no. 3 (September 1, 2018): 469–74, https://doi.org/10.1007/s11007-018-9447-7. My thanks to Adam Blair for directing me to Beith's work.

48. This is an extreme version of dead constitutionalism, but before deciding that it is an anachronism, a caricature, or a merely logical exercise, see the dissenting opinion authored by Justice Clarence Thomas of the US Supreme Court in *Brown v. Entertainment Merchants Association*, 2011. https://www.law.cornell.edu/supct/html/08-1448.ZD.html.

49. Letter to Colonel Smith, November 13, 1787.

50. This is Popper's concern. The term *paradox of democracy* is the expression of his worry about what this might lead to. See Karl R. Popper, *The Open Society and Its Enemies*, new one-volume ed. (Princeton, NJ: Princeton University Press, 2013), 118, 581–82.

51. Joan C. Tronto, *Moral Boundaries: A Political Argument for an Ethic of Care* (Hove: Psychology Press, 1993), 103; Walter Benjamin, "Theses on the Philosophy of History," in *Illuminations*, ed. Hannah Arendt, trans. Harry Zohn (New York: Schocken, 1969), 261, 264; Hans Jonas, *The Imperative of Responsibility: In Search of an Ethics for the Technological Age* (Chicago: University Of Chicago Press, 1985).

52. The French Revolution presents a different generational profile. Robespierre, Danton, King Louis XVI, and Marie-Antoinette were all in their early thirties in 1789, and the revolutionaries became still younger as the Terror progressed. Saint Just died in 1794, aged twenty-seven.

53. Adams writes: "I fear there will be greater difficulty to preserve our Union than You and I, our Fathers Brothers Disciples and Sons have had to form it." Adams to Jefferson, February 2, 1816, quoted in Joseph Ellis, *Founding Brothers: The Revolutionary Generation* (New York: Knopf, 2003), 238n56.

54. James R. Martel, *The Misinterpellated Subject* (Durham, NC: Duke University Press, 2017).

55. See Glenn Wallach, *Obedient Sons: The Discourse of Youth and Generations in American Culture, 1630–1860* (Amherst: University of Massachusetts Press, 1997), esp. 46–54.

56. Jefferson to Adams, January 20, 1821, quoted in Ellis, *Founding Brothers*, 240n58.

57. Jacques Derrida, "Declarations of Independence," *New Political Science* 7, no. 1 (1986): 9–11.

58. Remember that Jefferson's family included his white, legally acknowledged daughters and their offspring as well as his Black, unacknowledged sons and daughters and their offspring.

59. See the Third Draft by Jefferson (before June 1776) at https://founders .archives.gov.

60. As Samir Haddad puts it: "The 'good people' are never present, indeed cannot be if the Declaration is to retain its meaning and effect. Instead, the authority they are supposed to provide is constituted according to the temporal logic of the future perfect—the people have the authority to sign the Declaration only if they will have been seen to have it in their future." Samir Haddad, "Fundaciones Politicas y Derecho a La Filosofia," trans. Jorge Laplace, in *Escenas de escritura. Sobre filosofia y literatura*, ed. Cristóbal Olivares Molina, trans. Jorge Laplace (Santiago de Chile: Pólvora Editorial, 2020), 127–52.

61. Arendt regrets that the American Revolution did not overcome the rift that has been in place since the time of Pericles, the rift between the men of action and the thinkers, which latter could have given the revolution "conceptual clarity and precision with respect to existing realities and experiences." Hannah Arendt, *On Revolution* (New York: Penguin, 1963), 168. It is unclear which realities and experiences she has in mind, since her analysis of the American Revolution is remarkable in its neglect of the realities of racism and slavery. See Shmuel Lederman, *Hannah Arendt and Participatory Democracy: A People's Utopia* (Springer, 2019), 98.

62. Jürgen Habermas, "Constitutional Democracy: A Paradoxical Union of Contradictory Principles?," *Political Theory* 29, no. 6 (December 2001): 775.

63. Habermas, "Constitutional Democracy." I do not agree with Honig's additional argument that the mere fact of using the language of familial generation condemns Habermas to a conservative position that cannot take account of trauma or transformation. Families, as Honig also seems to appreciate with her references to Mendelssohn and Freud, are the familiar sites of both. Bonnie Honig, *Emergency Politics: Paradox, Law, Democracy* (Princeton, NJ: Princeton University Press, 2009), 46.

64. Jean-Luc Nancy, *The Truth of Democracy* (New York: Fordham University Press, 2010), 32.

65. This is where Arendt's understanding of the realm of politics as the place where one shows *who* rather than *what* one is runs up against her insistence that "If one is attacked as a Jew, one must defend oneself as a Jew." Hannah Arendt, "'What Remains? The Language Remains': A Conversation with Günther Gaus," in *Hannah Arendt: The Last Interview and Other Conversations*, trans. Joan Stambaugh (Brooklyn: Melville House, 2013).

66. Martin Luther King Jr., *Where Do We Go from Here: Chaos or Community?* (Boston: Beacon, 2010).

67. See Eddie S. Glaude, *Democracy in Black: How Race Still Enslaves the American Soul* (New York: Broadway, 2017).

## Conclusion: The Antigenocidal Democracy

1. Samuel Scheffler, *Death and the Afterlife*, ed. Niko Kolodny, 1st ed. (New York: Oxford University Press, 2013), 34.

2. See Christopher Macleod, "An Alternative Approach to the Harm of Genocide," *Politics* 32, no. 3 (2012).

3. Shmuel Lederman, "A Nation Destroyed: An Existential Approach to the Distinctive Harm of Genocide," *Journal of Genocide Research* 19, no. 1 (January 2, 2017): 112–32, https://doi.org/10.1080/14623528.2016.1250473.

4. Democracy is a world of worlds; the argument that follows could also be made in terms of protecting worlds, world-survival, and saving the world. See Derrida's late seminars: Jacques Derrida, *The Beast and the Sovereign*, 2 vols., trans. Geoffrey Bennington (Chicago: University of Chicago Press, 2011); Jacques Derrida, *The Death Penalty*, vol. 1, trans. Peggy Kamuf (Chicago: University of Chicago Press, 2013); Jacques Derrida, *The Death Penalty* vol. 2, trans. Elizabeth G. Rottenberg (Chicago: University of Chicago Press, 2017). See also Michael Naas, *Derrida: From Now On* (New York: Fordham University Press, 2008); Patrick O'Connor, "Derrida Saves the World: A Rope at the End of the Tunnel," unpublished paper.

5. Hannah Arendt, *Between Past and Future: Eight Exercises in Political Thought* (New York: Penguin, 1968).

6. *Afterlife* is used here in the way it is used in Scheffler, *Death and the Afterlife*, and in Lisa Guenther, *Solitary Confinement: Social Death and Its Afterlives* (Minneapolis: University of Minnesota Press, 2013).

7. See Hannah Arendt, *The Promise of Politics* (New York: Knopf, 2009).

8. Hannah Arendt, "Collective Responsibility," in *Essays in Understanding, 1930–1945* (New York: Schocken, 1994), 147, 148.

9. See Hannah Arendt, "The Crisis in Education," in *Between Past and Future* (New York: Penguin, 1968), 173–96.

10. See *Politics* 2.2 1216a, 3.16, 1287a.

11. Fritsch works out the Aristotelian insight brilliantly in generational terms in Matthias Fritsch, *Taking Turns with the Earth: Phenomenology, Deconstruction, and Intergenerational Justice* (Stanford, CA: Stanford University Press, 2018), 170–79.

12. See Lederman, "A Nation Destroyed," 125; Hannah Arendt, "Truth and Politics," in *Between Past and Future: Eight Exercises in Political Thought* (New York: Penguin, 1968), 243; Hannah Arendt, *The Origins of Totalitarianism* (New York: Houghton Mifflin Harcourt, 1973), 301.

13. See Lederman, "A Nation Destroyed," 123; and also Jennifer Gaffney, "Another Origin of Totalitarianism: Arendt on the Loneliness of Liberal Citizens," *Journal of British Society for Phenomenology* 47, no. 1 (2016): 1.

14. Note that we can take this on as an expression of the desire for the survival of a world we could recognize even though we must reject the hierarchy. For example, in "The Crisis in Culture," the temporary tents of nomadic cultures are enough to show their creators' lack of culture and the poverty of their world. Hannah Arendt, "The Crisis in Culture," in *Between Past and Future: Eight Exercises in Political Thought* (New York: Penguin, 1968), 205–26. It is a hierarchy that makes possible a comparison of evils she finds troubling elsewhere, though she leaves the trouble unresolved.

In *Eichmann in Jerusalem* she reports the musings of Harry Mulisch as follows. The historian Salo W. Baron had given testimony about the rich history of the Jews, leading Mulisch to ask: "'Would the death of the Jews have been less of an evil if they were a people without a culture, such as the Gypsies who were also exterminated? Is Eichmann on trial as a destroyer of human beings or as an annihilator of culture? Is a murderer of human beings more guilty when a culture is also destroyed in the process?' And when he put the questions to the Attorney General, it turned out—'He [Hausner] thinks yes, I [Mulisch] think no.'" Hannah Arendt, *Eichmann in Jerusalem* (New York: Penguin, 1963), 96–97.

15. After all, Athenian law addressed each of these elements of life in various ways. See Ilias Arnaoutoglou, *Ancient Greek Laws: A Sourcebook* (London: Routledge, 1998).

16. Marc Crépon frames the existential condition in stark terms: "Insofar as we cannot avoid the eclipse or the suspension of the principle that attaches us to the vulnerability and mortality of the other . . . we must begin by recognizing that no-one *in good conscience* can consider his or her life, as being-in-the-world, immune from murderous consent." Crépon considers ways in which this comes to have particular historical—and implicitly generational—content in the work and testimony of Emmanuel Levinas, Günther Anders, Kenzaburo Oe, and others. See Marc Crépon, *Murderous Consent: On the Accommodation of Violent Death*, trans. Michael Loriaux and Jacob Levi (New York: Fordham University Press, 2019), 6.

17. Lederman, "A Nation Destroyed," 126–27.

18. See Anya Topolski, *Arendt, Levinas, and a Politics of Relationality* (London: Rowman & Littlefield, 2015).

19. Hannah Arendt, "Introduction into Politics," in *The Promise of Politics* (New York: Knopf, 2009), 176.

20. See Jacques Derrida, *Rogues: Two Essays on Reason* (Stanford, CA: Stanford University Press, 2005); Jacques Derrida, *The Politics of Friendship* (London: Verso, 2020). See also Michael Naas, "'One Nation . . . Indivisible': Jacques Derrida on the Autoimmunity of Democracy and the Sovereignty of God," *Research in Phenomenology* 36, no. 1 (January 1, 2006): 15–44, https://doi.org/10.1163/1569164406779165818; Samir Haddad, *Derrida and the Inheritance of Democracy* (Bloomington: Indiana University Press, 2013).

21. United Nations High Commissioner for Refugees, "Refworld | Burma Citizenship Law," *Refworld*, https://www.refworld.org/docid/3ae6b4f71b.html.

22. Benjamin Zawacki, "Defining Myanmar's 'Rohingya Problem,'" *Human Rights Brief* 20, no. 3 (2013): 18–25.

23. "White Americans to Be Minority by 2042," *Telegraph*, August 14, 2008.

24. Commonwealth submission, 1996, 30; quoted in John Frow, "A Politics of Stolen Time," in *Timespace: Geographies of Temporality*, ed. Jon May and Nigel Thrift (New York: Routledge, 2003), 83.

25. Frow, "A Politics of Stolen Time," 83.

26. Ranjana Khanna, "Post-Palliative: Coloniality's Affective Dissonance," *Postcolonial Text* 2, no. 1 (December 31, 2005), https://www.postcolonial.org/index.php/pct/article/view/385.

27. Jonathan Lear, *Radical Hope: Ethics in the Face of Cultural Devastation* (Cambridge, MA: Harvard University Press, 2006), 2.

28. For an analysis of the cosmological and epistemological import of *pacha*, see Omar Rivera, *Andean Aesthetics and Anticolonial Resistance: A Cosmology of Unsociable Bodies* (New York: Bloomsbury, 2021), 20–25.

29. Catherine Allen, "Time, Place, and Narrative in an Andean Community," *Societé Suisse des Américanistes* 57–58 (1994 1993): 93.

30. Catherine Brun confronts the same question in her study of the conflicting temporalities of humanitarian institutions, humanitarian workers, and the refugees they work with in conditions of protracted displacement, e.g., Syrian refugees living in cities in Jordan in 2015: "Currently, humanitarian ethics and practices seem to advocate an understanding of what counts as responsible action in a way that privileges the interests of the present and, thus, puts at risk the interests of future generations." Cathrine Brun, "There Is No Future in Humanitarianism: Emergency, Temporality, and Protracted Displacement," *History and Anthropology* 27, no. 4 (August 7, 2016): 393–410, https://doi.org/10.1080/02757206.2016.1207637.406.

31. Dolleen Tisawii'ashii Manning, "The Murmuration of Birds: An Anishinaabe Ontology of Mnidoo-Worlding," in *Feminist Phenomenology Futures*, ed. Helen A. Fielding and Dorothea E. Olkowski (Bloomington: Indiana University Press, 2017), 174. Manning's essay also offers the resources of a shift from *world* to *worlding* and from universal models to "metamorphoses en route to an elsewhere."

32. Baraitser, "Touching Time: Maintenance, Endurance, Care," 27.

33. Joan C. Tronto, *Moral Boundaries: A Political Argument for an Ethic of Care* (Hove, U.K.: Psychology Press, 1993), 103.

34. Lisa Baraitser, "Touching Time: Maintenance, Endurance, Care," in *Psychosocial Imaginaries*, ed. Stephen Frosh (London: Palgrave Macmillan, 2015), 28.

35. See Gail Lewis, "Birthing Racial Difference: Conversations with My Mother and Others," *Studies in the Maternal* 1, no. 1 (January 1, 2009): 1–21. Cited in Baraitser, "Touching Time," 29. Regarding the connection between the Arendtian thought of natality and the political significance of care, see Adriana Cavarero, "'A Child Has Been Born unto Us': Arendt on Birth," trans. Silvia Guslandi and Cosette Bruhns, *PhiloSOPHIA* 4, no. 1 (2014). For the connection between the division of societal labor and political theory's ability to ignore generational dependencies, see Eva Feder Kittay, *Love's Labor: Essays on Women, Equality, and Dependency* (New York: Routledge, 2013). For a fine-grained consideration of the treatment of old people as belonging on a spectrum of genocidal violence, see Nancy Scheper-Hughes, "The Genocidal Continuum: Peace-Time Crimes," in *Power and the Self*, ed. Jeannette Marie Mageo (Cambridge: Cambridge University Press, 2002), 29–47.

36. James R. Martel, *The Misinterpellated Subject* (Durham, NC: Duke University Press, 2017), 273.

37. Mierle Laderman Ukeles, "Manifesto for Maintenance Art 1969! Proposal for an Exhibition 'CARE.'" *Journal of Contemporary Painting*, October 1, 2018.

38. Robert Nixon, *Slow Violence and the Environmentalism of the Poor* (Cambridge, MA: Harvard University Press, 2011), 2, 102; Elizabeth A. Povinelli, *Economies of Abandonment: Social Belonging and Endurance in Late Liberalism* (Durham, NC: Duke University Press, 2011), 145.

39. Nancy Scheper-Hughes, "Small Wars and Invisible Genocides," *Social Science and Medicine* 43, no. 5 (1996): 889–900.

40. Scheper-Hughes, "The Genocidal Continuum," 44.

41. Scheper-Hughes, "The Genocidal Continuum," 33.

42. We can think of this as what Lauren Berlant calls "worlding." Lauren Berlant and Lee Edelman, *Sex, or the Unbearable* (Durham, NC: Duke University Press, 2014), 111.

43. For an Arendtian analysis of the public sphere's resistance to violence and its character as the rightful place for the question of violence, see Richard J. Bernstein, *Violence: Thinking without Banisters* (London: John Wiley & Sons, 2013).

# Bibliography

23andMe. "Customer Stories—23andMe." https://www.23andme.com/stories/.

"1998 AAA Statement on 'Race.'" *Anthropology Newsletter* 39, no. 9 (1998): 3.

Abed, Mohammed. "Clarifying the Concept of Genocide." *Metaphilosophy* 37, no. 3–4 (July 1, 2006): 308–30. https://doi.org/10.1111/j.1467-9973.2006 .00443.x.

Abtahi, Hirad, and Philippa Webb. *The Genocide Convention: The Travaux Préparatoires.* 2 vols. New York: Brill, 2008.

———. "Secrets and Surprises in the Travaux Préparatoires of the Genocide Convention." In *Arcs of Global Justice: Essays in Honour of William A. Schabas.* Oxford: Oxford University Press, 2018. https://www.oxfordscholarship.com/ view/10.1093/oso/9780190272654.001.0001/oso-9780190272654-chapter-17.

Adorno, Theodor. *Negative Dialectics.* New York: Routledge, 2003.

Agamben, Giorgio. *Remnants of Auschwitz: The Witness and the Archive.* Brooklyn: Zone, 1999.

Akhavan, Payam. *Reducing Genocide to Law: Definition, Meaning, and the Ultimate Crime.* Cambridge: Cambridge University Press, 2012.

Alexander, Michelle. *The New Jim Crow: Mass Incarceration in the Age of Colorblindness.* New York: New Press, 2012.

Allen, Amy. *The End of Progress: Decolonizing the Normative Foundations of Critical Theory.* New York: Columbia University Press, n.d. https://www .degruyter.com/document/doi/10.7312/alle17324/html.

Allen, Catherine. "Time, Place, and Narrative in an Andean Community." *Société Suisse des Américanistes* 57–58 (1993–1994): 89–95.

Al-Saji, Alia. "A Phenomenology of Hesitation: Interrupting Racializing Habits of Seeing." In *Living Alterities: Phenomenology, Embodiment, and Race,* 133–72. Albany: State University of New York Press, 2014.

Améry, Jean. "How Much Home Does a Person Need?" In *At the Mind's Limit*, trans. Sidney Rosenfeld and Stella P. Rosenfeld, 41–61. Bloomington: Indiana University Press, 1980.

Anidjar, Gil. *Blood: A Critique of Christianity*. New York: Columbia University Press, 2014.

Anzaldúa, Gloria. *Borderlands/La Frontera: The New Mestiza*. San Francisco: Aunt Lute, 2012.

Appiah, Anthony. "The Uncompleted Argument: Du Bois and the Illusion of Race." *Critical Inquiry* 12, no. 1 (1985): 21–37. https://doi.org/10.2307/1343460.

Arendt, Hannah. *Between Past and Future: Eight Exercises in Political Thought*. New York: Penguin, 1968.

——. "Collective Responsibility." In *Essays in Understanding, 1930–1945*. New York: Schocken Books, 1994.

——. "The Crisis in Culture." In *Between Past and Future: Eight Exercises in Political Thought*, 205–26. New York: Penguin, 1968.

——. "The Crisis in Education." In *Between Past and Future*, 173–96. New York: Penguin, 1968.

——. *Eichmann in Jerusalem*. New York: Penguin, 1963.

——. *The Human Condition*. 2nd ed. Chicago: University of Chicago Press, 1998.

——. "Introduction into Politics." In *The Promise of Politics*, 93–200. New York: Knopf, 2009.

——. *Love and Saint Augustine*. Chicago: University of Chicago Press, 2014.

——. *On Revolution*. New York: Penguin, 1963.

——. *The Origins of Totalitarianism*. New York: Houghton Mifflin Harcourt, 1973.

——. "Personal Responsibility under Dictatorship." In *Responsibility and Judgment*, 17–49. New York: Schocken, 2005.

——. *The Promise of Politics*. New York: Knopf Doubleday, 2009.

——. *Responsibility and Judgment*. New York: Schocken, 2005.

——. "Truth and Politics." In *Between Past and Future: Eight Exercises in Political Thought*, 223–59. New York: Penguin, 1968.

——. "'What Remains? The Language Remains': A Conversation with Günther Gaus." In *Hannah Arendt: The Last Interview and Other Conversations*, trans. Joan Stambaugh. Brooklyn: Melville House, 2013.

Aristotle. *Categories*. Trans. W. D. Ross. London: Methuen, 1971.

Arnaoutoglou, Ilias. *Ancient Greek Laws: A Sourcebook*. London: Routledge, 1998. https://doi.org/10.4324/9780203011744.

Badiou, Alain. *Ethics: An Essay on the Understanding of Evil*. Trans. P. Hallward. London: Verso, 2002.

Badiou, Alain, Judith Butler, Georges Didi-Huberman, Sadri Khiari, Jacques Rancière, and Pierre Bourdieu. *What Is a People?* New York: Columbia University Press, 2016.

Balibar, Etienne. "(De)Constructing the Human as Human Institution: A Reflection on the Coherence of Hannah Arendt's Practical Philosophy." *Social Research* 74, no. 3 (2007): 727–38.

Balibar, Etienne, and Immanuel Wallerstein. *Race, Nation, Class: Ambiguous Identities.* New York: Verso, 1991.

Balter, Michael. "Geneticists Decry Book on Race and Evolution." *Science | AAAS*, August 8, 2014. http://www.sciencemag.org/news/2014/08/geneticists -decry-book-race-and-evolution.

Baraitser, Lisa. "Touching Time: Maintenance, Endurance, Care." In *Psychosocial Imaginaries*, ed. Stephen Frosh, 21–47. London: Palgrave Macmillan, 2015.

Barlow, Alex, et al. "Partial Genomic Survival of Cave Bears in Living Brown Bears." *Nature: Ecology and Evolution*, August 27, 2018. https://doi.org/10 .1038/s41559-018-0654-8.

Barnard, Alan. "Rules and Prohibitions: The Form and Content of Human Kinship." In *Companion Encyclopedia of Anthropology*, ed. Tim Ingold, 783–812. London: Taylor & Francis, 1994.

Barnett, Clive. "Deconstructing Radical Democracy: Articulation, Representation, and Being-with-Others." *Political Geography* 23, no. 5 (2004): 503–28. https://doi.org/10.1016/j.polgeo.2004.01.004.

———. "Temporality and the Paradoxes of Democracy." *Political Geography* 24, no. 5 (2006): 641–47.

Barta, Tony. "Relations of Genocide: Land and Lives in the Colonization of Australia." In *Genocide and the Modern Age: Etiology and Case Studies of Mass Death*, 237–51. Syracuse, NY: Syracuse University Press, 2000.

Bauman, Zygmunt. *Postmodernity and Its Discontents.* New York: New York University Press, 1997.

Beith, Don. *The Birth of Sense: Generative Passivity in Merleau-Ponty's Philosophy.* Athens: Ohio University Press, 2018.

Benhabib, Seyla. *The Reluctant Modernism of Hannah Arendt.* Lanham, MD: Rowman & Littlefield, 2003.

Benjamin, Walter. "Theses on the Philosophy of History." In *Illuminations*, ed. Hannah Arendt, trans. Harry Zohn, 253–64. New York: Schocken, 1969.

Benveniste, Emile. *Indo-European Language and Society.* Trans. Elizabeth Palmer. London: Faber and Faber, 1973.

Bergoffen, Debra. *Contesting the Politics of Genocidal Rape: Affirming the Dignity of the Vulnerable Body.* New York: Routledge, 2012.

Berlant, Lauren, and Lee Edelman. *Sex, or the Unbearable.* Durham, NC: Duke University Press, 2014.

Bernasconi, Robert. "Kant as an Unfamiliar Source of Racism." In *Philosophers on Race: Critical Essays*, 145–65. Oxford: Wiley-Blackwell, 2002.

———. "Rousseau and the Supplement to the Social Contract: Deconstruction and the Possibility of Democracy." *Cardozo Law Review* 11, no. 5/6 (August 1990): 1539–64.

Bernstein, J. M. *Adorno Disenchantment and Ethics*. Cambridge: Cambridge University Press, 2001.

Bernstein, Richard J. *Violence: Thinking without Banisters*. London: John Wiley & Sons, 2013.

Bersani, Leo. *Homos*. Cambridge, MA: Harvard University Press, 1996.

Bettelheim, Bruno. *The Informed Heart: Autonomy in a Mass Age*. New York: Free Press, 1960.

Bianchi, Emanuela. "Genos and Kratos: Kinship between Nature and Power." New York University, November 21, 2016.

Bird, Greg. *Containing Community: From Political Economy to Ontology in Agamben, Esposito, and Nancy*. Albany: SUNY Press, 2016.

Blair, Adam. "Review of Don Beith's *The Birth of Sense: Generative Passivity in Merleau-Ponty's Philosophy* (978-0-8214-2310-3)." *Continental Philosophy Review* 51, no. 3 (September 1, 2018): 469–74. https://doi.org/10.1007/s11007-018-9447-7.

Bleichmar, Daniela. "Botanical Conquistadors." In *Worlds of Natural History*, ed. H. A. Curry, N. Jardine, J. A. Secord, and E. C. Spary, 236–54. Cambridge: Cambridge University Press, 2018.

Blight, David W. *Frederick Douglass: Prophet of Freedom*. New York: Simon and Schuster, 2018.

Bloxham, Donald, and A. Dirk Moses, eds. *The Oxford Handbook of Genocide Studies*. Oxford: Oxford University Press, 2010.

Blunt, Wilfrid. *Linnaeus: The Compleat Naturalist*. Princeton, NJ: Princeton University Press, 2001.

Bodenhorn, Barbara. "'He Used to Be My Relative': Exploring the Bases of Relatedness among Inupiat of Northern Alaska." In *Cultures of Relatedness*, ed. Janet Carsten, 128–48. Cambridge: Cambridge University Press, 2000.

Bogdanović, Mira. "The Rift in the Praxis Group: Between Nationalism and Liberalism." *Critique* 43, no. 3–4 (October 2, 2015): 461–83. https://doi.org/10.1080/03017605.2015.1099850.

Bredecamp, Horst. "From Walter Benjamin to Carl Schmitt, via Thomas Hobbes." Trans. Melissa Thorson Hause and Jackson Bond. *Critical Inquiry* 25, no. 2 (Winter 1999): 247–66.

Broberg, Gunnar. "Homo Sapiens: Linnaeus's Classification of Man." In *Linnaeus: The Man and His Work*, ed. Tore Frangsmyr, 156–94. Canton, MA: Science History Publications, 1994.

Brophy, Sarah. *Witnessing AIDS: Writing, Testimony, and the Work of Mourning*. Toronto: University of Toronto Press, 2004.

Brown, Vincent. *The Reaper's Garden: Death and Power in the World of Atlantic Slavery*. Cambridge, MA: Harvard University Press, 2008.

Browning, Christopher R. *Ordinary Men: Reserve Police Battalion 101 and the Final Solution in Poland*. New York: HarperCollins, 2017.

Brun, Cathrine. "There Is No Future in Humanitarianism: Emergency, Temporality, and Protracted Displacement." *History and Anthropology* 27, no. 4 (August 7, 2016): 393–410. https://doi.org/10.1080/02757206.2016.1207637.

Burton, Annie L., et al. *Women's Slave Narratives*. Mineola, NY: Dover, 2006.

Butler, Judith. *Frames of War: When Is Life Grievable?* New York: Verso, 2016.

———. *Precarious Life: The Powers of Mourning and Violence*. New York: Verso, 2004.

Canguilhem, Georges. *Knowledge of Life*. New York: Fordham University Press, 2008.

Card, Claudia. "Genocide and Social Death." *Hypatia* 18, no. 1 (February 1, 2003): 63–79. https://doi.org/10.1111/j.1527-2001.2003.tb00779.x.

Casey, E. *The Fate of Place: A Philosophical History*. Berkeley: University of California Press, 2013.

Cassin, Barbara, Emily Apter, Jacques Lezra, and Michael Wood. *Dictionary of Untranslatables: A Philosophical Lexicon*. Princeton, NJ: Princeton University Press, 2014.

Cassirer, Ernst. *The Problem of Knowledge: Philosophy, Science, and History since Hegel*. Trans. William H. Woglom and Charles W. Hendel. New Haven, CT: Yale University Press, 1950.

Cavalli-Sforza, Luigi Luca, Paolo Menozzi, and Alberto Piazza. *The History and Geography of Human Genes*. Princeton, NJ: Princeton University Press, 1994.

Cavarero, Adriana. "'A Child Has Been Born unto Us': Arendt on Birth." Trans. Silvia Guslandi and Cosette Bruhns. *PhiloSOPHIA* 4, no. 1 (2014): 12–30.

Cleef, Alfred van. *De Verloren Wereld van de Familie Berberovic*. Taal: Meulenhoff Boekerij, 1999.

Clifford, James. "Taking Identity Politics Seriously: 'The Contradictory, Stony Ground . . .'." In *Without Guarantees: In Honor of Stuart Hall*, ed. Paul Gilroy, Lawrence Grossberg, and Angela McRobbie, 94–112. London: Verso, 2000.

Connolly, William. *Identity/Difference: Democratic Negotiations of Political Paradox*. Minneapolis: University of Minnesota Press, 2002.

———. *A World of Becoming*. Durham, NC: Duke University Press, 2011.

Crépon, Marc. *Murderous Consent: On the Accommodation of Violent Death*. Trans. Michael Loriaux and Jacob Levi. New York: Fordham University Press, 2019.

Critchley, Simon. *Infinitely Demanding: Ethics of Commitment, Politics of Resistance*. London: Verso, 2014.

Darwin, Charles. *The Origin of Species*. London: John Murray, 1859.

Davis, Mike. *Late Victorian Holocausts*. London: Verso, 2001.

Delaney, Carol. "Cutting the Ties That Bind: The Sacrifice of Abraham and Patriarchal Kinship." In *Relative Values: Reconfiguring Kinship Studies*, 445–67. Durham, NC: Duke University Press, n.d.

Derrida, Jacques. *The Beast and the Sovereign*. 2 vols. Trans. Geoffrey Bennington. Chicago: University of Chicago Press, 2011.

———. *The Death Penalty*. 2 vols. Trans. Peggy Kamuf and Elizabeth G. Rottenberg. Chicago: University of Chicago Press, 2013, 2017.

———. "Declarations of Independence." *New Political Science* 7, no. 1 (1986): 7–15.

———. *The Politics of Friendship*. London: Verso, 2020.

———. *Rogues: Two Essays on Reason*. Stanford, CA: Stanford University Press, 2005.

Deutschkron, Inge. *Ich Trug Den Gelben Stern*. Verlag Wissenschaft und Politik, 1983.

Dinshaw, Carolyn, Lee Edelman, Roderick A. Ferguson, Carla Freccero, Elizabeth Freeman, Judith Halberstam, Annamarie Jagose, Christopher Nealon, and Nguyen Tan Hoang. "Theorizing Queer Temporalities: A Roundtable Discussion." *GLQ* 13, no. 2–3 (n.d.): 177–95.

Douglass, Frederick. *Autobiographies*. New York: Library of America, 1994.

Dronamraju, Krishna R. *If I Am to Be Remembered: The Life and Work of Julian Huxley*. Singapore: World Scientific, 1993.

Dunbar, R. I. M. "Sociality among Humans and Non-Human Animals." In *Companion Encyclopedia of Anthropology*, ed. Tim Ingold, 756–82. London: Taylor & Francis, 1994.

Dunn, John. "How Democracies Succeed." *Economy and Society* 25, no. 4 (1996): 511–28.

Duve, Thierry de. "Aesthetics as the Transcendental Ground of Democracy." *Critical Inquiry* 42, no. 1 (September 1, 2015): 149–65. https://doi.org/10.1086/682999.

DuVernay, Ava, dir. *Thirteenth*. Netflix, 2016. https://www.netflix.com/title/80091741.

Eco, Umberto. *Semiotics and the Philosophy of Language*. Bloomington: Indiana University Press, 1986.

Edelman, Lee. *No Future: Queer Theory and the Death Drive*. Durham, NC: Duke University Press, 2004.

Edwards, Jeanette, and Marilyn Strathern. "Including Our Own." In *Cultures of Relatedness*, ed. Janet Carsten, 149–66. Cambridge: Cambridge University Press, 2000.

Eilberg-Schwartz, Howard. *The Savage in Judaism: An Anthropology of Israelite Religion and Ancient Judaism*. Bloomington: Indiana University Press, 1990.

Elden, Stuart. *Foucault: The Birth of Power*. Hoboken, NJ: John Wiley & Sons, 2017.

Ellis, Joseph J. *Founding Brothers: The Revolutionary Generation*. New York: Knopf, 2003.

Evens, T. M. S. *Two Kinds of Rationality: Kibbutz Democracy and Generational Conflict*. Minneapolis: University of Minnesota Press, 1995.

Eze, Emmanuel Chukwudi. *Achieving Our Humanity: The Idea of the Postracial Future*. New York: Routledge, 2001.

Fanon, Frantz. *Black Skin, White Masks*. Trans. Richard Philcox. New York: Grove, 2008.

Finchelstein, Federico. "The Holocaust as Ideology: Borges and the Meaning of Transnational Fascism." *Dapim: Studies on the Shoah* 25 (2011): 273–300.

Finding Your Roots. "Video: Educator Geoffrey Canada on His Complicated Slave Ancestry." March 27, 2012. http://ec2-54-235-253-171.compute-1
.amazonaws.com/weta/finding-your-roots/both-sides-of-slavery/1330/.

"First DNA Exoneration, Center on Wrongful Convictions: Bluhm Legal Clinic,
Northwestern Pritzker School of Law." http://www.law.northwestern.edu/
legalclinic/wrongfulconvictions/exonerations/il/gary-dotson.html.

Forster, Georg. "Guiding Thread to a Future History of Humankind (1789)."
In *Georg Forsters Werke*, ed. Akademie der Wissenschaften der DDR, later
Berlin-Brandenburgische Akademie der Wissenschaften, 8:193. Berlin:
Akademie Verlag, 1958.

Foucault, Michel. *The Archaeology of Knowledge*. New York: Knopf, 2012.

———. *The History of Sexuality*. Vol. 1: *The Will to Knowledge*. New York: Penguin, 2008.

———. *The Order of Things: An Archaeology of Human Sciences*. New York:
Knopf, 2012.

———. *Society Must Be Defended: Lectures at the College de France, 1975–1976*.
New York: Picador, 2003.

Frangsmyr, Tore, ed. *Linnaeus: The Man and His Work*. Canton, MA: Science
History Publications, 1994, 1994.

Franklin, Sarah, and Susan McKinnon. *Relative Values: Reconfiguring Kinship
Studies*. Durham, NC: Duke University Press, 2002.

Freud, Sigmund. *Civilization and Its Discontents*. New York: Norton, 1989.

———. "Family Romances." In *The Standard Edition of the Complete Psychological Works of Sigmund Freud*, trans. James Strachey, 9:238. London: Hogarth,
1959.

———. *Totem and Taboo and Other Works*. In *The Standard Edition of the Complete Psychological Works of Sigmund Freud*, vol. 13. London: Hogarth, 1955.

Fritsch, Matthias. "Natal Alienation and Intergenerational Relations." Presented
at the Annual Meeting of the Society for Phenomenology and Existential
Philosophy, Atlanta, GA, October 2015.

———. *Taking Turns with the Earth: Phenomenology, Deconstruction, and Intergenerational Justice*. Stanford, CA: Stanford University Press, 2018.

Frow, John. "A Politics of Stolen Time." In *Timespace: Geographies of Temporality*, ed. Jon May and Nigel Thrift, 73–87. New York: Routledge, 2003.

Gadamer, Hans-Georg. *Truth and Method*. London: A&C Black, 2013.

Gaffney, Jennifer. "Another Origin of Totalitarianism: Arendt on the Loneliness
of Liberal Citizens." *Journal of British Society for Phenomenology* 47, no. 1
(2016): 1–17.

Garber, Marjorie, Beatrice Hanssen, and Rebecca L. Walkowitz, eds. *The Turn to
Ethics*. New York: Routledge, 2013.

Garland, Theodore, and Scott A. Kelly. "Phenotypic Plasticity and Experimental
Evolution." *Journal of Experimental Biology* 209 (2006): 2344–61. https://doi
.org/10.1242/jeb.02244.

George, Alexander. *Western State Terrorism*. London: Polity, 1991.

Glaude, Eddie S. *Democracy in Black: How Race Still Enslaves the American Soul*. New York: Broadway, 2017.

Gordon, Lewis R. *Freedom, Justice, and Decolonization*. New York: Routledge, 2020.

Gould, Carol. *Marx's Social Ontology: Individuality and Community in Marx's Theory of Social Reality*. Cambridge, MA: MIT Press, 1978.

Gould, Stephen Jay. "Evolution and the Triumph of Homology." *American Scientist* 74, no. 1 (1986): 60–69.

Green, R. E., et al. "A Draft Sequence of the Neandertal Genome." *Science* 328 (2010): 710–22.

Guenther, Lisa. "Fecundity and Natal Alienation: Rethinking Kinship with Levinas and Orlando Patterson." *Levinas Studies* 7, no. 1 (June 13, 2014): 1–19.

———. "Six Senses of Critique for Critical Phenomenology." *Puncta* 4, no. 2 (2021): 5–23. https://doi.org/10.5399/PJCP.V4I2.2.

———. *Solitary Confinement: Social Death and Its Afterlives*. Minneapolis: University of Minnesota Press, 2013.

———. "Critical Phenomenology." In *Fifty Concepts for a Critical Phenomenology*, ed. Weiss et al., 11–16. Evanston, IL: Northwestern University Press, 2020.

Guerrero Hernández, Juan Carlos. "Mutilated Bodies and Memories of Violence: Displacements and Contestations of Representations of Violence, in Contemporary Video Art and Photography in Colombia, 1993–1998." PhD diss., Stony Brook University, Department of Art and Art History, 2015.

Gündoğdu, Ayten. *Rightlessness in an Age of Rights: Hannah Arendt and the Contemporary Struggles of Migrants*. Oxford: Oxford University Press, 2015.

Habermas, Jürgen. "Constitutional Democracy: A Paradoxical Union of Contradictory Principles?" *Political Theory* 29, no. 6 (December 2001): 766–81.

Hacking, Ian. "Trees of Logic, Trees of Porphyry." In *Advancements of Learning: Essays in Honour of Paolo Rossi*, ed. J. Heilbron, 219–61. Florence: Olshki, 2007.

Haddad, Samir. *Derrida and the Inheritance of Democracy*. Indiana University Press, 2013.

———. "Fundaciones Politicas y Derecho a La Filosofia", Translated by Jorge Laplace, in, Ed. Cristóbal Olivares Molina (Santiago de Chile:" In *Escenas de Escritura: Sobre Filosofia y Literatura*, edited by Cristóbal Olivares Molina, translated by Jorge Laplace, 127–52. Santiago de Chile: Pólvora Editorial, 2020.

Halberstam, Jack. *In a Queer Time and Place: Transgender Bodies, Subcultural Lives*. New York: New York University Press, 2005.

Hamilton, Rebecca. "Inside Colin Powell's Decision to Declare Genocide in Darfur." *Atlantic*, August 17, 2011. http://www.theatlantic.com/international/

archive/2011/08/inside-colin-powells-decision-to-declare-genocide-in
-darfur/243560/.

Hampton, Jean. "Defining Wrong and Defining Rape." In *A Most Detestable Crime: New Philosophical Essays on Rape*, 118–56. Oxford: Oxford University Press, 1999.

Haraway, Donna J. *Staying with the Trouble: Making Kin in the Chthulucene*. Durham, NC: Duke University Press, 2016.

Harry, Debra, and Frank Dukepoo. *Indians, Genes, and Genetics: What Indians Should Know about the New Biotechnology*. Nixon, NV: Indigenous Peoples Coalition against Biopiracy, 1998.

Harvey, Robert. *Witnessness: Beckett, Dante, Levi, and the Foundations of Responsibility*. New York: Bloomsbury Publishing USA, 2010.

Hatley, James. *Suffering Witness: The Quandry of Responsibility after the Irreparable*. Albany: State University of New York Press, 2012.

Hatzfeld, Jean. *Life Laid Bare: The Survivors in Rwanda Speak*. London: Other, 2013.

Heidegger, Martin. *Being and Time*. Trans. John Macquarrie and Edward Robinson. New York: Harper & Row, 1962.

Hobbes, Thomas. *The English Works of Thomas Hobbes of Malmesbury*. Vol. 2. Bohn, 1841.

Hocquenghem, Guy. *Homosexual Desire*. Durham, NC: Duke University Press, 1993.

Hoff, Shannon. "Rights and Worlds: On the Political Significance of Belonging." *Philosophical Forum* 45, no. 4 (2014): 355–73.

Honig, Bonnie. *Emergency Politics: Paradox, Law, Democracy*. Princeton, NJ: Princeton University Press, 2009.

Hursthouse, Rosalind. *On Virtue Ethics*. Oxford: Oxford University Press, 1999.

Isin, Engin. *Being Political: Genealogies of Citizenship*. Minneapolis: University of Minnesota Press, 2002.

Jacob, François. *The Logic of Life: A History of Heredity*. New York: Vintage, 1976.

Jarman, Derek. *Modern Nature*. Minneapolis: University of Minnesota Press, 1992.

Johnston, Mark David. *The Spiritual Logic of Ramon Llull*. London: Clarendon, 1987.

Jonas, Hans. *The Imperative of Responsibility: In Search of an Ethics for the Technological Age*. Chicago: University of Chicago Press, 1985.

———. "Toward an Ontological Grounding of an Ethics for the Future." In *Mortality and Morality: A Search for Good after Auschwitz*, 99–111. Chicago: Northwestern University Press, 1996.

Jones, Adam. *Genocide, War Crimes, and the West*. London: Zed, 2004.

Kant, Immanuel. *Critique of Judgment*. Trans. Werner S. Pluhar. Indianapolis: Hackett, 1987.

———. *Critique of Pure Reason*. Ed. and trans. Paul Guyer and Allen Wood. Cambridge: Cambridge University Press, 1998.

———. "Of the Different Races of Human Beings." In *Anthropology, History, and Education*, ed. Günter Zöller and Robert B. Louden. Cambridge: Cambridge University Press, 2007.

Keenan, Brian. *An Evil Cradling*. London: Random House, 2015.

Keller, Evelyn Fox. "Nature, Nurture, and the Human Genome Project." In *The Code of Codes*, ed. Daniel J. Kevles and Leroy Hood, 281–99. Cambridge, MA: Harvard University Press, 1992.

Khanna, Ranjana. "Post-Palliative: Coloniality's Affective Dissonance." *Postcolonial Text* 2, no. 1 (December 31, 2005). https://www.postcolonial.org/index.php/pct/article/view/385.

King, Martin Luther, Jr. *Where Do We Go from Here: Chaos or Community?* Boston: Beacon, 2010.

Kittay, Eva Feder. *Love's Labor: Essays on Women, Equality, and Dependency*. New York: Routledge, 2013.

Koerner, Lisbet. *Linnaeus: Nature and Nation*. Cambridge, MA: Harvard University Press, 2009.

Kristof, Nicholas. "A Journey through Atrocities." *New York Times*, June 13, 2021.

Lagier, Raphael. *Les races humaines selon Kant*. Paris: PUF, 2004.

Lang, Berel. *Genocide: The Act as Idea*. Philadelphia: University of Pennsylvania Press, 2017.

Lear, Jonathan. *Radical Hope: Ethics in the Face of Cultural Devastation*. Cambridge, MA: Harvard University Press, 2006.

Lederman, Shmuel. *Hannah Arendt and Participatory Democracy: A People's Utopia*. Springer, 2019.

———. "A Nation Destroyed: An Existential Approach to the Distinctive Harm of Genocide." *Journal of Genocide Research* 19, no. 1 (January 2, 2017): 112–32. https://doi.org/10.1080/14623528.2016.1250473.

———. "What's So Bad about Genocide, Anyway?" *Journal of Genocide Research* 20, no. 3 (July 3, 2018): 429–33. https://doi.org/10.1080/14623528.2018.1445421.

Lefort, Claude. *Democracy and Political Theory*. Trans. David Macey. Oxford: Oxford University Press, 1988.

Leighton, Kimberly. "Addressing the Harms of Not Knowing One's Heredity: Lessons from Genealogical Bewilderment." *Adoption & Culture* 3, no. 1 (2012): 63–107. https://doi.org/10.1353/ado.2012.0010.

Lemkin, R. *Axis Rule in Occupied Europe: Laws of Occupation, Analysis of Government, Proposals for Redress*. Washington, DC: Carnegie Endowment for International Peace, Division of International Law, 1944.

———. *Totally Unofficial: The Autobiography of Raphael Lemkin*. Ed. D. L. Frieze. New Haven, CT: Yale University Press, 2013.

Lemos, Ramon M. "The Concept of Natural Right." *Midwest Studies in Philosophy* 7, no. 1 (1982): 133–50.

Levi, Primo. *The Drowned and the Saved*. New York: Summit, 1988.

———. *Survival in Auschwitz* and *The Reawakening*. New York: Summit, 1986.

Lévi-Strauss, Claude. *The Elementary Structures of Kinship*. Red. ed. Boston: Beacon, 1969.

Lewis, C. T., and C. Short. *Latin Dictionary: Based on Andrews's Edition of Freund's Latin Dictionary*. Oxford: Oxford University Press, 1963.

Lewis, Gail. "Birthing Racial Difference: Conversations with My Mother and Others." *Studies in the Maternal* 1, no. 1 (January 1, 2009): 1–21.

Lewontin, R. C. "The Apportionment of Human Diversity." In *Evolutionary Biology*, ed. T. Dobzhansky, M. K. Hecht, and W. C. Steere. New York: Springer, 1972. https://doi.org/10.1007/978-1-4684-9063-3_14.

Lewy, Guenter. "Can There Be Genocide without the Intent to Commit Genocide?" *Journal of Genocide Research* 9, no. 4 (December 1, 2007): 661–74. https://doi.org/10.1080/14623520701644457.

Linné, Carl von. *Linnaeus' Philosophia Botanica*. Trans. Stephen Freer. Oxford: Oxford University Press, 2005.

———. *Systema Naturae, 1735: Facsimile of the First Edition with an Introduction and a First English Translation of the "Observationes."* Ed. H. Engel, trans. M. S. J. Engel-Ledeboer. De Graaf, 1964.

Lomax, J. Harvey. "Nietzsche and the Eternal Recurrence." *Philosophy Now* 29 (November 2000): 20–22.

Loraux, Nicole. *Born of the Earth*. Trans. Selina Stewart. Ithaca, NY: Cornell University Press, 2000.

Lovejoy, A. O. *The Great Chain of Being: A Study of the History of an Idea*. Cambridge, MA: Harvard University Press, 2009.

Macleod, Christopher. "An Alternative Approach to the Harm of Genocide." *Politics* 32, no. 3 (2012).

Mahner, M., and M. Bunge, eds. *Foundations of Biophilosophy*. Berlin: Springer, 2013.

Malabou, Catherine. "Philosophers, Biologists: Some More Effort If You Wish to Become Revolutionaries!" *Critical Inquiry* 43 (Autumn 2016): 200–6.

Mann, Michael. *The Dark Side of Democracy: Explaining Ethnic Cleansing*. Cambridge: Cambridge University Press, 2005.

Manning, Dolleen Tisawii'ashii. "The Murmuration of Birds: An Anishinaabe Ontology of Mnidoo-Worlding." In *Feminist Phenomenology Futures*, ed. Helen A. Fielding and Dorothea E. Olkowski, 155–80. Bloomington: Indiana University Press, 2017.

Manville, Phillip Brooke. *The Origins of Citizenship in Ancient Athens*. Princeton, NJ: Princeton University Press, 1990.

Marks, Jonathan M. *Human Biodiversity: Genes, Race, and History*. New Brunswick, NJ: Transaction, 2001.

———. "'We're Going to Tell These People Who They Really Are': Science and Relatedness." In *Relative Values: Reconfiguring Kinship Studies*, ed. Sarah Franklin and Susan McKinnon. Durham, NC: Duke University Press, 2001.

Martel, James R. *The Misinterpellated Subject*. Durham, NC: Duke University Press, 2017.

May, Larry. *Genocide: A Normative Account*. Cambridge: Cambridge University Press, 2010.

May, Todd. *The Political Thought of Jacques Rancière: Creating Equality*. Edinburgh: Edinburgh University Press, 2008.

McCracken, Peggy. *The Curse of Eve, the Wound of the Hero: Blood, Gender, and Medieval Literature*. Philadelphia: University of Pennsylvania Press, 2010.

McLaughlin, Peter. "Kant on Heredity." In *Heredity Produced: At the Crossroads of Biology, Politics, and Culture, 1500–1870*, ed. S. Müller-Wille and H.-J. Rheinberger, 277–92. Cambridge, MA: MIT Press, 2007.

Medina, José M., John J. Stuhr, and Jessica Wahman. *Cosmopolitanism and Place*. Bloomington: Indiana University Press, 2017.

Meierhenrich, Jens. *Genocide: A Reader*. Oxford: Oxford University Press, 2014.

Meillassoux, Claude. *Mythes et limites de l'anthropologie. Le sang et les mots*. Page deux, 2001.

Mendieta, Eduardo. "From Imperial to Dialogical Cosmopolitanism." *Ethics & Global Politics* 2, no. 3 (January 1, 2009): 241–58. https://doi.org/10.3402/egp .v2i3.2044.

Mensch, Jennifer. *Kant's Organicism: Epigenesis and the Development of Critical Philosophy*. Chicago: University of Chicago Press, 2013.

Merleau-Ponty, Maurice. *Phenomenology of Perception*. Trans. Donald A. Landes. London: Routledge, 2013.

Mignolo, Walter. "Cosmopolitanism and the De-Colonial Option." *Studies in Philosophy and Education* 29, no. 2 (March 2010): 111–27. https://doi.org/10 .1007/s11217-009-9163-1.

Miller, Lulu. *Why Fish Don't Exist: A Story of Loss, Love, and the Hidden Order of Life*. New York: Simon and Schuster, 2021.

Miller, Sarah Clark. "Moral Injury and Relational Harm: Analyzing Rape in Darfur." *Journal of Social Philosophy* 40, no. 4 (2009): 504–23. https://doi.org/ 10.1111/j.1467-9833.2009.01468.x.

Monod, Jacques. *Chance and Necessity: An Essay on the Natural Philosophy of Modern Biology*. London: Penguin, 1997.

Moran, Dermot. "'Let's Look at It Objectively': Why Phenomenology Cannot Be Naturalized." *Royal Institute of Philosophy Supplement* 72 (2013): 89–115. https://doi.org/10.1017/S1358246113000064.

Morrison, Toni. *Beloved*. New York: Vintage, 2004.

Mouffe, Chantal. *The Democratic Paradox*. London: Verso, 2000.

"The Moynihan Report: An Annotated Edition." *Atlantic*, September 2015. https://www.theatlantic.com/politics/archive/2015/09/the-moynihan-report -an-annotated-edition/404632/.

Mudimbe, V. Y. *The Invention of Africa: Gnosis, Philosophy, and the Order of Knowledge*. Bloomington: Indiana University Press, 1988.

Mukherjee, Siddhartha. *The Gene: An Intimate History*. New York: Simon and Schuster, 2016.

Muller, Hermann. "Our Load of Mutations." *American Journal of Human Genetics* 2, no. 2 (1950): 111–76.

Müller-Wille, S., and H.-J. Rheinberger, eds. *Heredity Produced: At the Crossroads of Biology, Politics, and Culture, 1500–1870*. Cambridge, MA: MIT Press, 2007.

Müller-Wille, S., and H.-J. Rheinberger. *A Cultural History of Heredity*. Chicago: University of Chicago Press, 2012.

Myers, Ella. *Worldly Ethics: Democratic Politics and Care for the World*. Durham, NC: Duke University Press, 2013.

Naas, Michael. *Derrida: From Now On*. New York: Fordham University Press, 2008.

———. "'One Nation ... Indivisible': Jacques Derrida on the Autoimmunity of Democracy and the Sovereignty of God." *Research in Phenomenology* 36, no. 1 (January 1, 2006): 15–44. https://doi.org/10.1163/156916406779165818.

Nancy, Jean-Luc. *Being Singular Plural*. Stanford, CA: Stanford University Press, 2000.

———. *The Sense of the World*. Minneapolis: University of Minnesota Press, 1997.

———. *The Truth of Democracy*. New York: Fordham University Press, 2010.

Nancy, Jean-Luc, and Philippe Lacoue-Labarthe. *Scène*. Paris: Détroits, 2013.

Narayan, Uma. *Dislocating Cultures: Identities, Traditions, and Third World Feminism*. Routledge, 2013.

Nash, Catherine. "Genetic Kinship." *Cultural Studies* 18, no. 1 (January 1, 2004): 1–33. https://doi.org/10.1080/0950238042000181593.

Nelson, Alondra. *The Social Life of DNA: Race, Reparations, and Reconciliation after the Genome*. Boston: Beacon, 2016.

Nietzsche, Friedrich. *On the Genealogy of Morals*. Trans. Walter Kaufmann. New York: Knopf, 2010.

Nixon, Robert. *Slow Violence and the Environmentalism of the Poor*. Cambridge, MA: Harvard University Press, 2011.

Novick, Peter. *The Holocaust in American Life*. New York: Houghton Mifflin Harcourt, 2000.

Ó Tuama, Padraig. *In the Shelter: Finding a Home in the World*. London: Hodder, 2015.

O'Byrne, Anne. "Communitas and the Problem of Women." *Angelaki* 18, no. 3 (September 2013): 125–38.

———. *Natality and Finitude*. Bloomington: Indiana University Press, 2011.

———. "Possible: On Rodolphe Gasché's Deconstruction, Its Force, Its Violence." *Philosophy Today* 63, no. 1 (n.d.): 243–53. https://doi.org/10.5840/philtoday2019631257.

———. "Symbol, Exchange, and Birth." *Philosophy and Social Criticism* 30, no. 3 (May 2004): 355–73.

O'Byrne, Anne, and Martin Shuster, eds. *Logics of Genocide: The Structures of Violence and the Contemporary World*. New York: Routledge, 2020.

Oksala, Johanna. *Foucault on Freedom*. Cambridge: Cambridge University Press, 2005.

Olson, Maynard V. "When Less Is More: Gene Loss as an Engine of Evolutionary Change." *American Journal of Human Genetics* 64, no. 1 (January 1, 1999): 18–23. https://doi.org/10.1086/302219.

Palmié, Stephan. "Mixed Blessings and Sorrowful Mysteries: Second Thoughts About 'Hybridity.'" *Current Anthropology* 54, no. 4 (2013): 463–82. https://doi .org/10.1086/671196.

Patterson, Orlando. *Slavery and Social Death*. Cambridge, MA: Harvard University Press, 1982.

PBS. *Finding Your Roots: Deepak Chopra's Ancestral Pilgrimage*. PBS, 2014. https://www.youtube.com/watch?v=SHwlPTgmxOk.

Peralta, Jaime. "De 'delirios ignorantes' a 'cultas reflexiones': la Ilustración europea y la apropiación de los saberes de la periferia colonial." *Fronteras de la Historia* 19, no. 1 (2014).

Pigliucci, Massimo. "Phenotypic Plasticity." In *Evolution: The Extended Synthesis*, ed. Massimo Pigliucci and Gerd Müller. Cambridge, MA: MIT Press, 2010.

———. "Species as Family Resemblance: The (Dis)Solution of the Species Problem?" *BioEssays* 25, no. 6 (n.d.): 596–602.

Popper, Karl R. *The Open Society and Its Enemies*. New one-vol. ed. Princeton, NJ: Princeton University Press, 2013.

Porphyry. *Introduction*. Trans. Jonathan Barnes. London: Clarendon, 2006.

Povinelli, Elizabeth A. *Economies of Abandonment: Social Belonging and Endurance in Late Liberalism*. Durham, NC: Duke University Press, 2011.

Power, Samantha. *A Problem from Hell*. New York: Basic Books, 2013.

Protevi, John. *Life, War, Earth*. Minneapolis: University of Minnesota Press, 2013.

Rancière, Jacques. *Aesthetics and Its Discontents*. Trans. Steven Corcoran. Cambridge: Polity, 2009.

———. *Dissensus*. Trans. Steven Corcoran. London: Bloomsbury, 2010.

———. *Hatred of Democracy*. Trans. Steven Corcoran. London: Verso, 2006.

Rawls, John. *A Theory of Justice*. Original ed. Cambridge, MA: Harvard University Press, 2009.

Reardon, Jenny. *Race to the Finish: Identity and Governance in an Age of Genomics*. Princeton, NJ: Princeton University Press, 2009.

———. "Race without Salvation: Beyond the Science/Society Divide in Genomic Studies of Human Diversity." In *Revisiting Race in a Genomic Age*, ed. Barbara A. Koenig, Sandra Soo-Jin Lee, and Sarah S. Richardson, 304–19. New Brunswick, NJ: Rutgers University Press, 2008.

Restrepo, José Alejandro. *Musa paradisíaca: una video-instalación* [exhibition catalog]. Bogotá: Colombia: Instituto colombiano de cultura, 1997.

Rivera, Omar. *Andean Aesthetics and Anticolonial Resistance: A Cosmology of Unsociable Bodies*. New York: Bloomsbury, 2021.

Roberts, Dorothy. *Fatal Invention: How Science, Politics, and Big Business Re-Create Race in the Twenty-First Century*. New York: New Press, 2011.

Roth, John K. *Genocide and Human Rights: A Philosophical Guide*. New York: Palgrave Macmillan, 2005.

Rubin, Gayle. "Of Catamites and Kings: Reflections of Butch, Gender, and Boundaries." In *Transgender Studies Reader*, ed. Susan Stryker and Stephen Whittle, 471–89. New York: Routledge, 2006.

Ruin, Hans. *Being with the Dead: Burial, Ancestral Politics, and the Roots of Historical Consciousness*. Stanford, CA: Stanford University Press, 2019.

Rummel, R. J. *Power Kills: Democracy as a Method of Nonviolence*. Oxford: Transaction, 2003.

Rummel, R. J., and Irving Louis Horowitz. *Death by Government: Genocide and Mass Murder since 1900*. New York: Routledge, 2017.

Russell, Camisha. *The Assisted Reproduction of Race*. Bloomington: Indiana University Press, 2018.

Ryan, Lyndall. "Digital Map of Colonial Frontier Massacres in Australia 1788–1930." *Teaching History* 54, no. 3 (2020): 13–20. https://doi.org//doi/10.3316/informit.515797928995944.

Ryn, Zdzislaw and Stanslaw Klodzinski. *An der Grenze zwischen Leben und Tod. Eine Studie über die Erscheinung des Muselmanns" im Konzentrationslager, Auschwitz-Hefte*. Vol. 1. Weinheim: Beltz, 1987.

Salon Staff Writer. "Ben Affleck: 'I Didn't Want Any Television Show about My Family to Include a Guy Who Owned Slaves. I Was Embarrassed.'" *Salon*, April 22, 2015. http://www.salon.com/2015/04/22/ben_affleck_i_didnt_want_any_television_show_about_my_family_to_include_a_guy_who_owned_slaves_i_was_embarrassed/.

Sants, H. J. "Genealogical Bewilderment in Children with Substitute Parents." *British Journal of Medical Psychology* 37, no. 2 (June 1, 1964): 133–42. https://doi.org/10.1111/j.2044-8341.1964.tb01981.x.

Scarry, Elaine. *The Body in Pain: The Making and Unmaking of the World*. New York: Oxford University Press, 1985.

Schebinger, Londa. *Plants and Empire: Colonial Bioprospecting in the Atlantic World*. Cambridge, MA: Harvard University Press, 2004.

Scheffler, Samuel. *Death and the Afterlife*. Ed. Niko Kolodny. 1st ed. New York: Oxford University Press, 2013.

Scheper-Hughes, Nancy. "The Genocidal Continuum: Peace-Time Crimes." In *Power and the Self*, ed. Jeannette Marie Mageo, 29–47. Cambridge: Cambridge University Press, 2002.

———. "Small Wars and Invisible Genocides." *Social Science and Medicine* 43, no. 5 (1996): 889–900.

Schmitt, Carl. *The Crisis of Parliamentary Democracy*. Trans. Ellen Kennedy. Cambridge, MA: MIT Press, 1988.

Schneider, David M. *A Critique of the Study of Kinship*. Ann Arbor: University of Michigan Press, 1984.

———. "The Kinship System and Village Organization of Yap, West Caroline Islands, Micronesia: A Structural and Functional Account." Harvard University, 1949.

———. "What Is Kinship All About?" In *Kinship Studies in the Morgan Centennial Year*, ed. Priscilla Reining, 88–112. Washington, DC: Anthropological Society of Washington, 1972.

———. "Yap Kinship Terminology and Kin Groups." *American Anthropologist* 55, no. 2.1 (June 1953).

Schott, Robin M. "War Rape, Social Death, and Political Evil." *Development Dialogue* 55 (March 2011): 47–62.

"Season Wrap-Up: Finally! DNA Takes Center Stage | Finding Your Roots." PBS. http://www.pbs.org/weta/finding-your-roots/blog/season-wrap-finally-dna-takes-center-stage/.

Sforza, Luigi Luca Cavalli, and Francesco Cavalli-Sforza. *The Great Human Diasporas: The History of Diversity and Evolution*. New York: Basic Books, 1995.

Shange, Savannah. "Play Aunties and Dyke Bitches: Gender, Generation, and the Ethics of Black Queer Kinship." *Black Scholar* 49, no. 1 (2019): 40–54. https://doi.org/10.1080/00064246.2019.1548058.

Shuster, Martin. "A Phenomenology of Home: Jean Améry on Homesickness." *Journal of French and Francophone Philosophy* 24, no. 3 (February 24, 2017): 117–27.

———. "Philosophy and Genocide." In *Oxford Handbook of Genocide Studies*, ed. Donald Bloxham and A. Dirk Moses. New York: Oxford University Press, 2010.

Simpson, G. G. *Principles of Animal Taxonomy*. New York: Columbia University Press, 1961.

Siraj, Nasrin, and Ellen Bal. "'Hunger Has Brought Us into This Jungle': Understanding Mobility and Immobility of Bengali Immigrants in the Chittagong Hills of Bangladesh." *Social Identities* 23, no. 4 (July 4, 2017): 396–412. https://doi.org/10.1080/13504630.2017.1281443.

Skallerud, E. S. "'Acts Shocking to the Conscience of Mankind': Why Norway Voted to Delete Cultural Genocide from the 1948 Genocide Convention." University of Olso, 2019. https://www.duo.uio.no/bitstream/handle/10852/75292/1/HUMR5200-Candidate-8008.pdf.

Smith, Larry Douglas. "Fitzroy and the Fuegians: A Clash of Cultures." *Anglican and Episcopal History* 59, no. 3 (1990): 386–403.

Sontag, Susan. *Regarding the Pain of Others*. New York: Macmillan, 2004.

Spillers, Hortense J. "Mama's Baby, Papa's Maybe: An American Grammar Book." *Diacritics* 17, no. 2 (1987): 65–81. https://doi.org/10.2307/464747.

Stauffer, Jill. *Ethical Loneliness: The Injustice of Not Being Heard*. New York: Columbia University Press, 2015.

Stepan, Nancy. *Idea of Race in Science: Great Britain, 1800–1960*. New York, 1982.

Stevens, Jacqueline. "The Friends of War and Genocide." In *Logics of Genocide*. New York: Routledge, 2020.

———. "Methods of Adoption: Eliminating the Genetic Privilege." In *Adoption Matters: Philosophical and Feminist Essays*, ed. Sally Anne Haslanger and Charlotte Witt, 68–94. Ithaca, NY: Cornell University Press, 2005.

Stiassny, Melanie L. J. "Atavisms, Phylogenetic Character Reversals, and the Origin of Evolutionary Novelties." *Netherlands Journal of Zoology* 42, no. 2 (1991): 260–76. https://doi.org/10.1163/156854291X00324.

Stocking, George W. *Race, Culture, and Evolution: Essays in the History of Anthropology.* Chicago: University of Chicago Press, 1968.

Straus, Scott. *The Order of Genocide: Race, Power, and War in Rwanda.* Ithaca, NY: Cornell University Press, 2013.

Talcott, Samuel. "Errant Life, Molecular Biology, and Biopower: Canguilhem, Jacob, and Foucault." *History and Philosophy of the Life Sciences* 36, no. 2 (October 1, 2014): 254–79.

TallBear, Kimberly. *Native American DNA: Tribal Belonging and the False Promise of Genetic Science.* Minneapolis: University of Minnesota Press, 2013.

Thorley, John. *Athenian Democracy.* London: Routledge, 1996.

Topolski, Anya. *Arendt, Levinas, and a Politics of Relationality.* London: Rowman & Littlefield, 2015.

Tronto, Joan C. *Moral Boundaries: A Political Argument for an Ethic of Care.* Hove: Psychology Press, 1993.

Ukeles, Mierle Laderman. "Manifesto for Maintenance Art 1969! Proposal for an Exhibition 'CARE.'" *Journal of Contemporary Painting*, October 1, 2018. https://doi.org/10.1386/jcp.4.2.233_7.

United Nations High Commissioner for Refugees. "Refworld | Burma Citizenship Law." *Refworld.* https://www.refworld.org/docid/3ae6b4f71b.html.

United Nations Secretary-General. "Draft Convention on the Crime of Genocide." June 26, 1947. https://digitallibrary.un.org/record/611058?ln=en#record-files-collapse-header.

"Universal Declaration of Human Rights," October 6, 2015. http://www.un.org/en/universal-declaration-human-rights/.

Velleman, J. David. "Family History." *Philosophical Papers* 34, no. 3 (November 1, 2005): 357–78. https://doi.org/10.1080/05568640509485163.

Venter, Craig. "SPIEGEL Interview with Craig Venter: 'We Have Learned Nothing from the Genome.'" *Spiegel Online*, July 29, 2010. http://www.spiegel.de/international/world/spiegel-interview-with-craig-venter-we-have-learned-nothing-from-the-genome-a-709174-2.html.

Verboon, Annemieke. "The Medieval Tree of Porphyry: An Organic Structure of Logic." In *The Tree: Symbol, Allegory, and Structural Device in Medieval Art and Thought*, ed. A. Worm and P. Salonis, 95–116. Brepols: Turnhout, 2014.

Visker, Rudi. *Truth and Singularity: Taking Foucault into Phenomenology.* Berlin: Springer Science & Business Media, 2000.

Wade, Nicholas. *A Troublesome Inheritance: Genes, Race, and Human History.* New York: Penguin, 2015.

Wallach, Glenn. *Obedient Sons: The Discourse of Youth and Generations in American Culture, 1630–1860*. Amherst: University of Massachusetts Press, 1997.

Waxman, Zoe. "Testimony and Representation." In *The Historiography of the Holocaust*, ed. Dan Stone. London: Palgrave Macmillan, 2004.

Weschler, Lawrence. *Vermeer in Bosnia*. New York: Knopf, 2007.

Weinbaum, Alys Eve. *Wayward Reproductions: Genealogies of Race and Nation in Transatlantic Modern Thought*. Durham, NC: Duke University Press, 2004.

Weinstein, Jami. "Vital Ethics: On Life and In/Difference." In *Against Life*, ed. Alastair Hunt and Stephanie Youngblood, 87–118. Evanston, IL: Northwestern University Press, 2016.

Wellisch, E. "Children without Genealogy—A Problem of Adoption." *Mental Health* 12, no. 1 (1952): 41–42.

Wentzer, Thomas Schwarz. "Approaching Philosophical Anthropology: Human, the Responsive Being." In *Finite but Unbounded: New Approaches in Philosophical Anthropology*, 25–46. Berlin: De Gruyter, 2017. https://doi.org/10.1515/9783110523812-003.

West-Eberhard, Mary Jane. *Developmental Plasticity and Evolution*. Oxford: Oxford University Press, 2003.

Weston, Kath. *Families We Choose: Lesbians, Gays, Kinship*. New York: Columbia University Press, 1991.

"White Americans to Be Minority by 2042." *Telegraph*, August 14, 2008.

Whitehead, David. *The Demes of Attica, 508/7–ca. 250 B.C.: A Political and Social Study*. Princeton, NJ: Princeton University Press, 2014.

"Whose Genome Is It Anyway?" *Genome News Network*. http://www.genomenewsnetwork.org/articles/02_01/Whose_genome.shtml.

Wilshire, Bruce. *Get 'Em All! Kill 'Em!* Lanham, MD: Lexington, 2005.

Wittgenstein, Ludwig. "I: A Lecture on Ethics." *Philosophical Review* 74, no. 1 (1965): 3–12. https://doi.org/10.2307/2183526.

———. *Notebooks, 1914–1916*. Chicago: University of Chicago Press, 1984.

Yoon, Carol Kaesuk. *Naming Nature: The Clash between Instinct and Science*. New York: Norton, 2010.

Zambrana, Rocío. "Genocide and Agency in the Americas: Methodological Considerations." In *Logics of Genocide*, ed. Anne O'Byrne and Martin Shuster. New York: Routledge, 2020.

Zawacki, Benjamin. "Defining Myanmar's 'Rohingya Problem.'" *Human Rights Brief* 20, no. 3 (2013): 18–25.

Zerilli, Linda M. G. *A Democratic Theory of Judgment*. Chicago: University of Chicago Press, 2016.

———. *Feminism and the Abyss of Freedom*. Chicago: University of Chicago Press, 2005.

Ziarek, Ewa Plonowska. *An Ethics of Dissensus: Postmodernity, Feminism, and the Politics of Radical Democracy*. Stanford, CA: Stanford University Press, 2001.

# Index

absolute belonging, 29, 65, 68–73
action: capacity for, 14, 71, 86, 96, 120–21; distance from one's own, 110–11; responsibility and, 16; into world, 14
actions, ethical, 106, 201n30
actions, political, 156
Adams, John, 144, 197n53
Adorno, Theodor, 22, 114–15
aenocide, 22, 98–102
Affleck, Ben, 84
Africa, 81, 90–91, 100
African Americans, 79, 84, 90–91, 95, 100, 145–46, 186n60. See also Black Americans
African people, 69, 80–81, 128, 163
AfricanAncestry.com, 90, 91
afterlife, 151–54, 156, 199n6
afterworld, 151–54, 156
Agamben, Giorgio, 111–12, 113, 192n31
agency, 21, 109, 134, 135, 170n52, 195n11
alienation, natal, 14, 93–94
American Anthropological Association, 61
American Revolution, 198n61
Améry, Jean, 112, 153; "How Much Home Does a Person Need?" 67–68
anarchism, 127, 138, 140, 141–44
anarchist temporality, 141–42
ancestor, common, 51, 60, 62, 64, 179n105
ancestor veneration, 15, 88
ancestors, 70–73, 83–84, 88, 91–92, 99, 160, 184n24

ancestral charts, 63, 72, 182n154
ancestry: movement to race from, 91–92
Anidjar, Gil, 74
annihilation camps, 105, 109–15, 173n12, 193n49. See also Auschwitz, Poland
Anthony, Aaron, 93
anthropology: culture and, 99, 100, 152–53, 156, 189n122; kinship and, 63, 73, 86–87, 96, 134–35; race and, 81
anthropos, 99
anticipation within generation, 10–11, 16–17, 34
antifoundationalism, 122
antigenocidal democracy, 23, 30, 151–64, 153–54, 162–64
antimiscegenation laws, 188n94
anxiety, existential, 28, 34, 35–36
Anzaldúa, Gloria, 98
appearance, 25, 26, 27, 35: of blood, 74–77, 82; of DNA, 79, 82–83; of victims of rape, 118
appropriation, 65–66
arbores juris (Trees of Consanguinity), 174n25
Arendt, Hannah: American Revolution, 198n61; ancestor veneration, 15; antifoundationalism, 122; antimiscegenation laws, 188n94; birth, 11, 14, 26, 120; capacity for action, 14, 120–21; "Collective Responsibility," 105; cultures, 156–57, 199n14; death, 11; dictatorship, 109–10;

Arendt, Hannah (*continued*)
    Eichmann, 116; extermination camps,
    105, 109–10, 114, 173n12; generational
    time, 100; *The Human Condition*, 26,
    157; human groups, 153; human social
    nature, 64; human temporalities, 155–57;
    natality, 118, 120–21; politics, 25, 26,
    105, 120–22, 130, 153–57, 160–61, 198n65;
    Rights of Man, 136, 195n21; superfluity,
    192n28; sustaining the world, 12; tragic
    choices, 192n24; treating adults as adults,
    144; wrongness of genocide, 120
Aristotle, 2, 7, 74, 138, 140, 155: *Categories*, 28,
    36–37, 38, 39–40, 173n17, 174n27–28
Armenian genocide, 5
Assembling the Tree of Life (ATOL), 29, 52,
    62, 63, 181n150, 182n151
*atavus, atavia*, 72
Athenians, ancient, 1–2, 72, 137–41, 196n36,
    200n15
Augustine, 74
Augustynka, Tadeusz, 101
Auschwitz, Poland, 13, 112, 114–15, 193n49
Australia, 124, 158–59. *See also* Australian
    Aboriginal genocide
Australian Aboriginal genocide, 108, 127–28,
    158–59, 162, 171n64, 175n46
Australian Reconciliation Convention,
    158–59
Austria, 153

Badiou, Alain, 192n43
Bailey, Harriet, 93–94, 96
Balibar, Etienne, 122, 195n21
Balkans, 9. *See also* Yugoslavia
Bangladesh, 108–9
Baraitser, Lisa, 160–61
Barnard, Alan, 86–87
Barnett, Clive, 196n30
basic science, 62, 181nn148–49
Bauman, Zygmunt, 65
*Beagle*, HMS, 49–50
being. *See* being-with; existence; genera-
    tional being
being-with, 11, 12, 14, 160
belonging: ancestors and, 70–73, 88, 184n24;
    definitions of, 65–66, 153; democracy
    and, 1–2, 3, 126–27, 130–31, 140, 196n36;
    difference in, 70; *genos* and, 28, 64–65;
    groups and, 65, 152; Hoff, 85–86; Kant,
    64; necessity of, 85–89, 136; not belong-
    ing and, 67

risks of, 163; world and, 66–67
belonging, absolute, 29, 65, 68–73
belonging, cosmopolitan, 135
Benhabib, Seyla, 121
Benjamin, Walter, 144
Berberovic family, Yugoslavia, 104–5
Bergen-Belsen, Germany, 103
Berlant, Lauren, 31, 142, 202n42
Bernasconi, Robert, 126, 177n78
Bernstein, J. M., 115
Bernstein, Richard, 170n45
Bersani, Leo, 97, 98, 189n120
Bettelheim, Bruno, 110–11
bewilderment, genealogical, 85–91
biological change, 58
biological genocide, 123
biological inheritance, 5–6, 48–57, 70
biological race, 84–85
biological time, 99
biology, 29, 58, 59, 61, 136, 179n113
biopolitics, 25, 29, 49, 54, 60, 61, 84, 171n65
*bios*, 51, 99, 136, 155, 156
birth: alienation at, 93–94; Arendt, 11, 14,
    26, 120; blood and, 73–74; in democratic
    nation-states, 4; differences of, 188n94;
    genocide and, 14, 19; natality and, 13–14,
    19, 26
Black Americans, 128, 163. *See also* African
    Americans
Blair, Adam, 71–72
Bleichmar, Daniela, 175n46
blood, 73–77, 82, 85, 94, 188n104. *See also*
    families; kinship
blood relations, 29, 52, 73–77. *See also* fami-
    lies; kinship
bloodlines, 76, 77, 85
Bloxham, Donald, 109
Blumenbach, Johann Friedrich, 61
Boer people, 128
Boethius, 38
Borges, Jorge Luis: "Of Exactitude in Sci-
    ence," 62–63
Borgesian tree, 62–63
Bosnian Serbs, 118–19
Bosnian War, 118–19, 190n6
botany, 40, 41–42, 175n46
Braun, Wernher von, 61
Brazil, 162
Britain. *See* United Kingdom
Broberg, Gunnar, 43, 176n55
Brown, Christopher, 21
Brown, Vincent, 100

Brown, Wendy, 167n3
Brun, Catherine, 201n30
Buffon, Comte de (Georges-Louis Leclerc), 46, 49, 57, 177n70, 179n108
Bunge, M., 179n109, 181n137
Butler, Judith, 143

camps, extermination, 105, 109–15, 173n12, 193n49. *See also* Auschwitz, Poland
Canada, 122, 127
Canada, Geoffrey, 83–84
Canguilhem, Georges, 35
capacity for action, 14, 71, 86, 96, 120–21
carceral violence, 117
Card, Claudia, 96, 100, 189n126
care, 161–62
Carsten, Janet, 96–97
Cassirer, Ernst, 45, 47, 52–53
categorical imperatives, 114–16
*Categories* (Aristotle), 28, 36–37, 38, 39–40, 174nn27–28
categorization, 33–40: Aristotle, 28, 36–37, 38, 39–40, 63, 174n23, 174nn27–28; Darwin, 52; Eco, 39; Kant, 39, 46, 61, 174n28; Linnaeus, 42–44; Llull, 39, 174n32; Ockham, 38, 39; Porphyry, 28, 36–40, 42, 173n17, 174nn22–23, 174n27, 174n30, 175n33. *See also* classification; order; systematization
Cavalli-Sforza, Luigi Luca, 61, 79–80–81, 185n47
celebrity genealogy, 68–69, 82–84
Cesalpino, Andrea, 175n33
change, biological, 58
Charlottesville, Virginia, 158
Child: figure of, 142–43
children: possibility of, 143
chiliagon (Descartes), 191n18, 195n14
China, 123
Chittagong Hill Tracts, Bangladesh, 108–9
choices, 4, 29, 71, 97, 109, 120, 192n24
Chopra, Deepak, 70
chosen families, 97
Christianity, 75–76
circumcision, 75–76, 77
citizenship: ancient Athens, 1–2, 137–41, 196n36; Myanmar, 158; United States, 144, 146–47. *See also* democratic citizenship
clades, 29, 59–60
cladistics, 59–60, 62, 181n137

classification, 45, 51, 53–54, 58–59, 61–62, 84, 86. *See also* categorization; order; systematization
Clinton, Bill, 24
collective rule, 2
colonization, 8, 69, 108, 128. *See also* settler-colonialism
common ancestor, 51, 60, 62, 64, 179n105
communities, 14, 21, 22, 51, 55, 97, 118–19, 140–41
completeness, 28, 31, 34, 41–45, 53, 76. *See also* continuity
Connolly, William, 3–4, 129
*consanguinitas*, 76
consanguinity, 73–77
consequentialism, 109
conservatism, 4–5, 142, 168n9
Constitution of the United States of America, 143, 144
constitutional democracy, 142–49
constitutional inheritance, 144–48
constitutional responsibility, 155
constitutions, 2, 142, 143–44, 148, 155, 197n48
contestation, 106–7, 130, 162, 164
contingency, 16–17, 27–28, 31, 51, 53, 55, 120, 138
continuity: in constitutions, 142, 148, 155; in democracies, 1–2, 23, 138–39, 141, 142, 155; in generations, 10–11, 59, 151–52; in genetics, 56–57; in heredity, 53; in humans, 42–43, 48, 53; in nature, 41–45, 53; in world, 12–13, 154, 156, 157–58, 160. *See also* completeness
Convention on the Prevention and Punishment of the Crime of Genocide (UN). *See* Genocide Convention (UN)
Cortés, Hernán, 34, 36, 173n5
cosmopolitan belonging, 135
cosmopolitanism, 3, 4, 7, 131–35
*cosmos*, 4–5, 126–27, 129, 131–37
*cosmos*-thinking, 3, 4–5, 7, 133–34
cousins, genetic, 92
creating kin, 93–99
Creator, 41, 112, 113
Crépon, Marc, 200n16
critical phenomenology, 10, 25–27, 171n65, 173n10. *See also* phenomenology
Croats, 117
Crow (people), 159
cultural genocide, 117, 122–24, 152, 194n78, 199n14
cultural kinship classifications, 86

cultures: anthropological view of, 99, 100, 152–53, 156, 189n122; Arendt, 156–57, 199n14; destruction of, 117, 122–24, 152, 194n78, 199n14; hierarchies in, 156–57, 199n14
curiosity, genealogical, 82–85

Darfur genocide, 20–21, 24, 117–18, 171n62
Darwin, Charles, 28–29, 44, 48–57, 62, 178n97, 181n150; *On the Origin of Species*, 50
Davis, Troy, 20, 170n44
de Duve, Thierry, 132–33, 136
death: Arendt, 11; in extermination camps, 114, 115, 193n49; of God, 113; Heidegger, 11, 13, 169n26; Nietzsche, 11, 168n18
death, moral, 109–11, 192n24
death, physical, 11, 26, 56–57, 151–52
death, social, 15, 20–21, 96, 117
Declaration of Independence, 145–46, 198n60
demes, 1–2, 137–41, 147, 196n28, 196n36
demesmen (*demotoi*), 2, 140
democracy: as anarchism plus generational life, 127, 141; in ancient Athens, 1–2, 137–41, 196n36; anticipated, 158, 160; Aristotle, 7; belonging and, 1–2, 3, 126–27, 130–31, 140, 196n36; citizenship in, 4, 129–30, 136; contestation in, 130, 162, 164; continuity in, 1–2, 23, 138–39, 141, 142, 155; *cosmos* and, 126–27; *demos* and, 126–27; descent and, 2; equality and, 130, 195n12; excluded people and, 107, 140, 144, 146–47; freedom and, 2, 127, 129, 132, 140, 154–55, 167n3, 195n12; generational being and, 127, 130, 141, 147; genocidal violence and, 8–9, 24, 158–60 (*see also* Genocide Convention (UN)); genocide and, 7, 8, 23, 30; *genos* and, 1–2, 126–27; history of, 1, 137–41, 196n36; human plurality and, 129; maintenance of, 161–62; necessity of, 73; place of, compared to space of, 139, 196n30; Plato, 144; political existence and, 138–39, 196n37; problem of time for, 1–2, 4–5, 7–8, 30, 126–49; purpose of, 154–55; Rancière, 127; rule of, 155; struggle and survival of, 126–29; temporal openness of, 102, 158, 160, 162, 164; tension between *demos* and *genos* in, 7–9, 23, 30, 124, 125, 129, 130, 137–41, 144–49, 194n8; violence and, 8–9, 23; world and, 157–58, 199n4. *See also* democratic politics

democracy, antigenocidal, 23, 30, 151–64, 153–54, 162–64
democracy, constitutional, 142–49
democracy, liberal, 2–3, 129, 159
democracy, radical, 3–4, 102, 127, 196n30
democratic citizenship, 4, 129–30, 136, 155, 157, 195n11
democratic freedom, 154–55
democratic institution, 143–44
democratic paradox, 2–4, 7–9, 30, 126–31, 167n3, 197n50, 199n4
democratic peoples, 2–4, 126–27, 129–30
democratic politics: Arendt, 25, 26, 105, 120–22, 130, 153–57, 160–61, 198n65; appearance and, 25; biology and, 136; Child as problem of, 142–43; conservative nature of, 4–5, 142, 168n9; contestation in, 106–7; ethics compared with, 105–7; genocide and, 6, 30, 105, 118–19; *genos* and, 1–2, 4–5; identity and, 3–4; ontology and, 119–25; place and, 138–39, 196n30; Plato, 144; relations and, 105; social existence and, 3–4; uncertainty in, 158; use of term, 172n77; violence and, 106–7. *See also* democracy
democratic responsibility, 154–55, 157, 164
democratic time, 1–2, 7, 139, 148–49
*demos*: in ancient Athens, 1, 137–41, 196n36; in antigenocidal democracy, 163; community as, 140–41; criterion for belonging to, 3; democracy and, 126–27; expansion of, 148; generation and, 147; *genos* and, 1–2, 7–9, 23, 30, 124, 125, 129, 130, 136–41, 144–49, 194n8; interruption of, 2, 126, 140, 141; organization by, 129–30; place of, compared to space of, 139, 196n30; political existence and, 138–39, 196n37; work of, 161–62
*demos*-thinking, 7, 23
*demos*-time, 141, 146
*demotoi* (demesmen), 2, 127, 140
Denmark, 123
deontology, 107, 109
Derrida, Jacques, 129, 145, 158, 193n62
Descartes, René, 191n18, 195n14
descent, 2, 28, 48–57, 62, 60, 70, 178n97
descent with modification, 51–54
determinism, genetic, 84–85
Deutschkron, Inge, 20
dictatorship, 109–10
difference: in belonging, 70; in biology, 58; of birth, 188n94; categorization and, 38; classification and, 58; cosmopolitanism

and, 3; Darwin, 51, 54; existence and, 35–36, 188n94; *genos* and, 37–39, 174n22; in groups, 153; in humans, 61, 120; Kant, 46; in living things, 42, 46, 174n27, 179n108; natural injustice and, 188n94; need for order within, 35–36; plurality of, 188n94; as political, 3–4; as social, 3; taxonomy and, 36; in temporal order, 54, 179n105; war as producer of, 119

differentia, 38, 39, 42, 43, 50, 174n23. *See also* difference

Dinshaw, Carolyn, 142

disruption, social, 117

diversity. *See* difference

DNA (deoxyribonucleic acid) analysis, 77–85, 90–92, 185n47

Dostoevsky, Fyodor, 112

Dotson, Gary, 78–79

Douglass, Frederick, 93–94, 96

drift, genetic, 55

Dunbar, R. I. M., 86, 184n24

Eco, Umberto, 39, 42, 62, 174nn22–23, 174n30

Edelman, Lee, 98, 142, 168n9

Edwards, Jeanette, 92

Egypt, Ophelia Settle, 94

Eichmann, Adolf, 116, 117

Eilberg-Schwarz, Howard, 75

Elden, Stuart, 180n131

end of ethics, 107–16, 119–22

end of humanity, 151–52

equality, 66, 95, 130, 133–34, 148, 164, 195n12

ethical actions, 106, 201n30

ethical categories, 106, 114

ethical thinking, 105–6

ethics, 6, 29–30, 103–16, 119–22

ethnic cleansing, 119

*ethos*, 29, 109

eugenics, 117

evil, 105, 114, 190n8, 192n43

excluded peoples, 107, 140, 144, 146–47

existence: choice and, 4, 71, 120; contingency in, 27–28, 120; difference and, 35–36, 188n94; extermination camps and, 109–10, 114. *See also* being-with; generational being

existence, cultural, 9

existence, legal, 109

existence, moral, 109

existence, plural, 6

existence, political, 3, 25, 26, 30, 35, 106, 120, 138–39, 196n37

existence, social, 3–4, 64, 71, 100

existence, worldly, 102

existential anxiety, 28, 34, 35–36

experience, 47, 86

extermination camps, 105, 109–15, 173n12, 193n49. *See also* Auschwitz, Poland

extinctions, 53, 55, 180n119

families, 29, 67, 72, 87–89, 93–98, 128–29, 132–35, 188n108

families, chosen, 97

families, gay, 97–98, 188n108

families, ideal, 67

family of man, 132–34, 135. *See also* families; humanity

family trees, 29, 48, 60, 62, 63

Fanon, Frantz, 64, 126

fantasies: of completeness, 28, 31, 34, 43, 76; of *genos*, 63, 65, 73, 98, 99

father blood, 75–77

fictive kin, 96, 184n28

Finchelstein, Federico, 170n52

*Finding Your Roots* (PBS), 82

Fischer, Kuno, 52

FitzRoy, Robert, 49–50

forced impregnation, 17, 118–19

forensic evidence, 78–79

Forster, Georg, 61

Foucault, Michel, 35, 36, 57, 58–59, 171n65, 173n10, 180n131

Fox Keller, Evelyn, 77, 78

France, 122

Franklin, Benjamin, 144

freedom: in Declaration of Independence, 146; democracy and, 2, 127, 129, 132, 140, 154–55, 167n3, 195n12

freedom, individual, 2, 141–42, 167n3

Freeman, Elizabeth, 142

French Revolution, 197n52

Freud, Sigmund, 70, 76, 88, 183n17

Fritsch, Matthias, 168n17, 172n69, 191n15, 193n62

future world, 151–54, 156

Gadamer, Hans-Georg, 66, 67

Gates, Henry Louis, Jr., 82, 186n60

gay activism, 98

gay families, 97–98, 188n108

gene pool, 56

genealogical analysis, 77–85, 90–92, 185n47

genealogical aspiration, 90

genealogical bewilderment, 85–91

genealogical curiosity, 82–85

genealogical exhaustion, 92–93
genealogical orientation and disorientation, 91–92
genealogical thinking, 81–93
genealogical trees, 181n150
genealogy, 29, 31, 68–69, 70, 82–84, 99, 183n14
Genealogy of Life (GoLife), 52, 181n150. *See also* Assembling the Tree of Life (ATOL)
*genera*: definitions of, 28, 104; Eco, 39; as enduring temporal relations, 103; Kant, 45, 47; Linnaeus, 34, 41, 42; Ockham, 38; Palmié, 65; Porphyry, 37; use of term, 31. See also *genos*; *genus*
generating. *See* generation
generation: anarchy and, 142; biopolitics and, 25; contingency in, 16–17, 51; critical phenomenology of, 171n65; definitions of, 64; *demos* and, 147; generational being and, 16–17; genocide and, 5–6, 9; *genos* and, 1, 64; *genos*-thinking and, 4; as ground of resistance, 100; meaning in, 101; possibility in, 10–11, 16–17, 34; practices of, 149; results of, 101, 189n128; science of, 54–55, 59; world and, 14–15
generational being, 10–17, 168n17; definitions of, 17; demands of, 122, 193n62; democracy and, 127, 130, 141, 147; fear of loss of, 30; generation and, 16–17; genocidal sexual violence and, 17; genocide and, 5–6, 157; *genos* and, 17; identity and, 88–89; kinship and, 68, 101; mortality and, 11, 12, 13, 17, 151–52; natality and, 11, 12, 13–14, 17; naturalization of, 57–63; phenomenology and, 11–12, 168n17; queerness and, 98, 189n120; relations and, 105; responsibility and, 11, 16; self-extension and, 17; value of, 6, 152; violence towards, 156–57, 200n16; world and, 11, 12–13
generational continuity, 10–11, 59, 151–52
generational overlap, 98, 99–100, 141–42
generational responsibility, 14, 16, 22, 100, 101–2, 169nn32–33
generational time, 99–100
genes, 55–56, 59, 98
Genesis, 74
genetic belonging, 86
genetic continuity, 56–57
genetic cousins, 92
genetic determinism, 84–85
genetic drift, 55
genetic kinship, 87, 92

genetic load, 56
genetic mutations, 53, 56, 78, 185n47
genetic parents, 86, 186n68
genetic predispositions, 77–78
genetic thinking, 57
genetic time, 56, 57
genetic variations, 59
genetics, 54–56, 59–62, 77–78, 81, 84, 98, 99, 179n110
genetics, classical, 54, 179n110
genocidal agency, 21, 109, 170n52
genocidal intention, 21, 25, 108, 170n49, 171n64c
genocidal sexual violence, 17, 20–21, 117–19
genocidal violence, 18–23; definitions of, 6, 24, 73, 157, 171n62; democracies' response to, 8–9, 24, 158–60 (*see also* Genocide Convention (UN)); insult of, 21–22; intergenerational relations and, 100–1; mortality and, 13; nation-states and, 6–7; perpetrators of, 21, 22–23; types of, 20–21, 100, 117, 189n126; United States and, 8, 15, 20, 24, 163
genocide: as aenocide, 98–102; birth and, 14, 19; definitions of, 5–6, 18–23, 24–25, 108, 122–25, 127–28, 152, 157, 162, 171n62; democracy and, 7, 8, 23, 30; democratic politics and, 118–19; deontology and, 107, 109; determination of violence as, 24, 171n62; ethics and, 6, 29–30, 103–16; generation and, 5–6, 9; generational being and, 5–6, 157; *genos* and, 6–7, 9, 105; groups targeted for, 6, 19–22, 157, 170n45; as legal problem, 6, 105; as moral problem, 6; obsession with, 23–24; philosophy on, 18, 24–25, 171n61; political thinking on, 119–25; as political problem, 6, 30, 105, 118–19; and possibility of every evil, 105, 114, 192n43; United States and, 128; use of term, 5, 19, 31, 33, 172n2; Wilshire, 24, 103; world and, 30, 117–18, 120; wrongness of, 5, 6, 9–10, 18, 24–25, 29–30, 103–25, 168n12
genocide, biological, 123
Genocide Convention (UN): Article II, 18; Article III, 9, 194n78; contracting parties to, 6, 7; definitions of genocide, 5, 18–23, 24, 108, 122–24, 127–28, 152, 157; nation-states and, 6, 135; Secretariat Draft of, 122, 123; United States and, 122, 123, 128
genocide, cultural, 117, 122–24, 152, 194n78, 199n14

genocide paradox, 7–9, 119, 122, 126–31, 136–37

genocide, physical, 123

*genofond* (gene fund), 55, 56

Genographic Project, 81, 85

*genos*, 33–63; as absolute, 65, 73; as affective order, 69; ancient Athenians and, 72; in antigenocidal democracy, 163; Aristotle, 140; belonging and, 28, 64–65; as category, 28, 38; as clade, 59; continuity of, 56; and *cosmos*, 4–5, 131–36; in Declaration of Independence, 145; definitions of, 1, 17, 28–29, 36–38, 64, 72, 101, 189n129; democracy and, 1–2, 126–27; democratic politics and, 1–2, 4–5; *demos* and, 1–2, 7–9, 23, 30, 124, 125, 129, 130, 136–41, 144–49, 194n8; difference and, 37–39, 174n22; differentia and, 50; experience of, 135; fantasy of, 63, 65, 73, 98, 99; genealogy and, 31; generation and, 1, 64; generational being and, 17; genetics and, 59, 98, 99; genocide and, 6–7, 9, 105; in human life, 28; Kant, 48; kinship and, 189n129; law of, 137; Lemkin, 33; in living things, 28, 40–48; in logical order, 28, 36–40; naturalization of, 23, 53, 134–35; order and, 28, 36–40, 129, 134–35; past and future and, 4, 56, 63, 146; possibility and, 28; purpose of, 39; race and, 36, 73, 101; reducing importance of, 131; relations and, 1, 28, 64; self-extension and, 28; in temporal order, 50–57, 179n105; use of term, 31, 33; violence and, 7, 130; war and, 7; world and, 28. See also *genera*; *genus*

*genos*, absolute, 65, 73

*genos*, pure, 116, 119

*genos*, self-generating, 48

*genos*-thinking, 3, 4, 7, 8, 23, 137

*genos*-time, 141, 146

genotypes, 55, 59

*genus*, 33–34, 38, 39, 42, 47, 174n22. See also *genera*; *genos*

Germany, 21, 103

Gobineau, Arthur de, 61

God, 41, 112, 113

Goethe, Johann Wolfgang von, 62

Gordon, Lewis, 4

Gould, Stephen Jay, 59, 60

groups: Arendt, 153; belonging and, 65, 152; community and, 14; continuity of, 152; destruction of, 20–21; differences among, 153; meaning in, 152, 157; social death in, 20–21; types targeted for genocide, 6, 19–22, 157, 170n45

groups, kinship, 73, 92, 184n24

groups, minority, 129, 194n8

groups, political, 122

Guerrero, Juan, 175n46

Habermas, Jürgen, 147–48, 198n63

Hacking, Ian, 173n17, 174n32, 175n33

Haddad, Samir, 198n60

Halberstam, Jack, 142

Hamlet, 139

Hampton, Jean, 190n2

Haraway, Donna, 189n130

Hatley, James, 22, 101, 102, 189n129

Hebrew patriarchs, 75–76, 100

Hegel, Georg Wilhelm Friedrich, 52

Heidegger, Martin, 11, 12, 13; *Being and Time*, 169n26

heredity, 48–59, 86, 89, 180n131

hermeneutics, 26–27, 68, 122. *See also* interpretation

heroes, 15, 156

Heyer, Heather, 158

hierarchies, cultural, 156–57, 199n14

Hippias the tyrant, 137

history, 11, 14–15, 50–51

Hobbes, Thomas, 16, 169nn32–33

Hoff, Shannon, 67, 71, 85–86, 87, 186n67

Holocaust, 5, 23–24, 170n52, 170n60

home, 67–68, 120, 139

*Homo sapiens*, 44

homosexuality, 97–98, 188n108

Honig, Bonnie, 161, 198n63

Howard, John, 158–59

human family, 132–34, 135. *See also* families; humanity

Human Genome Diversity Program, 80, 85

human genome project (Celera, completed 2000), 185n50

Human Genome Project (completed 2003), 52, 77, 85

human paradox, 4

human rights, 131–36, 195n21

human temporalities, 155–57

humanity: continuity of, 16, 42–43, 48, 53; in cosmopolitanism, 134; difference in, 61, 120; end of, 151–52; genetics and, 61–62; Linnaeus, 44; meaning making in, 157; plurality in, 6, 14, 25, 26, 120, 129, 155, 195n12; social nature of, 64

Hume, David, 26

Husserl, Edmund, 12, 26

Hutu, 110
hybridity, 65
hybridization, 54

ideas, regulative, 45, 116
identity, 3–4, 17, 20, 64–65, 88–89, 115, 119, 170n45
imperialism, 8, 36, 58, 128
impregnation, forced, 17, 118–19
Inca, 160
India, partition of, 128
indigenous peoples, 8, 80–81. *See also names of specific peoples*
individual freedom, 2, 141–42, 167n3
individual rights, 131–32
individual time, 56, 57
individualism, 152
inheritance, 5–6, 48–57, 70, 144–48, 154–56, 164. *See also* heredity
injustice, 93–95, 113, 187n93, 188n94, 192n41
injustice, natural, 93–94, 187n93, 188n94, 192n41
institution, 28, 71–72, 143–44
intention, genocidal, 21, 25, 108, 170n49, 171n64
intergenerational justice, 191n15
intermaterial relations, 85–90, 186n67, 187n69. *See also* Hoff, Shannon.
International Criminal Tribunal for former Yugoslavia, 103
interpretation, 27, 50, 59–61. *See also* hermeneutics
interruption of *demos*, 2, 126, 140, 141
Iran, 123–24
Ireland, 163
Isocrates, 196n27
Italy, 162

Jackson, Mattie J., 20
Jacob, François, 35, 48; *The Logic of Life*, 59
Jamaican sugar plantations, 100
Jarman, Derek, 98
Jefferson, Thomas, 143–45, 198n58
Jewish cemetery, Kazimierz Dolny, Poland, 101–2
Jewish genocides, 21, 101–2, 117
Johannsen, Wilhelm, 54, 55
Johnston, Mark David, 175n32
Jonas, Hans, 144; "Toward an Ontological Grounding of an Ethics for the Future," 121
Józéfów, Poland, 21

judgment, 5, 9–10, 23–28, 30, 111, 129, 130, 195n11
*jus sanguinis*, 4
*jus soli*, 4
justice, 95, 188n94, 191n15

Kafka, Franz, 153–54, 155; "Abraham," 146
Kant, Immanuel; belonging, 64; categorical imperative, 115–16; categorization, 39, 46, 61, 174n28; difference, 46; *genos*, 48; germ (*Keim*), 46–47, 69; on Linnaeus, 175n41; purposiveness of nature, 46, 47–48, 52, 64, 177n73, 182nn1–2; race, 48, 69, 177n78, 182n2; reason, 45–48; understanding of nature, 45–47, 176nn61–63, 177n70
*katagoria*, 36. *See also* categorization
Kazimierz Dolny, Poland, 101–2
Keenan, Brian, 22
Keller, Evelyn Fox. *See* Fox Keller, Evelyn
Khanna, Rajana, 159
kin, fictive, 96, 184n28
kin, real, 96
King, Martin Luther, Jr., 148
kinship: ancestors and, 184n24; anthropology and, 63, 73, 86–87, 96, 134–35; blood and, 188n104; of circumstance, 96–97, 188n104; classification in, 86; creation of, 93–99; definitions of, 63, 68, 73, 86–87, 101, 184n28, 189n129; and DNA analysis, 82; dynamism of, 189n130; generational being and, 68, 101; *genos* and, 189n129; natural injustice and, 94; necessity of, 29, 64–102; queering of, 97–98, 188n108; refusal of, 97, 98; requirements for, 92–93; responsibility and, 92–93, 101, 190n130; slavery and, 93–96, 188n97; structures of, 134–35. *See also* blood; blood relations; families
kinship, genetic, 87, 92
kinship groups, 73, 92, 184n24
kinship studies, anthropological, 134–35
Kleisthenes, 1–2, 4, 30, 137–41, 147, 196n28, 196n36
Klodzinski, Stanslaw, 112
Kristof, Nicholas, 168n12
Kurz, Doriane (Holocaust survivor), 103

language: taxonomy and, 40, 42, 175n46
law, 3, 6, 95, 105, 129, 137, 200n15
law, universal, 3, 129
Lear, Jonathan, 159
Lederman, Shmuel, 153, 157, 161

legal existence, 109
legal thinking, 105
legitimate rule, 2–3, 136
Leibniz, Gottfried Wilhelm, 28
Leighton, Kim, 88, 89
Lemkin, Raphael, 19, 31, 33, 172n2
lesbian families, 97–98, 188n108
Levi, Primo, 102, 112
Lévi-Strauss, Claude, 73
Lewis, Gail, 161
Lewontin, R. C., 61, 62
Lewsam (or Newsham), Amelia, 176n57
liberal democracy, 2–3, 129, 159
liberalism, 2
liberty. *See* freedom
Linnaeus, Carl: biopolitics, 60; family
    name, 177n80; Kant on, 175n41; Lewsam
    (or Newsham) and, 176n57; *Paradoxa*,
    42–44, 176n52; sexualism, 49, 178n84;
    species, 41, 42, 48, 177n79; *Systema
    Naturae*, 40–41, 42–43; taxonomy, 28,
    34, 40–49, 58, 61, 175n33, 175n41, 175n46,
    176n50, 176n52
Linné, Carl von. *See* Linnaeus, Carl
Llull, Ramon: "*Arbor naturalis, arbor logica-
    lis,*" 39, 174n32
load, genetic, 56
love, 133, 188n94
Lovejoy, A. O., 43, 53
Lynch, Thomas, Jr., 144

Mahner, M., 179n109, 181n137
maintenance, 161–62
majority rule, 129, 194n8
Malaysian migrant communities, 97
Mann, Michael, 22–23, 194n8
Manning, Dolleen Tisawii'ashii, 160, 201n31
Manville, Phillip, 137
Marks, Jonathan, 80–81
Martel, James, 146, 162
material relations, 85–86
maternity, 74–75, 76, 77
May, Larry, 23, 24, 170n60
May, Todd, 127
meaning, 26–28, 71–72, 151–57, 161, 183n20
Meillassoux, Claude, 74
melancholia, 57, 159
Mendel, Gregor, 54, 179n110
Mensch, Jennifer, 46–47, 177n70
Merleau-Ponty, Maurice, 186n67
microbes, 181n150
migrant communities, 97, 140, 147
Miller, Sarah, 21, 117–18

Milner, Jean-Claude le, 172n71
minority groups, 129, 194n8
misinterpellated people, 144, 146, 147
modification, descent with, 51–53
Moore, CeCe, 83
Moore, G. E., 26
moral death, 109–11, 192n24
moral existence, 109
moral philosophy, 25, 26. *See also* ethics
moral thinking, 6
morality: genocide as problem for, 6
Moran, Dermot, 26–27
Morgan, Henry Lewis, 135
Morison, Robert, 40
Morrison, Toni: *Beloved*, 100–1
mortality: generational being and, 11, 12,
    13, 17, 151–52; Heidegger, 11, 13, 169n26;
    physical death and, 26
Moses, Dirk, 109 mother blood, 74–75,
    76, 77
Mouffe, Chantal, 129
mourning, 56–57, 102, 114
Moynihan, Daniel Patrick, 95
Mukherjee, Siddhartha: *The Gene*, 61
Mulisch, Harry, 200n14
Müller-Wille, Staffan, 52, 54, 179n110,
    181n149
Munshi, Jonab Ali, 108–9
*Muselmann*, 111–12, 113, 192n31
mutations, genetic, 53, 56, 78, 185n47
Mutis, Jose Celestino, 175n46
Myanmar, 158

Nancy, Jean-Luc, 27, 184n20
Napoleon I, 155
Narayan, Uma, 189n122
Nash, Catherine, 183n14
natal alienation, 14, 93–94
natality: Arendt, 118, 120–21; birth and,
    13–14, 19, 26; generational being and, 11,
    12, 13–14, 17; genocidal sexual violence
    and, 118–19; human condition of, 120–21
nation-states, 4, 6–7, 129–30, 135, 136
National Science Foundation of the United
    States, 62, 182n151
Native Americans, 15, 117
natural injustice, 93–94, 187n93, 188n94,
    192n41
natural variation, 53, 58, 59, 80
naturalism, 25–27
naturalistic fallacy, 25–27
naturalization: of generational being, 57–63;
    of *genos*, 23, 53, 134–35

nature: continuity in, 41–45, 53; *cosmos* and, 135; mother's right over child in, 16, 169n32; purity in, 45–46, 51, 177n63; purposiveness in, 46, 47–48, 52, 64, 177n73, 182nn1–2; reason and, 45–48, 57; relations in, 62; understanding of, 45–47, 176nn61–63, 177n70
Nazism, 13, 21, 108, 109–10, 114, 120, 153, 192n28
Nelson, Alondra, 79, 91
Newsham (or Lewsam), Amelia, 176n57
Nietzsche, Friedrich, 11, 27, 121, 168n18
Nigeria, 162
Nixon, Rob, 22, 162

Ó Tuama, Padráig, 64
oblivion, 11
Ockham, William of, 38, 39
Ogoni, 162
old-age homes, 163
ontology, 23–28, 119–25
order, 28–29, 33–40, 44–45, 48–57, 129–30, 131, 134–35. *See also* categorization; classification; systematization
order, complete, 44–45
order, temporal, 48–57
organisms, 47, 53, 55, 60, 62
orientation, genealogical, 91–92
overlap of generations, 98, 99–100, 141–42

Pakistan, 123
Paley, William: *Natural Theology*, 49
Palmié, Stephan, 65
Parker, Sarah Jessica, 69
Pascal, Blaise, 34, 36
past and future: antigenocidal democracy and, 164; being between, 10–11, 68, 130, 152; being with, 160; democracy's problem of, 30 (*see also* time: problem for democracy of); of generations, 6, 101, 130, 146; *genos* and, 4, 56, 63, 146; kin and, 85; politics in gap between, 153–54, 155, 160–61
paternity, 75–77, 82–83
Patrick, Deval, 83, 90
Patterson, Orlando, 14, 93, 94, 188n94, 192n41
pedigrees, 29, 63, 72
Pericles, 156
permission, prohibition and, 112–14
Peru, 160
Peter of Spain, 38

phenomenology, 10–12, 25–27, 168n17, 171n65, 172n69, 173n10
phenomenology, critical, 10, 25–27, 171n65, 173n10
phenomenology, political, 26, 172n69
phenotypes, 55
phylogeny, 52, 182n151
physical death, 11, 26, 56–57, 151–52
physical genocide, 123
Pigliucci, Massimo, 179n113
plants (botanical), 40, 41–42, 175n46
plasticity, 55, 98
Plato, 11, 127, 144; *Laws*, 136
Plenty Coups (Crow chief), 159
plurality: of *demotoi*, 127; of differences, 188n94; human condition of, 6, 14, 25, 26, 120, 129, 155, 195n12; investigation of, 27
poisoning, 162
police violence, 117
political action, 156
political agency, 195n11
political difference, 3–4
political districts, 139
political existence, 3, 25, 26, 30, 35, 106, 120, 138–39, 196n37
political groups, 122
political hermeneutics, 122
political phenomenology, 26, 172n69
political thinking, 105–6, 119–25
politics. *See* democratic politics
polities, 2, 137–41, 196n36
Popper, Karl R., 144, 197n50
Porphyry: Aristotle's *Categories*, 37, 173n17; categorization, 28, 36–40, 42, 173n17, 174nn22–23, 174n27, 174n30, 175n33; *Introduction* (*Isagoge*), 37; Tree of Porphyry, 28, 36–40, 174nn22–23, 181n150
possibility: of children, 143; of every evil, 105, 114, 190n8, 192n43; of generation, 10–11, 16–17, 34; *genos* and, 28; of revolution, 143
poverty, 15
Povinelli, Elizabeth, 22
Powell, Colin, 24, 171n62
predications, 36–37, 38, 39
predispositions, genetic, 77–78
preformation, 57
privilege, white male, 98
probrium, 174n22
procreation, 41, 42, 97, 98
progressive temporality, 148–49

prohibition, permission and, 112–14
propriety, 60, 65–66
purity: in genetics, 54–55, 60, 84; hybridity
  and, 65; in nature, 45–46, 51, 177n63; in
  race, 80, 84, 116, 119
purity, racial, 80, 84, 116, 119
purposiveness of nature, 46, 47–48, 52, 64,
  177n73, 182nn1–2
Pygmies, 80–81

queer kinship, 97–98, 188n108
queerness and generational being, 98,
  189n120

race: ancestry and, 91–92; anthropology
  and, 81; biopolitics of, 84; classification
  of, 61–62, 84; genetics and, 61–62, 81; genos and, 36, 73, 101; Kant, 48, 69, 177n78,
  182n2; purity in, 80, 84, 116, 119
race, biological, 84–85
racial classification, 61–62, 84
racial purity, 80, 84, 116, 119
racism, 80–81, 82, 84
radical democracy, 3–4, 102, 127, 196n30
Ramus, Peter, 175n33
Rancière, Jacques, 127, 136, 172n77
rape, 17, 20–21, 117–19, 190n2, 190n8. See also
  genocidal sexual violence
rational demonstrability, 115, 116
Ray, John, 40; Wisdom of God Manifested in
  the Works of Creation, 49
real kin, 96
reason: nature and, 45–48, 57
Reed, Mr., 94–95
regulative ideas, 45, 116
relational harm, 21, 118
relations: being-with and, 14; care in, 161;
  democratic politics and, 105; destruction
  of, 20–21, 93–96, 100; ethics and, 105;
  genera and, 103; generational being and,
  17, 130, 163; between generations, 86–87,
  100; genos and, 1, 28, 64; genotype and
  phenotype, 55; institution of, among
  humans, 28; maintenance of, 161; modes
  of relatedness and, 92; in nature, 62; to
  old world, 15; relating compared with,
  157; of responsibility, 14, 100; sex as
  mode of, 118; slavery and, 93–96. See also
  kinship
relations, blood, 29, 52, 73–77
relations, genetic, 85, 90
relations, homosexual, 97–98

relations, intermaterial, 85–90, 186n67,
  187n69
relations, material, 85–86
relationships. See relations
reproduction, 16, 49, 53. See also generation
resemblances, 48, 51, 84
Reserve Police Battalion 101 of Hamburg,
  Germany, 21
respect, 121, 132–33
responsibility: actions and, 16; aenocide
  and, 101–2; of antigenocidal democracy,
  164; of democratic citizens, 155, 157; of
  democratic freedom, 154–55; generational being and, 11, 16; kinship and,
  92–93, 101, 190n130; relations of, 14, 100
responsibility, constitutional, 155
responsibility, generational, 14, 16, 22, 100,
  101–2, 169nn32–33
responsibility, moral, 159
responsibility, political, 154–55
Restrepo, José Alejandro, 176n46
revolutionary governments, 155
revolutions, 143–44, 147, 154, 162, 197n52
Rheinberger, Hans-Jörg, 52, 54, 179n110,
  181n149
rights, human, 131–36, 195n21
Rights of Man, 136, 195n21. See also rights,
  human
Roberts, Dorothy, 84–85
Rohingya, 158
Romans, ancient, 15, 72, 76
Ross, W. D., 39
Rousseau, Jean-Jacques, 2
Rubin, Gayle, 33
ruling, 2–3, 129, 136, 155, 194n8
Rutledge, Edward, 144
Rwandan genocide, 5, 24, 110, 192n28
Rwililiza, Innocent, 110, 192n28
Ryn, Zdzisław, 112

Sachs, Julian, 52, 178n97
same-sex marriage, 188n94
Sants, H. J., 87, 88, 89, 90
Scheffler, Samuel, 151–52, 153
Scheper-Hughes, Nancy, 162–63
Schmitt, Carl, 3, 140, 129, 141
Schneider, David, 73, 135
Schott, Robin May, 118–19, 190n8
science, 50–51, 54–55, 57, 59
science, basic, 62, 181nn148–49
scientism, 50–51
Scotus, Duns, 39

self-extension, 12, 14, 17, 28, 48
self-generating *genos*, 48
self-identity, 88–89
self-possession, 96
self-rule, 2–3
sense, 183n20. *See also* meaning
Serbs, 117
Sergeevich, Aleksandr, 55
settler-colonialism, 15, 108–9, 127–28, 158.
    *See also* colonization
sexual violence, 117–19
sexualism, 49, 178n84
Shange, Savannah, 98
Shay's Rebellion, 143
Shuster, Martin, 22
Silenus, 27–28
Simplicius, 37, 173n17
Simpson, G. G., 179n109
sin, 112–13
singular plurality, 6, 14
slavery, 14, 15, 17, 20, 83–84, 93–96, 145,
    188n97
slow violence, 22, 162
social belonging, 86
social death, 15, 20–21, 96, 117
social difference, 3
social disruption, 117
social exhaustion, 92–93
social existence, 3–4, 64, 71, 100
social identity, 3
social nature, 64
social paradox, 129
social realm, 120
Socrates, 11
Solon, 1, 137
Somerville, Margaret, 89
Sonqo community, 160
South Africa, 123, 162
Soviet Union, 122, 128
species: Aristotle, 174n27; Buffon, 46,
    177n70; Darwin on, 28–29, 62; difficulty
    in defining, 55, 182n153; Eco, 39; Lin-
    naeus, 41, 42, 48, 177n79; Lovejoy, 43;
    Ockham, 38; Porphyry, 174n27
Spillers, Hortense, 94, 95, 183n17
Stevens, Jacqueline, 186n68
Strathern, Marilyn, 92
Straus, Scott, 192n28
structural violence, 22–23
structuralism, 172n71
Styron, William: *Sophie's Choice*, 109
Suarez, Francisco, 39

Sudan. *See* Darfur genocide
suicide, 112–13
superfluity, 156, 192n28
surveillance, 117
Sweden, 124
systematization, 40–48, 51, 54, 57, 179n109.
    *See also* categorization; classification;
    order

Taft, William, IV, 171n62
TallBear, Kim, 81
taxonomy: biopolitics and, 60, 61; complete-
    ness in, 34, 43, 44–45; definition in,
    42, 43; descent with modification and,
    53–54; difference and, 36; emergence of,
    34, 35–36; Gobineau, 61; S. J. Gould, 60;
    identity and, 64–65; invented nature of,
    57; language in, 40, 42, 175n46; Lewon-
    tin, 62; Linnaeus, 28, 34, 40–49, 58, 61,
    175n33, 175n41, 175n46, 176n50, 176n52;
    not a basic science, 62, 181n148; reason
    and, 45; purpose of, 61
teleology, 182n1. *See also* purposiveness of
    nature
temporal order, 48–57
temporalities, 56–57, 99–100, 155–57; de-
    mocracy's openness to, 102, 158, 160, 162,
    164; democracy's problem with, 1–2, 4–5,
    7–8, 30, 126–49; *demos* and, 141, 146
temporalities, human, 155–57
territorial violence, 117
Thomas, Nicholas, 65
threatened violence, 117
Tierra del Fuego, 50
time: problem for democracy of, 1–2, 4–5,
    7–8, 30, 126–49. *See also* temporalities
torture, 21–22
tradition, 11, 154
tragic choices, 29, 109, 192n24
Trail of Tears, 117, 163
Tree of Life. *See* Assembling the Tree of Life
    (ATOL)
Tree of Porphyry, 28, 36–40, 174nn22–23,
    181n150
trees, family, 29, 48, 60, 62, 63
trees, genealogical, 181n150
Trees of Consanguinity (*arbores juris*),
    174n25
Tronto, Joan, 144, 161
Tutsi, 110, 192n28
types. *See* groups
tyranny, 144

Ukeles, Mierle Laderman, 162
UN. *See* United Nations (UN)
uncertainty, 31, 158
understanding of nature, 45–47, 176nn61–63, 177n70
Union of South Africa, 123
United Kingdom, 92, 128, 145, 146
United Nations (UN): General Assembly, 131–32; Universal Declaration of Human Rights, 131–33, 136. *See also* Genocide Convention (UN)
United States of America: citizenship of, 144, 146–47; Constitution, 143, 144; Declaration of Independence, 145–46, 198n60; DNA evidence used in exonerations in, 78–79; founding of, 144–49, 197n53; genocidal violence and, 8, 15, 20, 24, 163; genocide charge against, 128; Genocide Convention (UN) and, 122, 123, 128; slavery in, 145
Universal Declaration of Human Rights (UN), 131–33, 136
universal law, 3, 129
universality, 36
urban violence, 163
USSR (Union of Soviet Socialist Republics), 122, 128

"Vampire Project," 80–81
van Cleef, Alfred, 104–5
variations, natural, 53, 58, 59, 80
Venter, Craig, 186n65
Vienna, Austria, 117
violence: *cosmos*-thinking and, 7; democracy and, 8–9, 23; democratic politics and, 106–7; of enforced orders of things, 29; as genocide, 24, 171n62; towards generational being, 156–57, 200n16; *genos* and, 7, 130; sources of, 31; types of, 22–23, 117–19. *See also* genocidal sexual violence; genocidal violence
virtue ethics, 29, 109

Wade, Nicholas: *A Troublesome Inheritance*, 61, 186n65

war, 7, 119
war rape, 118–19, 190n8
Washington, Isiah, 90–91
Weinstein, Jami, 44
Wellisch, Erich, 87
Wells, Spencer, 81
Weston, Kath, 97
white Americans, 148, 158
white supremacy, 95, 145–46, 158
Whitehead, David, 139
*Who Do You Think You Are?* (BBC), 68–69
Wilshire, Bruce, 24, 103
Wilson, Allan, 80
Wittgenstein, Ludwig, 70, 112–13
Wolff, Caspar Friedrich, 178n84
Women's International Democratic Federation, 128
world: acting into, 14; antigenocidal democracy and, 164; belonging and, 66–67; choices and, 120; continuity of, 12–13, 154, 156, 157–58, 160; culture and, 100; democracy and, 157–58, 199n4; democratic politics and, 105–6; *demos* and, 129; destruction of, 102, 117, 159–60, 201n30; in future, 151–54, 156; generation and, 14–15; generational being and, 11, 12–13; genocide and, 30, 117–18, 120; *genos* and, 28; ways of inheriting, 154
World Council of Indigenous Peoples, 80
worldliness, 12, 117, 120, 143
worldly existence, 102
worldly groups, 163
worldly politics, 153–54
Wright, Sewall, 55
wrongness of genocide, 5, 6, 9–10, 18, 24–25, 29–30, 103–25, 168n12

Yap, Caroline Islands, 135
Yates, Frances, 175n32
Yoon, Carol Kaesuk, 60
Yugoslavia, 9, 104–5, 190n6

*zoe* (as distinct from *bios*), 155
*Zugehörigkeit* (belonging), 66

**Anne O'Byrne** is Associate Professor of Philosophy at Stony Brook University. She is the author of *Natality and Finitude* (Indiana, 2010), coeditor of *Logics of Genocide* (Routledge, 2020), and translator or cotranslator of four books by Jean-Luc Nancy.

www.ingramcontent.com/pod-product-compliance
Lightning Source LLC
Chambersburg PA
CBHW020251030426
42336CB00010B/709